MARCH FORTH

TREVOR GREENE
AND DEBBIE GREENE

MARCH
FORTH

THE INSPIRING TRUE STORY OF A
CANADIAN SOLDIER'S JOURNEY OF
LOVE, HOPE AND SURVIVAL

HarperCollins Publishers Ltd

HarperCollins books may be purchased for educational, business, or sales
promotional use through our Special Markets Department.

HarperCollins Publishers Ltd
2 Bloor Street East, 20th Floor
Toronto, Ontario, Canada
M4W 1A8

www.harpercollins.ca

Library and Archives Canada Cataloguing in Publication data
is available upon request.

ISBN: 978-1-44340-512-6

Printed and bound in Canada
DWF 9 8 7 6 5 4 3 2 1

This book is dedicated to all Canadians who served in Afghanistan, and especially to those who paid the supreme sacrifice. Stand down, Bill. We'll miss you.

CONTENTS

FOREWORD
BY GEN. RICK HILLIER

Iknew much of Trevor and Debbie's story early, starting with the savage attack on Trevor by a young and misguided man filled with such rage that he would abrogate Pashtunwali, the very code of behaviour that guides the young man's tribe so completely and guarantees the safety of guests. I had been briefed on the recovery process from the remote site of the attack and I followed, at a distance, Trevor's evacuation from Shah Wali Kot to Kandahar Airfield to the U.S. Army Regional Medical Center in Landstuhl, Germany, and then, finally, home to Canada. Our medical specialists, including those involved in Trevor's follow-up care, had walked me through the nature and extent of his terrible wound and the dire prognosis for any recovery beyond living incapacitated, essentially, unable to do much, if anything, in life as a man, son, husband and father.

What I did not know, however, was the kind of man that Trevor was and the kind of life partner that he had found in Debbie. It was only in meeting them personally, some long months after the attack, that I saw what sort of people they were and why their outcome would be different. Trevor was a beautiful, courageous man whose pale complexion and faint voice belied a drive and determination to recover that were quite literally out of this world. Debbie was a lioness, with courage and determination equal to if not greater than Trevor's and a willingness to savage anything, or anyone, that would arbitrarily place limits on her man, her life partner. Clearly they were different.

Together, they were also unbeatable, and they created a story from the journey they travelled that inspires me and will, I am certain, inspire you. It inspires me to ignore the various daily complaints, whines and groans that come from those around us, despite the awesome society in which we, who have won the lotto that makes us Canadian, live. Trevor and Debbie inspire me to live life each and every day to the absolute fullest, to appreciate everything we have and to have with my wife the deep love that a man and woman can have for each other, with its capacity for enabling so much. They inspire me with what can only be described as a miracle of recovery. Trevor Greene and Debbie Greene, and their very lives, inspire me.

That inspiration came from a common thread that captivated me throughout Trevor and Debbie's story. It is based on a most fundamental belief, one in which I myself believe: that of being part of something more and something bigger in life than ourselves as individuals. Trevor and Debbie believed in their responsibility to give more to others and to each other than they took, a belief that is evident in Trevor's selection of the "warrior path"; in the support that Debbie provided to her partner by standing beside and behind him; in the courage Debbie and Trevor took from strong families and many friends; and in the couple's belief in an inherently greater power with a plan for each of us. Their strong beliefs brought to mind a saying that originated in the Second World War: "There are no atheists in foxholes." The fundamentals that keep men and women sane, strong and focused, with an ability to carry on despite incredible fears and difficulties, are not always obvious in the lives that most of us live but are easily visible during times of fear and instability. Such is what marks both Debbie and Trevor in this most compelling of life stories. They, in their "foxhole," continued to believe what most others had long since given up, and they worked to make their belief a reality. There are lessons in how they did this for all of us.

It was Trevor's strong beliefs that brought him to Afghanistan. Living life to the fullest, appreciating each day, loving his friends and family and wanting to give (and give back) to others led Trevor after many years to push for a deployment into Afghanistan as a CIMIC (Civil-Military Co-operation) officer. Trevor was offered the position, and in early 2006, he joined the first Canadian battle group to return to southern Afghanistan. Connecting the hard military work with the rebuilding effort became part of his everyday routine until the attack. Surviving and returning home, he was all but dismissed by a medical and military system that assumed his grievous wounds were too much for anyone. Yet recover to an unbelievable extent he did, with Debbie pushing, pulling, encouraging, praying, sustaining and, yes, crying with him through the pain, setbacks, stifling bureaucracy, impersonal caregivers and every other challenge imaginable. Every Canadian would benefit from reading this life story, comparing his or her approach to life with that of Debbie and Trevor, and becoming inspired by what Debbie and Trevor have done and continue to do. Every Canadian would live life more completely as a result. God bless two great Canadians every day.

PROLOGUE

A baleful desert sun screamed down mercilessly on my helmet while the heat and dust wrapped around me like a monstrous, suffocating pillow. Through the sodden kaffiyeh desert scarf wrapped around my mouth and neck, the air was malodorous with the acrid stench of smoke and the burned-paper smell of ancient dust. Behind my sunglasses, my eyes blurred from the oily sweat oozing from my forehead. My saliva thickened, and dust coated my parched throat. My rifle was cumbersome and warm in my shooting gloves. The bottoms of my feet burned in my tan desert boots as I carefully stepped around ankle-breaking rocks of crumbling shale. We were on the third dusty day of foot patrol.

I was attached to One Platoon, Alpha Company, 1st Battalion PPCLI. Call sign Orion 11. Our mission was to patrol a five-hundred-square-kilometre area of operations in the foothills of the Hindu Kush, bounded in the east by a circle of jagged mountains we called the Belly Button. No foreign army had been in the Belly Button, the most dangerous real estate in Kandahar Province, since the fall of the Taliban in 2002.

The Red Devil Inn, so called for the Alpha Company nickname, was a wattled mud compound that had been converted into our forward operating base. Our home away from home was about seventy kilometres as the buzzard flies from the main coalition base at Kandahar Airfield but closer to a hundred after dusty swerves and switchbacks. The compound was the size of an elementary school gymnasium and was just outside the village of Gonbad, about seventy kilometres north of Kandahar City—right in the heart of Taliban country. A road led from the Red Devil Inn through the village and branched to the south. This branch came to be known as IED Alley because of the countless bombs that had been laced into the road by the Taliban.

The front entrance to the compound was a massive double-doored gate. A small hill in front of the gate was always crowded with villagers mesmerized by our vehicles. They were insatiably curious and would hang out on the hill for hours, seemingly in shifts. We wanted to maintain goodwill with the locals by being good neighbours, but their proximity to the Inn was of concern. Every morning, the villagers were frisked by three Afghan National Army (ANA) soldiers in the unlikely event they carried weapons or explosives.

The Red Devil Inn's surprisingly cool rooms were on the ground level and looked like they had been hewn out of bare sandstone. We slept two to a room on a packed-mud floor along with thousands of creepy-crawlies. The only ones we were concerned with were the scorpions and the hand-sized camel spiders. The mornings were teeth-chatteringly cold, and I needed a thermal fleece and a hat until the sun once again ruled the sky. The Inn was protected by our heavy machine guns, which stood perched on all four corners of the top level, protected by sandbags.

An oily diesel smell hung over us from the frequent burn-off of the excrement that accumulated in the latrines, which were alongside a beautiful apple orchard around the back. We ate our meals around a bonfire in the centre of the compound, swapping stories and food to and fro. We lived on tinfoil packets of over-preserved, artificially tasty food high in calories. Tabasco sauce was a necessity to overpower the medley of preservatives.

I always cleaned my rifle the night before a patrol. The greasy feel and acrid, industrial smell of the lubricant on my fingers brought back memories of the hundreds of times I had performed this task before. I listened for the reassuring dry click of the bolt smoothly sliding back and forth. I stuffed dry socks and foot powder, which are almost as important as a well-functioning weapon, into my rucksack before crawling into my sleeping bag for the night.

One morning like any other, we loaded up in the light armoured vehicle (LAV) under the watchful, curious gaze of the locals at the front gate. It was a tight, hip-to-hip fit on the benches of the LAV. I held my rifle between my legs and rested the brim of my helmet on the barrel. We travelled down a highway through dry riverbeds, or wadis, following faint truck paths in the dirt.

We carefully approached the first village of the day, stopping far enough away to achieve some standoff distance in case things went bad. As we entered the village, we were greeted with smiles and handshakes. Our presence usually garnered enough attention to draw a few people out, so we never had to knock on doors. At the edge of the village they invited us to sit down, so we sat cross-legged on the ground facing the elders and talked through an interpreter. These meetings with the village elders were called *shuras*. During the *shura*, our platoon commander, Kevin Schamuhn, probed for tactical information about Taliban presence in the area. As the Civil-Military Co-operation officer, I was responsible for determining the villagers' infrastructure needs, which would help in reconstruction planning. After the *shura*, we handed out a few gifts of tea for the adults and pens for the kids, thanked the men for meeting with us and slowly made our way back to our vehicles.

At about 1330 local time, our three LAVs splashed across a small creek running alongside the tiny village of Shinkay, our third *shura* of the day. A farmer worked in a field and some kids played near a grove of trees. They stopped to gawk at us. We dismounted and assembled on the ground near a grassy area, a rare sight in the desert. We approached the farmer and introduced ourselves. Through our interpreter, the farmer indicated he would go and get the elders. As we waited for them, our security section set up a perimeter around where we wanted to meet.

3

A few minutes later, a smiling group of elders emerged with outstretched hands. We congregated on that peaceful, grassy spot in the shade of trees by the gently flowing river. Kevin and I sat cross-legged on the ground on either side of our interpreter, facing the elders. I placed my helmet on the ground next to me, as did the others, and laid my rifle on top of it. Section Commander Rob Dolson positioned himself on my left, and a senior Afghan solider sat on Kevin's right. One of the elders waved at a young boy, who then disappeared for about ten minutes and brought back tea. The tea was freshly made and surprisingly refreshing. It was served in well-scrubbed water glasses carried on a silverish tray deeply scored with wide brown scratches.

A small group of young men and kids milled about curiously behind us. The rest of the members of One Platoon were fanned out behind them in defensive positions facing outward. I felt safe as usual with the superb soldiers of One Platoon watching my back. There was also the inviolable, centuries-old tradition of *Pashtunwali,* which guarantees the safety of guests and mandates they be shown every hospitality the village can muster.

The elders waited for us to initiate the conversation. Kevin opened the meeting as usual, speaking directly to the leader in English about our presence and their security situation. "We are here to support your country and help the people of Afghanistan," he began. The men leaned forward, as they usually did, squinting and trying to make sense of his words. Once the interpreter had translated, only one man spoke back to the translator. The others watched intently in silence.

I could hear the familiar sounds of scuffing sandals and the voices of children at play in the village, reminding me of my own daughter on the other side of the world. As Kevin wrapped up his questions and turned the meeting over to me, I could hear the stream ripple nearby and thought about the peacefulness of the setting amidst all this war. By the time my next memory flashed across my consciousness, my daughter was one year older.

PART 1: BEFORE

Life isn't about dawdling to the grave, arriving safely in an attractive, wrinkle-free body, but rather an adventure that ends skidding in sideways, champagne in one hand, strawberries in the other, totally worn out, screaming, "Yeehaaa, what a ride!"

—*Anonymous*

CHAPTER 1:
THE ODYSSEY

I was five years old and riding west on the plains, lance in hand, on my jet-black horse as huge herds of buffalo thundered past. We rode relentlessly through the rain, wind and snow. My imaginary red tunic was stained with sweat and my blue britches were stiff with mud. My high leather riding boots creaked in the stirrups. This reverie lasted only a few minutes until I heard my mother snap, "Trevor, pay attention!" as she handed me the prayer book open to the proper page.

My family went to church every Sunday at the RCMP training facility called Depot, where my father was posted in 1969. He was appointed to instruct law for three years at the police academy before retiring twenty-six years later as a staff sergeant, the RCMP's highest non-commissioned rank.

The small white church was always cool inside. As we entered the building, my gaze would be drawn to the crossed Mountie lances over the door. Dad told me they had been carried by horseback across the country as part of the 1874 March West, a push by the fledgling North-West Mounted Police to bring law and order to the frontier. I rarely paid attention during the service because I was always on the wrong page of the prayer book, leafing through it looking for stories and pictures. When my mother wasn't looking, I would crawl down under the pews and look at people's feet and study their shoes to see if they were shiny like Dad's. A shiny pair of shoes indicated the wearer was a Mountie. Mum would haul me back to my seat by the scruff of my neck. My sister, Suzanne, always sat through the entire service quiet and pretty in her dress, while I crawled around in itchy wool pants on my hunt for shoes.

Being a Mountie, Dad was very fit. He worked out all the time, running three to five kilometres every day at noon. He trained with the RCMP's emergency response team, and spent hours boxing and performing police holds in recruit training. In the summer, we would race each other down the sidewalk in front of our house. He would never let me win, but every time I lost, I would want to race again and again until I was exhausted. Dad would give me a head start of twice his height, but it never made much of a difference.

He would often take me to watch drill training. In the cavern-ous drill hall, buffalo heads were mounted everywhere under crossed lances. I loved hearing the sergeant major bawl com-mands at the recruits. The trainees would stamp their feet, turn in unison and march in perfect order. They looked tall, brave and stoic. I was in awe of the discipline and hard work that went into it. As I proudly polished Dad's boots, I wondered if I would ever have the right stuff to serve the country one day.

We would move every few years when Dad got promoted. I was ten when we were posted to Dartmouth, Nova Scotia, and eleven when we transferred to Ottawa. It was in Ottawa that I got my first basketball hoop and ball, a major turning point in my life. This is where I realized that the harder I worked at home, the better I played in the game. Mum often came out and played with me. She would try to teach me the two-handed shot she had used in her high school basketball days in the fifties. Fortunately, my cousin Mickey, fifteen years my senior, lived nearby and would teach me how to shoot properly when she was gone. During pickup games with the neighbourhood kids, I perfected my jump shot. There was an oil spot about five metres from the left of the basket, and I made endless jump shots from there. At my high school games, I would try to get to that same position for a sure two points.

High school was where I really blossomed as an athlete, playing basketball, volleyball and track and field. I was one of the tallest in my grade, so I had an easy advantage in most sports. High school was also where I blossomed as a partier. Most Friday nights, we would get beer from the older kids, walk into the woods at the back of the school, sit on the case and drink it. Mum worked as a nurse's aid in a nursing home. After a bachelor's supper of minute steak and salad with Dad on nights she worked, I would go and pick her up. I hated the atmosphere in the nursing home. It reeked of urine and times gone by. I had trepidations about going in because I knew the place was going to be unpleasant. It smelled institutional—unwashed laundry, unwashed bodies, failed hope. Old people abandoned by their families and left to rot. The smell stayed in my nose the entire ride home. It was like being allergic to the smell of despair and abandonment.

I was being constantly volunteered to drive to basketball tournaments around the Ottawa Valley. We had a brown van that my buddy and I called the Propane-Powered Portable Passion Pit. It never actually saw any passion, but it fitted all my basketball teammates (who were in their prime for wanting passion, I suppose). We would drink pop and eat chips and boast how we would score at the game and hopefully with the girls. One year, I had to part ways with the van, thus depriving the team of both transportation and hope for passion. In that year, we went farther afield than Ottawa. Our team went all the way to Nova Scotia in what felt like a homecoming of sorts for me. Ecstatically happy to be back in the Nova Scotia rain and wind, I raced around like a madman while my teammates shivered inside.

By grade ten I knew I wanted to go to university. In my final year of high school, my parents and I would discuss my future at the supper table. After just a short stint at university Dad had joined the Mounties. Mum had gone straight to work in fashion at a department store (and she also modelled on TV). I don't think they regretted their own choices, but they knew university could impact my life in a profound way. Still, I really didn't know what I wanted to study. Like most RCMP brats, I toyed with the idea of joining the force, but ultimately I couldn't reconcile myself to the life of constant motion between postings I had experienced in my younger days. In grade twelve, I serendipitously came across a copy of Joan Didion's 1968 nonfiction masterpiece, *Slouching Towards Bethlehem*. Her rich, poignant essays, on topics from the hippies of Haight-Ashbury to morality in the modern world, allowed me to see writing and journalism as art forms.

At the University of King's College in Halifax, Nova Scotia, I took a first-year course in great books as part of the Foundation Year Programme (FYP). The course ranged from the marble debating halls of ancient Greece to the machine guns of First World War. The first book of the program was Homer's *Odyssey*, which I read in the summer prior to the start of the school year. The story of Odysseus, who made his way home after fighting in the Trojan War, spoke to me. I admired his

12

fortitude in conquering any obstacle that stood in his way. The course gave me a world context for the first time in my life, and it allowed me to grasp esoteric ideas. It lengthened the reach of my mind to encompass the concepts of the world's greatest writers and thinkers. The professors were passionate and fascinating, and many had studied at Oxford, including Dr. Robert Crouse, who was visibly moved when he lectured on Dante. Whenever he taught, the sunny lecture hall would be filled with former FYP students, eager to let themselves be captured by his eloquence again. He was mild-mannered and unassuming and entranced by literature. King's was modelled on the Oxford/Cambridge, or Oxbridge, concept. Each residence had a don who lived in the first-floor suite. The don of my residence, Radical Bay, was a flamboyant Anglican priest named Father Hankey. He would sashay around the college grounds in a suit and academic robes, holding forth in the faint English accent he had acquired at Oxford.

After spending the summer after FYP scooping ice cream in Halifax, I was thrilled to receive an acceptance letter from the King's journalism program. To its credit, the university was renowned for the journalists it produced. Our professors taught us to trust our instincts in conducting interviews, and to pay attention to the little details that would colour our writing and make our readers feel like they were there. I was given an assignment to watch an object in the harbour for twenty-four hours and then write about it. I chose a splintery, beat-up old wharf. I pitched my tent on the walkway above it and carefully arranged my Thermos of coffee and my chocolate bars, grabbed my notebook and started watching at half hour intervals. I saw the sun set and rise over the wharf. I listened to the waves jostle the chains. When morning finally came and people started to wander by my tent and cast curious glances, I decided it was time to go. Bone-weary and bleary-eyed, I rolled up my tent, packed up my full book of notes and trudged back to King's. That experience taught me to look at events from every angle because they change as your perspective changes.

At university I played varsity basketball and volleyball, but the first time I rowed, the other sports faded to oblivion. Before classes, at 5:30 a.m., our crew would gather in the administration building, yawning and with sleep in our eyes. We would run along the sidewalks and through a field where leaves were falling from the dew-covered trees. There was a loamy smell of wet earth all the way to the rowing club. We could feel the moisture of the air on our skin as we breathed in the cold sea air. Training began at 6 a.m., six days a week. We went out at dawn along the Northwest Arm, an inlet of the Atlantic Ocean. Sometimes our oars wouldn't touch the water at all as we rose on the crest of the breakers. The gurgle of bubbles down the wooden hull was a sign we were dipping our oars in perfect unison. This would elicit a sense of perfect rhythm all through my body that brought out goosebumps. We would warm up with twenty minutes of steady-state rowing at about half pressure and then take it up to just below full power for the next ten minutes. It was then that the burn started, as the lactic acid built up in my body. When the coxswain called for full power, I didn't think I could muster any more strength, but my body obeyed every time. With the first full power stroke, the boat surged ahead. The coach, riding alongside in an aluminum boat, would bark, "Long and strong." I kept this mantra running in my head for the entire practice. By the end, I was physically exhausted but mentally exhilarated. After training on the water, we would devour breakfast in the dining hall like starving dogs.

In a class on feature writing, our professor had us research story ideas and pitch them to the local paper. I had read that former slaves established a settlement in Halifax after the War of 1812. The thriving 150-year-old community of Africville was destroyed in the 1960s to make way for a bridge. But the culture itself couldn't be destroyed, and former Africvillians fiercely clung to their traditions. I admired their tenacity and wanted to chronicle the injustices done to them by city hall, which had sent garbage trucks to move them out. The headline of my feature piece, which was published in the *Chronicle Herald* newspaper, was taken from a quote by a prominent former resident and activist: "We Are Still Africvillians."

In my final year, fuelled by whiskey and cigars in the wee hours of the morning, I wrote a thesis called "Brothers in Arms: The Military and Media in Halifax." I was inspired by the naval tradition of King's and the East Coast fleet in the harbour. In one of my interviews, a retired navy captain told me that once a ship sailed over the horizon, only the families and the admirals paid any attention to it.

After my four years at King's, I was convinced that I had all the tools for a writing career and was missing only a foreign correspondent adventure, preferably in some far-flung corner of the globe. My friend Mike, also a recent King's graduate, was going to Japan to study martial arts, and I thought that would be a great place to get my career started. I felt excited to be going halfway around the world with no definite plans.

It took six months to get the working-holiday visa and passport. During that time, I read every book on Japan I could get my hands on. I bought a basic phrasebook to pick up a few words and key phrases. I didn't want to appear ignorant. I wanted to become fluent in the culture and language because I thought it would impress the Japanese people to see a foreigner working so hard to learn about their country. In between studying about the country, its culture and its language, I donned a leather bowtie and white shirt for work as a busboy in a Greek restaurant. Before long, the white shirt became tainted with the stains of half-eaten Greek food. The six months flew by, but at last I was at the airport. I took most of my clothes because I knew it would be hard to find anything to fit my 6'4" frame in Japan. One-way ticket in hand, I left the comfort and stability of Canada behind me as I passed through security.

All through the flight, my mind churned. I wondered if I had just made the biggest mistake of my life. Most of my friends had jobs with small community newspapers and were building their journalistic careers the traditional way. I wondered if I would skulk home with my head hung low after crashing into a brick wall of totally alien culture and language. I didn't sleep at all on the flight. I tried to practise my rudimentary Japanese with the flight attendants, but they just smiled and nodded at me. Hours later, the plane landed at Narita airport, outside of Tokyo. I was to meet Mike at an inn in the northeast part of the city. Two bus rides later, I got off in front of the only English sign for miles around. After locating the inn, I checked in and was taken to the small room Mike and I would be temporarily sharing. Mike had arrived in Japan only the day before. That night, we went out to a pub to celebrate our arrival. We quickly learned that the Japanese word for two beers was *nihon*. The next morning, we went for our first breakfast: a small piece of fish, a bowl of rice and a bowl of brown liquid called miso soup. We drank litres of water because of the salt in the breakfast and too many *nihons* the previous night. After breakfast, we strolled around the neighbourhood and grabbed the only English newspapers we could find. A few days later, Mike would be heading north to pursue his martial arts training and I would be left on my own in Tokyo, a city of thirteen million people.

It was inevitable that my first job would be as an English teacher. When I went to meet my potential employer, a short Japanese man approached me, gave a slight bow and introduced himself: "Hello Greene-san, I am Kawakami." We shook hands and he gave me his business card. The cards determine at a quick glance who is senior, and consequently, the deference to be shown by the length and depth of the bow of the junior.

He asked me to start a week later. My job was to teach mid-level English by repetition to adults at the company. I would read sentences over and over and have the students follow along. At the end of the day, I was sick of speaking English and wanted to think in French or any other language. I dreaded the thought of the ninety-minute ritual of swaying in a packed train carriage back to my apartment. My only consolations were the cleanliness of the Japanese and the fact that I was above the average armpit level. In the heat of the Japanese summer, my suit became rather pungent. When I got home, I tore it off and hung it outside to dry out and freshen up for the following day. This system worked well until I went out one morning to get my fresh suit and found only the hanger. For days after, I watched for a much smaller facsimile of my suit walking around the neighbourhood.

After only a few months of teaching English, I was bored and frustrated. Luckily, I came across an advertisement offering a position with one of the English daily newspapers. I was ecstatic when I got the job, which was to edit articles that had been translated from the larger parent newspaper. This was my first real break into a newsroom. I always kept an eye out for feature articles I could write. Somehow I heard about a homeless quarter in Tokyo called Sanya. I couldn't believe that a prosperous nation like Japan could have homeless people. What intrigued me most was that all the men were from one generation: those who had worked preparing Tokyo for the 1964 Olympics. My article started with "If the wind is right—or wrong, as the case may be—you can smell Sanya long before you see it. The only homeless quarter in Tokyo emits a pong of stinky feet, wet dog and asphalt which assails the senses as you emerge from the station." This was my first published piece in Japan. The editor sent me a rare memo of congratulations. Unbelievably, I was the first foreign journalist to write about the homeless. I felt my story didn't do justice to the issue, however, or to the men themselves. I knew that I had only scratched the surface, and that a first-hand account was necessary.

During my time in Japan, I joined a rugby team and met a bunch of Australian guys. One day they invited me to go on a dive trip to the Philippines, but they were leaving in two weeks, which didn't allow me enough time to get a visa. I had the time off work and didn't want to waste it, so I booked passage on a freighter bound south for Okinawa, the birthplace of karate. The freighter was a cheaper and more adventurous way of travelling than flying. The cabins were spartan and the food terrible, but I loved to stand at the rail and breathe in the salt air. The trip took roughly three days, and I saw no land on the way down. It felt like I had dropped off the face of the earth. I was the only English-speaking passenger on board, so I spent the majority of the time reading and sleeping. I was happy to finally see Okinawa, which had been the scene of fierce battles during the Second World War; the scars were still visible but healing slowly. The agony of the islanders was obvious in some of the sights, such as one sandstone room with shrapnel pockmarks on the wall. Japanese propaganda had depicted the Americans as flesh-eaters, so when they began battling for the island, one desperate mother gathered her children around her and pulled the pin on a hand grenade, splattering their bodies all over the wall. American soldiers made the grisly discovery after defeating the Japanese.

I was staying in a hostel on the harbour and would often stroll through pineapple and mango plantations that had been rebuilt after the island was devastated. There were remains of machine-gun pillboxes and concrete bunkers strewn the length and breadth of the island. The Americans had landed in the south and fought their way north, taking huge casualties. It felt odd to be on the northern tip of the island, where the Japanese had made their last stand with their backs literally to the sea.

All too soon, my seven days of landlubbing were over. On the slow boat back to Tokyo, I thought about the heavy American military presence on Japan and what it must mean to be a modern-day soldier training day in and day out for a conflict you hope never comes. I thought about the island's legacy of death and destruction, not really knowing why I had gone there. As waves lapped the ship, I thought about the brutal history of a desperate war.

When I returned to Tokyo, I decided to start freelancing. I had heard of a famous Canadian writer and naturalist named C.W. Nicol who lived up north in Nagano Prefecture. I had heard he had a direct manner that did not fit in Japan, where direct talk was considered rude or tactless. His nickname was Aka Oni, or Red Devil, because of the scorn and anger he expressed for the government officials who were allowing once-pristine forests and waterways to be destroyed. He fought back by preserving forty-five hectares of land around his house. He had made several television documentaries on topics ranging from the birds of Okinawa to the breeding practices of seals in the High Arctic. He spent much of his time criss-crossing Japan by train and giving impassioned speeches to schools in fluent Japanese about the rich natural history of the country. He was even a member of a council advising the prime minister on the environment.

I decided to write a profile on Nicol. I thought he might like the idea of a Canadian writer profiling him for a Canadian magazine in Japan, so I hopped on a train for the three-hour ride north. Once there, I was struck by the ordinariness of his house, until I noticed how it blended in perfectly with the landscape. A cold rushing river flowed on the other side of the road in front of his modest two-story home. Unlike countless other rivers in

Japan, this one had water flowing over rocks instead of smooth concrete. On his front porch, the writer met me with congenial eyes and a firm handshake. I was immediately put at ease when he said to call him Nic.

We sat in his kitchen and talked for hours over tea. He spoke each word thoughtfully in an accent that I later learned was Welsh. He had been in Japan for approximately twenty years. Nic had been an infant in Wales when his father was captured by the Japanese in Singapore and never heard from again. At fourteen, he began studying judo. At seventeen, he signed up for an expedition to the Canadian Arctic. He forged his stepfather's signature, got a UK passport and left his parents a note saying that he was going camping. He was gone for eight months. While in Canada, he got a job with the Canadian Fisheries Research Board, observing Japanese and Norwegian whalers. At the age of twenty-two, he finally made his way to Japan, where he studied karate and went on to earn his fifth-degree black belt.

I told Nic about the article I had written on Sanya and asked his advice on expanding it into a book. His head came up sharply. I remember the urgency in his voice as he said, "Young man, listen for the heartbeat of the story, dig around, then pour your soul into it and you WILL have a book." What struck me most about Nic during our afternoon together was his soft-spoken passion for nature and writing. From then on, I became his protégé and good friend. On the train ride home, I realized that I had just met the man who would shape me as a writer and passionate social observer.

After about a year at the paper, I became restless and decided to move on. I got a series of menial, low-paying writing and editing jobs. They mostly involved sorting out tangled English. My favourite assignment was a package of coffee grounds that was called *Ease Your Bosoms*. The idea was roughly "Drink this coffee and relax." I hit pay dirt one day when I was hired by the Tokyo office of the Visa credit card company as a writer and editor. The job gave a significant boost to my income and allowed me to start saving. My goal was to make enough money to leave my job and write a book about the homeless men of Sanya. I had learned from Nic that in order to do justice to the story, I had to live among them.

While transferring trains in Yokohama station one day, I saw a young guy with a guitar case covered in Canadian flags. I wandered over and introduced myself. Dave was from Calgary and lived with an American naval officer in the resort town of Hayama, in a house on the beach. Dave and I exchanged phone numbers.

He called a week later and invited me to a party. His place turned out to be a ramshackle brown house across from a temple with beaches on both sides. The party was in full swing when I got there. It was an annual event called Carpfest, named after a bottom-dwelling, overgrown goldfish on steroids. Every year a carp was fish-napped and given a home in the bathtub, where it swam around and drank beer. Eventually I met Dave's roommate, Lieutenant Ed Murdock, whose nickname was Mud. Mud and I got along like a house on fire. He was laid-back, fun-loving and comical to the extreme. I think we got along so well because our personalities and outlook were similar. His Southern drawl would come back heavy whenever he told a story or a joke, which was often. His stories of foreign ports and storms at sea were riveting. Little did I know that I would write my first book on his second-floor balcony overlooking the temple.

The highlight of my second Carpfest was a kiss from Mud. He was from Georgia, and that year the Atlanta Braves were playing the Toronto Blue Jays in the World Series. Obviously a bet was in order between the Canuck and the Yank, and we decided that the loser would have to kiss the winner's ass. When the Blue Jays won, Mud stayed true to his word and puckered up in front of a large, delirious crowd in his living room. Despite the hijinks of Mud's friends, I was impressed with their dedication to the navy and how hard they had trained.

Mud had somehow befriended a Nepalese bartender nick-named Beeno. One summer, Beeno acquired a coveted permit to run a bar on Morito beach, two beaches down from Mud's house. We built the bar out of thick bamboo poles with a sheet-metal roof covered in palm leaves. It was at the back of the beach on a slight slope. There were no walls, only a roof with a bar in the corner. The bar's name was Sloppy Joe's. Mud got plastic tables and chairs from his navy base, and Sloppy Joe's was in business. We blasted music all day and through the night. Our regular customers were mostly foreigners who lived nearby. At night, the waves glowed phosphorescent green. We would stand in the surf up to our calves, drinking beer and howling at a bright moon. When typhoon season came mid-summer, we would body-surf the mighty waves. Mud's description: being tossed end over end and winding up on the beach with a pound of sand jammed into your rectum.

After washing the weekend sand off, I reluctantly knotted a tie around my neck and took the train back into Tokyo for work. I would often blow off steam and work-related frustration with my good friend Peter Fuchs. Peter shared my passion for tell-ing the story of the homeless men. "Pierre," as I affectionately called him, was a journalist, an entrepreneur, a fiercely passion-ate and intelligent writer, and the editor of a Tokyo magazine for which I freelanced. We would often get together to drink beer and smoke cigarettes at a filthy, stinky pub under the rail-road tracks that we called the Rat. In the summer, we would sit outside at "tables" consisting of scrap pieces of wood on top of two beer crates, with the trains rumbling above us and the ground shaking below us. We would talk passionately about the stories of the day, writing, philosophy and rowing. Peter had rowed competitively in university. We had both become addicted to the early morning slogging on the water in the fresh air—and the pain that came with it. We would flex our writing muscles at each other by email.

my brother Pierre,

we make the hard call on each other and on things and on situations when it is warranted. we stick in. we don't really know why we get so goddamn stuck in but we do. we grunt thru. we think too much, we get even less credit for thinking hard, for being a bit clever . . . then the peer landscape gets barren before we even realize it.

we wait for coxie to call for a hard 10, as many hard 10s as it takes. eeeeeeeyyyyyyyaaaaaaaaahhhh. and we wait for the lactic acid to course through.

the bad 72 hours is just bad. full stop.

we band together sometimes when we don't even know why. we suck it up for reasons we don't even know about and can barely articulate.

then we walk down to the beach.

and then we just shut the hell up and go surfing in mid-July. we walk to the beer machine ruminating on how the beautiful but eternal mother ocean took us for a ride, how she toyed with us on our fibreglass shields, how she let us ride until she tired of us and then effortlessly gathered us in and said "puny rider, you ride my moon-ruled ripples because I deign to not kill you today."

Sanya was not on the social or cultural radar of the Japanese mainstream. Tokyo was settled in the 1600s like a nautilus shell around the shogun's castle at the centre of the city. The most powerful and rich lived close to the castle. The lesser chiefs had to live farther out. The area where Sanya is today was on the extreme outer edge of the shell. In feudal times, the area was an execution ground. It was basically a swamp with a bridge called Namidabashi, or Bridge of Tears. The condemned were led over the bridge to be executed.

I had arranged to stay in Sanya with Charlie McJilton, whom I had heard about through a professor at Sophia University, where I did most of my research on the homeless. Charlie knew the local chapter of Missionaries of Charity, the order founded by Mother Teresa of Calcutta. The missionary brothers were all from India. I found it ironic that missionaries from one of the poorest countries in the world had come to one of the richest countries to tend to the outcasts.

Because the homeless men didn't follow the tightly structured societal patterns laid out in Japan, they were quite literally written off. Every family in every village is registered by name with the local government. Most of the men in Sanya were the sons of farmers and had been expected to grow rice, as their fathers and grandfathers had done before them. The men were attracted to Tokyo because of the prospect of easy money and street life. It was rumoured there was big money to be made building infrastructure for the 1964 Summer Olympics. When the men left their villages, their names were literally erased from these lists and they were shunned.

I stayed in Sanya for three months. I would often join Charlie and the missionaries on their nightly "rice patrol," handing out rice balls and blankets to the men on the streets. The men would burn garbage to stay warm, so there was always a pall of smoke hanging over the night. I was awakened most mornings at 6 o'clock. by the sound of truck doors slamming as job brokers gathered the men for another day of labour. The ten thousand or so homeless day labourers of Sanya were referred to by the Japanese, with a mixture of awe and distaste, as *furosha*. They were the invisible subjects of the richest empire on earth. The men did dangerous jobs that no one else wanted. They earned roughly the daily equivalent of food and alcohol for a ten-hour shift, never enough to cross back over the bridge. They would spend their day's wages by nightfall. The booze would anesthetize them for another night on the streets and help them forget one more time the desperate lives they were leading.

One night, I put on all the sweaters I owned, got some quilts and set out to sleep on the streets. I settled in the doorway of a ceramics shop. Not far away, I saw two men sitting around a fire of garbage. The smoke wreathed their faces and made them look like vengeful Hindu gods. No sooner had I settled in when a light rain started to fall, soaking my quilts and hair. After about an hour of staring up at the sky, I fell asleep. At about 5 a.m. I awoke, stiff and so cold I felt like I was smuggling ice cubes in my testicles. The men I had seen the previous night were heading toward the main street, where job brokers were filling up their trucks. The brokers took a cut of the homeless men's pay for the day. The job brokers were members of the Japanese mafia, *yakuza*.

My mission in Sanya was to discover if any of the men had gone back to their former lives. I thought there could be an underground railway of sorts, like the one that had spirited the slaves out of the American South. What I found instead was a major intersection whose name means "bridge of tears." This used to be a bridge over a swamp where, four hundred years ago, prisoners said their final farewells en route to the execution grounds. Those who crossed the bridge had their lives ripped from them, their bodies hurled away with contempt. Those who crossed the bridge never returned. The bridge is still there and it still leads to doom, but it is a drawn-out, almost casual doom. Instead of a swift executioner's blade, death comes gradually from alcoholism, tuberculosis, exposure, neglect and loneliness. I made a stunning discovery. I asked if anybody who had lived in Sanya for more than a few months had ever made his way back home. To my astonishment, I found that the answer was no.

I knew I needed to get far away from the squalor of Sanya to pour my heart and soul into writing the story. I went to live with Mud in Hayama, where I wrote most mornings on his second-floor balcony. I would write the whole morning and then ride my bike to the beach bar to unwind. The summer passed quickly and my manuscript got longer.

When I felt the manuscript was complete, I took it to Nic's house and waited. After about three hours, he gave it back. He was beaming. He said it was a terrible story to be told, but he loved my writing. He asked if he could submit it for an esteemed book competition for foreigners writing about Japan. I agreed, and my book was short-listed. I was not quite thirty-three and my first book-length writing effort had been recognized.

By the end of the summer, my money had run out and I was back to scouring the Monday classified ads. I missed Canada very much and knew I wanted to return, but I didn't know what I wanted to do. As I looked back on my seven years in Japan, I realized that I had not served anybody but myself. I had reached my goals of immersing myself in a foreign culture and language. I'd made many good friends and written many articles and my first book. I'd pursued my passion for rowing, rugby and surfing. My life was full, but something was missing. I wanted to give back to my home and native land. I realized there was a common military thread through my life, starting with my years at university, which had been a naval officer–training base during the Second World War. I also reaffirmed my desire to turn the spotlight on the dispossessed, ignored and persecuted of the world through my writing. I knew that in order to get a good grasp on the issues, I would have to further my studies.

I completed two vastly different applications—one with the Canadian Forces recruiting centre and the other with Scotland's

University of Edinburgh for a master's degree. I also applied to Oxford University, only because of its prestigious boat race on the Thames, which had been the benchmark for me when I rowed in university. I would let fate decide my course and, ultimately, my destiny. A few weeks later I received two letters, literally one day apart. The first postmark was from Scotland, the second from Canada. I had been accepted by both. I chose the Canadian Forces.

My friend Mark Darbyshire asked why I decided to return to Canada and join the military. It was a fine summer day in 1995, and we were sitting in the backyard of his house in Kamakura, talking and watching his daughter, Adina, trying to catch butterflies in the garden. He had a point. Why should I leave? After all, I had launched a budding writing career, learned a language and was looking at a bright future. But after a massive sayonara party involving a lot of friends, many drinks and lip-syncing to ABBA, I knew I was ready to go home.

Because I wanted to continue the tradition of service to my country begun by my grandfather in the First World War. Because I wanted to help put an end to psychotic tyrants who keep the citizens of their torture states under their thumb and deny them rule of law and basic human rights. Because I wanted to push my extremes, both mentally and physically. Because I wanted to lead the best troops in the world, and I knew I had to do it while I was still relatively young.

I felt a deep sense of satisfaction on the flight back. I had met my goals and was ready to pursue the next challenges in my life. After completing my *Bridge of Tears* manuscript, I felt my journalistic hunger was sated for the time being.

CHAPTER 2:
THE PLEDGE

When I arrived home in Halifax, I met with a recruiting officer who had reviewed my application and said he could
swear me in as a direct entry officer with a minimum of fuss.
He advised me to get very fit. That afternoon I began a regimen
of running, push-ups, sit-ups and chin-ups, starting with an ex-
hausting thirty-minute uphill run to cure my jet lag. I was determined not to fail. I knew I would be a few years older than most
of the others, but I would make it. My parents were proud,
but my friends were flabbergasted. They had assumed I would
come home and leverage my experiences abroad to advance my
career, not "throw it all away" in the armed forces.

My heart pounded when I was sworn in a few weeks later.
I knew that once I put my hand on the Bible and pledged my
allegiance to her Majesty the Queen, there would be no turning

back. I swore that I would protect Canada at all costs. With that, I was officially a member of the regular force navy. I had no second thoughts or regrets about putting my journalism career on hold to embark on an unknown journey. I just knew that I would give my life for my country. A few days later, I received a plane ticket and orders to report for basic training in St. Jean, Quebec, in the middle of December.

After landing in Montreal three months later, I was shown to a bus with twenty other recruits all dressed in suits for the hour-long ride to the base. Once there, we pulled up beside a massive brick building with multiple wings. Immediately a man in combats burst in the door of the bus and ordered us to grab our luggage, get outside and give him twenty push-ups. I could see my tie lying on the top of the snow and I felt the snow scratching my hands as I broke through its crust while hammering out twenty of my best. I was glad I had done literally hundreds of push-ups on my own in preparation for this moment. Like a shark smelling blood, the sergeant was on the unlucky few who faltered. It was a chilling precursor to the next six months of our lives.

We were formed into ranks and marched into the building, where we met our full training cadre. We were informed that we were the nucleus of Two Platoon. Our platoon commander was an air force officer who didn't brook any bullshit. Our drill instructor was a tough-as-nails infantry sergeant. The sergeant ordered us to grab our bags and run up the six flights of stairs to our floor. By the time we reached it, we were sweaty and panting in our suits. The sergeant ran up behind us like a dog herding sheep. He barked out our room assignments and told us to unpack only our toiletries. We wouldn't be needing our civilian clothing for a long time.

My room was small and austere, with plain white walls and a tile floor. The only furniture was a desk and a black cast-iron single bed with a pillow and an itchy wool blanket with a stripe showing where your feet went. Across the room stood a large closet with a tangle of wire hangers under a shelf. I heard a startling yell come echoing down the hallway, demanding that we muster outside our rooms. As I stood loosely at attention outside my doorway, I got my first good look at my fellow masochists.

We were banned from taking the elevators for the duration of our basic training. We were issued three combat uniforms, a pair of boots and a pair of shoes in two large green duffle bags. We were told we would be inspected the next morning. The instructors showed us, with great precision, how our toiletries and uniforms should be laid out and our beds made. We were to fold our pillows into a perfect cube and fold the white sheet overtop of the grey blanket exactly twelve inches square. My white naval shirts had to be ironed with creases down the back and arms and hung exactly two inches apart. We had been issued ankle-high boots called barrack boots and shoes for everyday wear. Both were to be polished to a high gleam. (We never wore the barrack boots—they were meant to hone our polishing skills and suck up precious minutes in our inspection preparation.) The boots and shoes had to be placed just so on the blanket. We were then herded into the bathroom and shown how it should be kept to a high standard of cleanliness, which included fishing pubic hairs out of the urinals. Inspection was at 6 a.m. sharp. To maximize my sleep time, I would iron the sheet on the bed, lay the carefully folded pillow on the floor on one of my dirty T-shirts and then sleep on top of the bed in my T-shirt and underwear.

It wasn't all housekeeping, though. After inspection we would go for a three-kilometre run and then tackle the green monster, a huge wall marking the beginning of the obstacle course. Someone, usually me, would scramble up the wall and lie on top to help the rest of the platoon over one by one. The next obstacle was swinging hand over hand on the monkey bars. We would finish with a sprint to the end of the obstacle course. All this fresh air and effort left us exhausted. We wolfed down our breakfast in the allotted fifteen minutes.

Every day, the drill hall rang with the sound of our stamping feet. We were taught how to march in formation, come to attention and salute smartly. When outside, we had to run or march everywhere. We were tested on our decision-making and leadership abilities. The instructors would set up a series of stands posing different problems. One of my "favourite" tasks was setting up a tent under a tight time restriction. The objective wasn't only to set up the tent properly but also to light a stove inside it. If we went over our time limit, the instructors would tell us to tear down the tent, muscle it a few hundred yards away and then set it up again. After six months of this regimen, we started drill practice for basic training graduation.

My first posting was to Esquimalt on the West Coast. When I first saw Canada's West Coast fleet in the harbour, I knew I had made the right decision in not choosing academia. I was a navy acting sub-lieutenant, which is basically the lowest of the low for officers. I was indoctrinated into the mysteries of navigation, ship steering and damage control. As part of our navigation training, we sailed up the coast of Vancouver Island in fifty-foot yard maintenance ships called "yags." Standing on the deck, I took in great lungfuls of the salty air. I understood how the siren call of the sea had beckoned boys and men for centuries. Looking west, as my eyes travelled over the green and brown terrain of the land, I could imagine a retreating glacier carving a furrow that would become a strait deep into the frozen ground. I was on duty on the homeward leg of a trip that involved a port visit in Vancouver. As I was fixing our position at night I could see lights in the near distance, both at ocean level and up higher, as if on a mountain. One of my shipmates told me that the lower ones were the city lights and the higher ones ski hills. I made a mental note to see about living in this incredible city one day.

My first operational posting was to the tall ship HMCS *Oriole,* a hundred-foot, double-masted ketch and the oldest ship in the navy. My first deployment would take me across the Pacific Ocean to Australia over a period of three months. In the weeks leading up to the sailing date, I pondered our route: Victoria to San Francisco, Pearl Harbor, Palmyra Atoll, Western Samoa, Fiji and finally to Sydney. I got my first sight of *Oriole* on the day of our deployment. My berth was a sleeping bag on a small plastic mattress that rested on a rack chained to the side of the ship—basically a steel slab about the size of an autopsy table. We were organized into watches, six hours on, six hours off. As we motored slowly away from Vancouver Island and into the Juan de Fuca Strait, we met the full strength of the ocean for the first time. I was on deck with my legs braced against the roll of the ship as the bow leaped up and the stern plunged down on the swells. I was awestruck by the almost casual might of the blue ocean.

After making port in San Francisco and Pearl Harbor, we sailed for almost two thousand kilometres southeast to what was to be the most adventurous port of call of the journey. Palmyra Atoll is just a speck in the ocean between Hawaii and Western Samoa with, at that time, a population of one: a manic Frenchman named Roger Lextrait. Roger had been an executive chef for Sheraton hotels until the urge to wander took him over completely and brought him to Palmyra. The tiny horseshoe-shaped atoll is the rim of a volcano that nosed out of the water a zillion years ago and started adorning itself with coral to become thirty small islets. The island got its name in the early 1800s, when the good ship *Palmyra* sought shelter there from a storm. There are still unexploded bombs and mines from when the U.S. Navy occupied the island during the Second World War. We were the first Canadian sailors ever to set foot on Palmyra.

A pod of five dolphins gave us our welcome, cavorting grey

and swift down our port side. To starboard, the rusting hulk of a Second World War landing craft arched its broken back on a long fold of coral. As we entered the lagoon, we sensed a lightening as the dark blue sea gave way abruptly to frothy aquamarine shallows. A small blue-and-white sailboat with a plastic awning shading the deck was muzzled to shore by long mooring lines. Crowding the shores were other remnants of the U.S. Navy's wartime occupation: hundreds of rusty concrete bunkers and pyramid-shaped ammo dumps scattered like disused war game toys of the gods. The island is rife with palm trees. They thrust out of the thin soil at the very edge of the water and drape loopy, bushy fronds on the air.

When we dropped our hook into what we later learned was the West Lagoon, we heard the motor of an inflatable boat, and the island caretaker, Roger, exploded into our midst, talking a mile a minute—as you might expect from the lone occupant of a tiny island in the middle of the Pacific. His appearance was also just what I would expect: long brown ponytail under a battered Jimmy Buffett straw hat, faded muscle shirt, crab-eaten shorts, mismatched rubber sandals and a perfect tan on a fit, medium build. In a thick Parisian accent, Roger bid, "Welcome to Palme-ra, guys. Welcome to paradise."

The sight of Roger with his dreadlocks and crushed straw hat was irresistible to me. As soon as we secured ship and I got permission to leave, I was over the side, swimming for the beach. I found Roger on the other side of a small aluminum building, looking through his flip-flop collection. When I asked him where he had got them, he invited me for a walk to the windward side of the island. We came to a beach that looked like a lost-and-found bin for the whole ocean. Plastic bottles, flip-flops, buoys and various odds and sods littered the sand. He explained that the atoll is at the point where southern and northern currents meet, and that all the boat detritus winds up on this beach. He then showed me where his resupply came in every month: the original Second World War–era airstrip. Roger advised me not to tiptoe around the island too much because there were things that could "go boom." On the way back to the ramp, he pointed out a massive column of gooney birds spiralling over an inner lagoon like a tight tornado of muscular sheets of paper. It was one of the most impressive natural sights I had ever seen. Roger told me he slept on his yacht floating at anchor in the lagoon and said, "I don't wanna be crab shit, so I sleep on my boat." He spoke of the thousands of coconut crabs that hide during the day and come out at night to feed.

After two days on Palmyra, we bade farewell to Roger, pulled up our anchor and continued south to Western Samoa, Fiji and New Caledonia. Canadian sailors have an affectionate nickname for the ocean, "the oggie." The only time I saw the oggie turn violent was on that trip between Western Samoa and Fiji, when I saw what appeared to be a white curtain on the water. The skipper told us it was a white squall. We had heard that white squalls could swallow up ships and sailors. The skipper ordered a course correction to give the white squall a wide berth. We could hear the wind singing in our rigging as we sailed by.

Finally the Sydney harbour headlands loomed over our bow. We secured ship and *Oriole* was still at last. Another crew would take the ship home, so I said a final goodbye to her. My first Vietnamese Canadian friend, Vu Tran, whom I had met in basic training, had also made the journey across the Pacific on *Oriole*. Back in Victoria, Vu had taken me to Vietnamese noodle shops, where he introduced me to the world of Pho (pronounced *faa*), a noodle soup to which I soon became addicted. We began a tradition of eating Pho in every port we visited. Vu and I spent many a night watch lying on the sail bags midships, watching the stars and telling stories. Vu spoke of how his father had been interned on a North Vietnamese prison farm. He described how his family had escaped Vietnam after the war on a rickety fishing boat. I asked Vu how his parents felt about him making a career in the navy. He said they were both appalled and proud. Appalled because crossing the ocean had been such a desperate ordeal for them and proud because their boy had joined the ranks of the Canadian elite. I was sure that by contrast, my stories, which were somewhat interesting to others, seemed downright boring to Vu.

Looking back on the voyage of the *Oriole*, I am struck by the feelings I didn't have. I never felt lonely or insignificant, even though I was a puny creature on a puny craft on the massive oggie. I never felt fear, even when sliding over the first giant swells or being touched by the wild wind of the white squall. As I flew home to Victoria at hundreds of knots high above the track of the *Oriole*, pride and exhaustion washed over me, but not the same kind I had felt on graduating from basic training. These were more seasoned, more mature emotions. I had succumbed to the romance and adventure of the sea, but I knew the voyage of the *Oriole* had not satisfied my craving to serve Canada. I needed a more human mission where I could actually interact with the people I was defending.

About a month after returning from Australia, I was in Vancouver at the end of a navigation cruise up the coast. While off duty, I found an advertisement for a reporting job with the Bloomberg News wire service agency. I set up a meeting with the bureau chief at a restaurant on the water not far from our ship. A friend ferried me over to the restaurant on the ship's Zodiac. I was in my navy combats, which consisted of a blue shirt with blue trousers and leather sea boots. Not the ideal outfit for an important interview, but it was the best I had. My CV also wasn't ideal, with all my journalism experience ending abruptly when I went off to basic training. But Tim Moore and

I hit it off instantly over a couple of beers. Despite my unorthodox method of travel and my salt-streaked appearance, I was invited back a few weeks later to take a writing test. I nailed it and was offered a job. After I was released from the navy, I impulsively packed up and moved to Vancouver. My life thus far had been not so much about careful deliberation and planning but about acting on instinct.

The Bloomberg position got me back into the world of writing, but I found business journalism staid and impersonal. One day at work, I felt a jolt when I read the headline "Burmese Pro-Democracy Leader Detained Under House Arrest." As I read further, I learned that Aung San Suu Kyi had been elected president of Burma in a landslide, but the military junta disregarded the will of the people and placed Suu Kyi, now a Nobel Peace Prize laureate, under house arrest. It incensed me that a bunch of murderous thugs had seized control of a country and arbitrarily disregarded the rule of law. This was my first taste of indignation toward regimes that denied democracy to their people. But it wouldn't be the last. I decided that I had to go to Burma and write about this first-hand. I booked vacation time and a flight to Chiang Mai, the main Thai city closest to Burma.

In Thailand, I stayed in a cheap hotel with concrete walls that sweated so much they appeared to be weeping. During the day, I walked around and asked people about Burma. I met two young men, Dack and Theo, who were part of a group of students that had risen up in arms against the regime. I listened to their stories of humping ammunition and ancient hand-me-down weapons through the jungle and battling the modern weapons of the Burmese army.

Dack and Theo talked about the constant shortage of food. They told me a story about how they once had to abandon a position in a hurry. When they came back they found maggots in their rice, but they were so hungry they ate it anyway, maggots and all. Many of them got sick and had to be carried out. During the retreat, Theo's foot and calf were shredded when he stepped on a land mine. Fortunately, there was a medical student among them who stopped the worst of the bleeding. They carried Theo to a nearby Doctors Without Borders camp. The doctors wanted to cut off his foot, but he felt he had to fight on and asked them to fix it up the best they could. The injury left him with a permanent disability, but despite this, he kept soldiering. Dack told me about the Karen, an ethnic Burmese people who sought independence and were persecuted by the authorities. As a result, they armed themselves and furtively took the warpath against the army. They were ruthlessly crushed. No prisoners were taken when the Burmese army savaged the Karen people. The refugees from the slaughter fled into Thailand and were rounded up into internment camps.

My student contacts had told me about a refugee camp for Burmese outside of Chiang Mai. I talked my way into the camp using a patois of Japanese and English. After thirty minutes of talking, the gate was opened for me. Word spread quickly that there was a foreigner in the village. Children swarmed me as I was shown into the home of the headman. He asked me my name in English. I found out that he had studied English at a college in Bangkok and practised it using a well-worn copy of Plato's *Republic*. I could tell that the book was his prized possession. We shared tea and discussed literature. Our worlds could not have been further apart, but we found common ground talking about freedom and peace. The man asked me to sign his book, which I did. He said, "Friends forever, Canada." After a couple of hours, I sensed it was time to leave. I was escorted to the front gates by some of my new friends. I thought this was a polite gesture, but I also suspected it was dangerous for the headman to be seen speaking to a foreigner. I think the refugees wanted to make sure I left before nightfall.

I returned to my hotel, collected my things and started the trip back to Vancouver. As I gathered my belongings, I was assailed by two emotions I had rarely felt: rage at the callous disregard for human dignity by the Burmese army, and impotence. All I could offer the student fighters, the Karen and the Burmese who were suffering under the thumb of the army was a couple of newspaper column inches that would be largely ignored by an apathetic Western world.

I have always wondered, had I been of the generation that fought in the Second World War, if I would have stepped up and gone overseas. I knew Canada's long democratic history probably wouldn't be threatened in my lifetime, but in countries like Burma, democracy would always be under fire. When I saw how the democratic freedoms paid for in Canadian blood were being taken for granted, I thought of the freedom fighters I had met doing battle and dying in the jungle. When I got home to Vancouver, I decided to join a reserve infantry unit to further my military career. This part-time soldiering would allow me to continue with my journalism while I trained on weekends in leadership and infantry tactics. Because of my Scottish heritage and the fact that the armoury was next to a brewery, it was natural that I would join the Seaforth Highlanders of Canada. I was taught the mysteries of the Highlander uniform one night at the home of a fellow officer, an authentic Scotsman named John Milne. When John saw me in the kilt, he said in a thick Scottish brogue, "You've nowt got your kaks on, do you?" I guessed that *kaks* meant underwear, so I nodded in affirmation. John retorted, "Well, get them off, then. You're regimental now!" Strolling home later in the cool evening air, I felt oddly vulnerable, yet clean and free.

CHAPTER 3:
A STATE OF GRACE

As I adjusted to being back in Canada, I could feel my social consciousness growing. One day I came across a story of the mystery of the missing prostitutes of the Downtown Eastside of Vancouver. Their stroll was called Low Track. It was the last refuge of drug-addicted prostitutes who sold their bodies for a fix. High Track, by comparison, was a street with prostitutes of the "pretty woman" calibre, all with pimps. The women of the Downtown Eastside had a different kind of beauty. Ravaged outside, they had gone deep inside themselves to claim the last vestiges of their pride and dreams. This was all that kept them sane in the hardscrabble life they led. The women of Low Track were often beaten by johns who picked them up for just that purpose. These beatings were called "bad dates." I wrote an article on these tragedies for a news agency, but I couldn't get the saga off my mind. It was like a vision that stayed with me long after I had seen it. I wanted to bring Low Track out of the shadows by writing a book about it.

Every day after work, I walked to the Downtown Eastside to interview these sad, shy women. I would buy them a cup of coffee and we would talk. When I asked the women on the streets what they thought had happened to the missing women, their eyes would dart around nervously. They all had different theories, some of which were too far-fetched to be believable. Perhaps naively, I hoped the missing women had skipped the streets and gone home, because there was no trace of the bodies. Every day when I was done with interviews, I walked back across the bridge to my flat and wrote furiously until I had emptied. I poured everything I had into the book because I felt these broken women needed a voice. I felt numb when I typed the last word, but I couldn't send the manuscript off without reading it through. I biked to a nearby beach, let the ocean breeze wash over me and hefted my words. I sent it off to the publisher the next day, June 15, 2001.

The following evening, my friends and I marked the occasion by going out for drinks after work at a downtown pub. A beautiful blonde with a bubbly laugh who looked to be in her late twenties was a few tables away doing the same thing with her friends. My friends and I were trying to find a way to engage the women in conversation when I noticed that her sweater had fallen on the floor. Gallantly, I walked over, picked it up and asked if it was hers. When she turned around, I was struck by her beautiful brown eyes and her smile as she said, "Yes, thank you." Seizing my opportunity, I said the sweater was actually mine and jokingly put it on. Of course, it only came up to my elbows. To my utter relief, a small smile played across her lips, so I squatted down and introduced myself. I soon got her laughing. In the short time we spoke, I knew I needed to see her again. She and her friends were going to a nearby nightclub for a farewell party for a colleague. I made a command decision and changed our plans so I could keep in contact with her.

When we got to the club, it was so crowded that it took me a while to pick her out of the crowd. I finally spotted her and was about to go talk to her when I realized that I had forgotten her name. I asked my buddy to introduce himself and get her name for me. He did and quickly whispered "Debbie" in my ear. As I introduced myself again, I could sense that the connection was mutual. We danced and talked the rest of the night.

Debbie was articling at a large public accounting firm and said she would soon be writing her final professional exams to become a chartered accountant. When I told her I was a soldier, she didn't believe me, so I fished out my military ID card to prove it. I found out that she was from Nanaimo, a small city on the West Coast. She had moved away after high school to pursue her career. When the night ended, we went for a long walk. She didn't live far away, so I walked her home. It felt comfortable and natural to be walking down the street hand in hand, laughing and telling stories. When we finally reached her apartment building, I pulled her in close and drank in the sweet scent of her hair. I whispered in her ear, "I can't wait to see you again." She looked at me with a smile and nodded her agreement. As I walked across the bridge to my own apartment in the wee hours of the night, I mulled over my day. I had met a fabulous woman who had dared me to get closer and had just submitted the manuscript for what would be my first published book, since Japanese publishers wouldn't touch *Bridge of Tears*.

Our first date was the following night at a tapas restaurant near Debbie's apartment. We talked for hours, shared mussels and Ahi tuna, and sipped red wine on the patio. After we left the restaurant, we went for a walk along the seawall. We sat down on a bench and it seemed natural as she settled in next to me. I put my arms around her and kissed the back of her neck. She turned to face me, and our lips met for the first time. I knew she was different from any other woman I had dated: she was unpretentious and sensitive, yet impulsive and full of spirit. Naturally I wanted to give her a nickname, but I found "Deb" to be common and somehow too trivial. I decided to call her Bee.

That summer I wanted to spend more time near the ocean, so I decided to buy a thirty-two-foot weathered houseboat to live on. Debbie was studying for her final professional exams, and I prepared meals for her as she studied. At night we would sit on the top deck, staring at the stars and talking. She came to watch me play rugby without even remotely understanding the game. After a few months, I finally got to meet her family, including her eighty-two-year-old grandmother, Muriel, who lived on a narrow strip of land with a rustic woodshed that offered hours of wood-chopping. Having never known my own grandparents, I was taken with Muriel from our first meeting. She was everything I thought a grandmother should be: warm, loving, a fabulous cook and full of stories from the old days. She was well informed and could discuss any topic under the sun. The house was full of pictures of family. Debbie walked me to the back of the small acreage under huge old-growth pines and talked of her childhood memories. They were as idyllic as she was. As I got to know her, I came to love her honesty, compassion and loyalty, as well as the way she kept her cup half full. She had the same sense of wonder and adventure as I did, and I was impressed by the depth and spirit of her determination.

When my publisher sent me writer's copies of *Bad Date: The Lost Girls of Vancouver's Low Track,* I knew who would get my first one. I called Debbie to step out of her building and ran down to her with the book behind my back. With mounting excitement, I proudly showed her the book. Her face lit up when she saw it and read the inscription: "My darling Bee, my first edition! The first of many. Love, Maqua." Maqua was a playful nickname Debbie had given me from the book *The Last of the Mohicans*.

On September 11, 2001, as Debbie nervously got ready for the second of four days of CA exams, I turned on the TV and watched in horror as the tragedy in New York unfolded again and again. When Debbie came into the living room, I wordlessly motioned for her to sit on the couch and stammered, "We're going to war."

"Will *you* be going to war?" she asked.

"I didn't join the army to march around in a kilt in Canada, and I've always wanted an overseas deployment . . . so maybe."

Shock waves from that horrific moment would reverberate forever in our lives and set me on a path toward Afghanistan. Airplanes had been turned into weapons by terrorists, and the world would never be the same. I couldn't fathom the depths of the hatred of these fanatics. I knew the reaction from the West would be swift and decisive. I hoped Canada would not stand idly by watching the war on terrorism from the sidelines. In order to successfully soldier in Afghanistan, I knew I that would have to study about the country. I soon learned that Afghanistan had been invaded by enemies through the ages but never held. Ever.

By winter, Debbie and I were still sharing the same meal in the same tapas restaurant, but now we huddled together under the heaters on the patio watching the rainfall. At night, I would read to her as she curled up next to me in bed. But now my path to Afghanistan was inexorable.

In 2002, I turned my focus to my part-time army career. There is an expectation in the Canadian Forces that officers and non-commissioned officers (NCOs) will advance to command positions. The road to command led through the largest army base in Canada. CFB Gagetown was talked about with a mixture of awe and pain. I was told it had swamps on top of hills and tank ruts so deep they would swallow you up. I spent three months the following summer in the Gagetown heat and mud. My barrack mates and I started out as strangers, but the gruelling summer forged us into blood brothers.

When we were attending classes on base, we would muster each morning outside the barracks at 6 a.m. in PT kit, shivering in the early morning air. Our platoon commander led the runs while the second-in-command or warrant officer took up the rear to gather stragglers. The path ran through the woods with chin-up bars strategically set every fifty metres. We did push-ups and chin-ups until our elbows creaked. If the instructors were pissed at us, as was usually the case, the runs would be longer and harder. We would have to wait for stragglers in push-up position. When we did tactical training in the field, we would bushwhack all day, moving through various attack scenarios, and bivouac at night. We came to fear the night, when the instructors would attack us again and again. A chatter of automatic rifle fire would light up the trees, and shouts would ring out from all directions, jolting us out of an exhausted sleep. Not knowing what was going on, I still mustered the presence of mind to roll out of my sleeping bag, put on my boots and grab my rifle. My heart beat in my temples and my palms sweat. My hands shook as I loaded magazine after magazine of blank rounds into my rifle. Finally the instructors broke off the attack. We looked around at the stunned expressions on each other's faces, too tired and shaky from adrenaline withdrawal to bask in our victory.

The training was meant to test our ability to operate under extreme fatigue and extreme weather conditions. We were taught how to dig trenches and defend them. We practised patrols in pouring rain and blazing sun, sometimes on the same day. We were trained to balance stealth with aggression on patrol. We were taught to go to ground and, while lying absolutely still, try to locate the enemy. I remember flinging myself face-first into swamp water and then watching clusters of bloodthirsty mosquitoes and thunderous horseflies feed on my hands with impunity. One night we dug into a hillside under a bright moon. We had spent the previous night fighting off the enemy, so we were bone-tired and ragged. Somehow, we got our trenches dug and settled in for the night. I struggled to stay awake. I couldn't keep my eyes open and nodded off over my rifle. I was startled awake by the shouts from an angry warrant officer who had caught me snoring away. I was ordered to report to the camp commandant in the morning for disciplinary action. I knew this could result in my being kicked off the course due to dereliction of duty. It would mean going back to my unit in shame, and it would derail my promotion to platoon commander. I was driven back to camp and marched in to the board of inquiry to appear before three impeccably dressed officers. I came to attention in seven-day-old mud-covered green combats. I stood nervously at attention as I waited for them to decide my fate. I thought of how I'd slogged through these three months of tortuous tactical training and I desperately didn't want it to be in vain. Fortunately, since this was my first offence, they gave me a warning and said a second time would be my last. I returned to the field determined to excel. The summer pushed me to the breaking point, but it gave me my first taste of army leadership. The physical and mental training had been severe, but I had learned much more about my limits and knew I could lead. When I returned to my unit as a newly minted lieutenant, I was given command of a platoon. I looked forward to the leadership challenge. I couldn't wait to go on exercise with my men and actually lead them in the field.

After I'd been with the Seaforth Highlanders for about three years, I heard about a new specialized unit called Civil-Military

Co-operation, or CIMIC. CIMIC's mission was to liaise with civilians in a war zone and help bring them necessities such as medical care, clean water and food. When I read the job description, I learned that international experience would be an asset. CIMIC seemed to offer exactly what I had been looking for in my military career. It could also lead to my ultimate goal: a position as a CMCoord (Civil-Military Co-operation officer), the UN equivalent of a CIMIC officer.

CIMIC positions were meant to be filled by reservists, part-time soldiers who combined civilian and military careers, and they seemed to be a great way to get on-the-job training for the UN. But I was loath to take on another role that would mean time away from my hard-won duties commanding a platoon. When Debbie and I talked it over, I said it would probably mean more time away from home because I didn't want to neglect my platoon. She reassured me that I had committed to serving Canada—first with the navy, now with the army—and that my past experiences suited the position perfectly. She said I needed to pursue everything I'd set out to do in life, because, as she put it, "You'll only get one chance. I will be fine." Our talk gave me the reassurance and confidence I needed to apply.

CIMIC officers were selected from every branch and occupation in the reserves. I was confident of my chances. I had proven myself as a platoon commander, had travelled extensively and could speak and write well. I was told that the CIMIC commanding officer, Lt.-Col. Grant MacLean, would interview me. I found him to be brusque but charming and very knowledgeable. Seated at his desk, he pushed my file aside and told me to talk about my life and why I thought I was qualified for CIMIC. I started with my experiences in Japan and Burma and crossing the Pacific with the navy. I told him I spoke Japanese and French. With a hint of a smile, he said he would get in touch after reviewing my training files.

I was elated when I heard that I had been selected to train as a CIMIC officer. It brought me one step closer to working directly on the ground with the people I was defending. CIMIC training involved learning how to effectively coordinate emergency response agencies for domestic and international crises. We learned how to work with different first-responder agencies to get the affected people their most basic needs. When I heard that CIMIC personnel would be deploying to Afghanistan, I put my name forward. In order to qualify, I needed to take a NATO course. I was sent to an Italian army base in a small town outside Venice. My NATO colleagues shared their insights and experiences from dozens of missions. I learned how to assess civilian populations and their needs for health care, housing, food and clean drinking water, and to liaise with nongovernmental organizations to meet those needs. On the plane ride home from Italy, I felt I finally had all the tools and, just as important, the confidence to meet my military and humanitarian ambitions to serve on an international mission, boots on the ground. All I needed now was the mission itself.

Three years after Debbie and I met, my life changed irrevocably on a sunny day in May 2004. We met for dinner after work at our favourite tapas restaurant. During the meal, I asked her why she wasn't drinking her wine. Her answer knocked my world askew: "I'm pregnant." My first reaction wasn't ecstatic joy. That would come later. Up until then, I had choreographed the events in my life leading to a tour overseas, which was the last stepping stone to my goal to be a CMCoord with the UN. I also knew I wanted to spend my life with Debbie. We had talked about starting a family after my deployment, when life was a little more settled. We had even bought an empty lot in a new subdivision next to Debbie's sister and brother-in-law as a potential home for the future. After seven months of doctor's visits and cooking nutritious meals for Debbie and the growing baby, I was by her side in the delivery room on January 13, 2005, holding her hand and coaching her breathing. In fact, I was so caught up with helping her breathe that I became light-headed myself and had to be taken out of the room to be coached on my own breathing. A few hours later, I was cutting the umbilical cord of Grace Elizabeth Muriel Greene, and my fierce protective instinct was born. As I held her in my arms and looked down at her perfect little face and hands, I wondered if all my military training had been in vain. How could I put myself in harm's way and possibly deprive this sweet child of her father?

In the weeks after Grace was born, Debbie and I adjusted to being new parents. Hanging over this idyllic phase of my life like a cloud was the knowledge that at some point in the next year, I could be in the Afghanistan desert, rifle in hand. Over the previous year, my good friend and former basketball teammate Richard Provencher and I had talked at length about my UN aspirations and my preoccupation with Afghanistan. He had parlayed his broadcasting career into a position as a UN public information officer in Kabul. He had forwarded me several job postings with the UN, and I applied to a number of positions without any response. Finally, I was offered an interview with the United Nations Development Programme (UNDP) in Afghanistan, and I was overjoyed. It would be the foot in the door I needed to move up with the UN and was just the position for a new family man: safe behind a desk. After a lengthy long-distance panel interview, I received an email offering me a six-month stint as a public information officer in Kabul. That night, Debbie and I discussed the job and how it would be the start to fulfilling my lifelong dream and a chance to give Grace a global perspective from an early age. We rationalized that my six-month absence was a small price to pay for a potential career helping to empower the citizens of the least developed countries. We both agreed that I would accept the position.

The next day, I was reading to Grace when the phone rang. It was Lieutenant-Colonel McLean informing me that I had been selected for the first CIMIC rotation to Afghanistan, deploying in January 2006. My gut told me that turning down the deployment would be the biggest regret of my life. Training would begin across Canada immediately.

Chapter 4:
A NEW SENSE OF URGENCY

Our CIMIC training shifted into high gear with the focus on information gathering from *shuras,* meetings with village elders. As I would come to learn, the training ground in the rolling farmlands of Alberta bore no resemblance to the Afghanistan deserts. In training scenarios, soldiers played the roles of obstinate village elders with whom we had to negotiate through an interpreter.

With respect bordering on reverence, Afghan village elders are called *spin giri,* or white beards. Their beards are matted, squared at the bottom and hang halfway down their chests. They have seen everything, twice. White beards are the living history of a village, and their word is law. If we wanted to get familiar with a village, we had to go through them.

Shuras are cited in the Koran as the method used by the

Prophet Muhammed to gather information from his followers when making decisions. They are considered a critical component of gaining trust and building relationships. Since our group was the first CIMIC detachment to deploy to Afghanistan, we didn't get the benefit of handover briefings from the previous deployment. We worked around this by preparing research papers on aspects of the Afghan culture and traditions. The first paper I chose to write was on the tradition of *Pashtunwali*. Under this sacred code of honour, guests are to be protected and given food and water. It was comforting to know that this centuries-old tradition would safeguard us.

As I continued to study about Afghanistan, I found my preconceptions falling away. Before the 1979 Soviet invasion, life was rich and carefree. Food was plentiful, women worked outside the home and attended school, and burkas had long been relegated to history. Children's kites swooped and dipped in the sky, and music played freely. Farming was a respected and lucrative profession that was passed down from fathers to sons. Elaborate irrigation systems gushed water to the crops. Afghanistan was the world's largest exporter of dried fruit.

All that changed during the occupation. Women crouched in their houses, fearful of being raped by Soviet soldiers. Many Afghans paid large sums of money to be smuggled to neighbouring Pakistan, leaving their homes and possessions behind. For the first time, Afghanistan couldn't feed her people.

When the Soviets retreated in 1989, they left behind an estimated forty-five thousand soldiers in the ground and thousands of battle-hardened Afghan tribesmen called Mujahideen in the mountains. Victory over the Soviets ushered in a decade of civil war as the struggle for the cities began. The Mujahideen warlords knew how to fight but not how to rule. They attempted to govern the country but couldn't break down friction between tribes. Into this anarchy marched a group of students of a radical

Islamic sect made up mostly of Pashtuns, the dominant tribe in Afghanistan and Pakistan. The group, known as the Taliban (student of Islam), was dedicated to removing the warlords, returning the country to law and order, and imposing strict Islamic Sharia law on the country. Many of the young men had studied under radical teachers at the hardline Islamic schools, or *madrassas,* scattered up and down the border with Pakistan. Their goal was to defeat the unorganized, unruly Mujahideen and restore stability under what they called a "true Islamic order." They were led by a radical teacher called Mullah Omar, who based himself at Kandahar Airfield.

The decade of the Soviet invasion and occupation had been a dark time for Afghans, especially young men and women hungry for education. The Communist ideology is godless, and therefore traditional Islamic schools, which teach the Koran to young men, were shut down. These *madrassas* were reorganized just over the border in Pakistan, where they began preaching an extreme form of Islam based on a radical interpretation of the Koran. They became a spawning ground for the Taliban. News of the growth of the Taliban spread through the Muslim world and attracted hundreds of young extremists willing to die for their faith. The Taliban wore distinctive black turbans and were given weapons and ammunition from Pakistan and financial support from Saudi Arabia.

In 1994, the Taliban scored its first major victory: the capture of Kandahar City and Jalalabad. When the Taliban took Kabul in 1996, it hanged Mohammad Najibullah, the former Communist president, from a lamppost. The following year, Pakistan recognized the Taliban as the legitimate government of Afghanistan, and within three years, the Taliban ruled 95 percent of the country. Under the oppressive Taliban regime, women bore the brunt of the fundamentalist lunacy. They were forbidden to show their faces, work outside the home or go out without a male relative.

By the time girls turned eight, their education was over. Listening to music, playing cards and flying kites were forbidden. Thieves lost a hand. Adulterers lost their lives. Anyone could be publicly flogged or executed for flouting these rules. Laws were enforced by gangs of men who patrolled the streets whipping offenders and staging public executions in stadiums. The Taliban outraged and appalled the entire world when it destroyed priceless relics of Islam and blew up two ancient Buddhist statues.

Mullah Omar invited Osama bin Laden to Kandahar in 1994. Bin Laden, heir to a Saudi construction empire, had been trained by the U.S. in insurgency tactics and spent the 1980s leading a group of Mujahideen fighters against the Soviets. He later founded a group of hardline Islamists who called themselves Al-Qaeda (the base). Bin Laden funded Omar's fight against the other warlords for control of the country. From a house near Kandahar Airfield, he planned the horrific 9/11 attacks that changed history. Two weeks after those attacks, President George Bush demanded the Taliban hand over bin Laden and other Al-Qaeda leaders or face war. Omar refused. On October 7, 2001, the U.S. Army invaded Afghanistan. Canada entered the fight in 2002 in support of the U.S.-led mission, called Operation Enduring Freedom.

After learning about the history of the Taliban and reflecting on the monumental losses of 9/11, I felt a new sense of urgency toward my field training in Alberta. Yet again, I found myself sharing a tent with nine other guys farting and burping away. We encountered situations that tested our skills of negotiation, persuasion and diplomacy. The "actors" were soldiers dressed in civilian clothing. In one scenario, we were called on to negotiate a truckload of our wounded through a roadblock. The "partisans" demanded liquor, money and our weapons. One combat scenario involved vehicles striking an improvised explosive device (IED). Soldiers emerged from their vehicles looking dazed and confused.

Every day, we returned to base in high spirits but low on sleep. After the field training, we had to prepare for the final two hurdles to deployment: the battle fitness test and the rifle range rundown.

The battle fitness test was a three-kilometre march with a full thirty-kilogram rucksack and rifle. Before we set off, the sergeant major hefted our rucks to make sure they were heavy enough. The straps dug into my shoulders and the pack swayed with every step. I started off carrying my rifle properly, with both hands in front of me. Near the end, I was swinging it from hand to hand like a heavy suitcase. After the hot march, we gathered in the end zone of the base football field. It was now high noon and the sun was brutally hot. Each soldier was paired up with another man of about equal size and weight for the wounded carry. I got my huge partner off the ground in a fireman's lift, then bent down and took his rifle in my other hand. The goal was to carry him to the fifty-yard line and then switch. My legs started to tremble as soon as he was over my shoulders and the combined weight of the rifles seemed to pull my arm out of its socket, but I made it. He then carried me back to the end zone, where we fell to the ground exhausted.

The next day was the rundown. We were trucked to the longest rifle range I had ever seen, where we were issued six magazines of live ammunition. My first shot was from the four-hundred-metre mark. I had my elbows braced on sandbags. My white man-sized target on the green hillside looked about the size of a shimmering toadstool. After firing about twenty rounds, I leaped to my feet, ran a hundred metres and shot again. This time, the target toadstool was no longer shimmering. After firing, I ran to the two-hundred-metre mark, crouched and fired again. The target had by now coalesced into something that really was the size of a man. I changed magazines as I hustled to the hundred-metre mark, which I was happy to discover was a proper trench where I could stabilize and hopefully fire six rounds into the target. I changed the magazine as I ran to the fifty-metre mark, kneeled and carefully fired off more rounds. My target was now distinct and life-sized. I slapped a new magazine into my rifle and fired off ten rounds standing, then ran to the twenty-five-metre mark and blew off the rest of my rounds on semi-automatic. Slumped in an exhausted sweat, I could feel the adrenaline slowly leaving my bloodstream. I checked that my rifle was clear and trudged off the range. This final test marked the end of our training for deployment. I felt a mix of fatigue and anticipation at the prospect of putting the past nine months of training into action as part of Operation Archer, Task Force Orion—the first rotation to Afghanistan that would include a CIMIC team. I knew from the books I had read on Greek mythology in university that Orion was a hunter. At night I would find the constellation Orion, named after the giant hunter in the *Odyssey,* and ask to survive the war.

During workup training we were told that we had to keep our game faces on for the training and eventually for the mission itself. This would put us in the proper frame of mind to mentally and psychologically endure the six long months the mission demanded, and more important, it would keep us alive. Because the training was at a base in another city, I had already spent half of the year away. When I came home every other week, I found it difficult to really engage in normal life with Debbie and Grace. The mission—and the possibility that I wouldn't come home to them—was very real and raw for me. As my deployment date got closer, it struck me that I was distancing myself from the two girls I loved more than anything else. The thought of leaving Grace without a father and Debbie without a life partner made me sick to my stomach. I realized that I had already started the process of teaching them to live without me. Fortunately, we would have two uninterrupted weeks over the Christmas holidays before I departed in January for eight months.

Those weeks were just the time we needed to reconnect. Debbie and I spent the evenings talking and recording videos of me reading Grace's stories, singing the ABCs and just talking into a camera for her. Debbie insisted that I constantly use the word "daddy" so the fragile bond we had developed in her first year of life wouldn't be broken. I tried to spend as much time as possible with Grace. She was learning to walk, so I spent most of the time hunched over holding her up.

On January 13, 2006, the house was full of family and friends for Grace's first birthday party and my departure later that day. I sat on the couch watching the tendrils of grey smoke from Grace's birthday cake scatter on the ceiling. My gaze wandered around the living room, touching on the photos and the toys, and came to rest on the glass-topped coffee table, where my can of beer was getting warm. I loathed that coffee table—not for any fancy aesthetic reasons, but for the sharp corners, which I saw as a threat to Grace's safety every time she teetered toward them. For the eight months of my deployment, I would not be there to catch her when she fell. But there was something I could do now to protect my little girl from harm. I cut strips from a padded cardboard box and duct-taped them around the edges of the table. It certainly didn't do much to the décor, but it eased my mind immensely.

After most people had left, I trudged wearily up the stairs to the bedroom, where my new desert-tan uniform was lying out on the bed. We had been issued the rough, starchy uniform two weeks before we deployed. It was a tangible confirmation that I would be part of the mission in Afghanistan. I felt vindication that all my efforts and the sacrifices of my family had been worthwhile. The combats felt soft in my rough, bruised and callused hands. The new cloth buttoned up stiffly and was awkward on my arms and shoulders. I tied my desert boots as I had a thousand times before, but this time there was an air of finality about it. I went into Grace's room; she was napping in her crib entwined in her fluffy pink blanket. I desperately wanted to hold her in my arms, fill my nostrils with her baby scent and murmur into her ear that I was going away but would be back home safe. Instead, I put my hand lightly on her back and whispered, "I'm going away for a long time, but I promise I will come home to you. I love you, Little Wabbit." I hefted my heavy duffel bag and rucksack to my shoulders and walked downstairs.

Debbie and I had set the ground rules for our goodbye. To keep it as painless as possible, we'd agreed that she would not come into the terminal to see me off. We had already said everything that needed to be said. After saying our goodbyes in the car at the airport as planned, I climbed out to get my bags. As soon as the familiar weight of my rucksack and duffel bag had settled on my shoulders, Debbie was out of the car in a flash for a final goodbye. She held me tight and said she didn't want to let me go. I hugged her tightly and said, "Let's not make this more difficult than it has to be. It will be over in no time. I'll call and email as soon as I'm able. I love you." We had one final hug and kiss, and I turned, settled my beret on my head and went into the airport for the short flight to the base. I made it to the ticket counter before I felt the lump in my throat.

As part of the paperwork we had to complete to deploy, we were given an official form on which to record a last will and testament. As the last written communication to my loved ones, it felt too sterile and impersonal. In the long months before deployment, I tried to avoid any conversations about leaving, as if it weren't really happening. I had been avoiding the "what if" conversations—what if I died or was severely wounded. I didn't want to talk about these things for fear it would give the words power to become reality. But I realized that I desperately needed to share with Debbie how I felt and what was going through my mind when I decided to leave her and Grace for eight months to serve our country. It would be the hardest letter I ever wrote. I could imagine Debbie reading the words and telling Grace about how her daddy had stepped up and fought for kids like her, for their future. I folded up the letter and wrote on the back of the envelope, "Stick this in a drawer and forget about it. You will never need to read it. Only read it if something happens to me. I love you, Maqua."

The night before departing for Afghanistan, I dropped the letter into a mailbox. I felt a sense of melancholy as it left my fingers and slipped down the slot. Not discussing death or injury was like not admitting to myself that I was going off to war, but now I had written a whole letter about it.

A few hours later, I was staring at a monotone grey C-130 transport plane with black maple leaves. It looked like any other airbus on the tarmac, except for the soldiers filing on board. The austerity of the cabin was oddly reassuring—as if we had left all the frills behind for the civilians. No TVs or flight safety cards explaining where the oxygen mask will drop from. The aircraft took off like all the others I had been on, but as the wheels came up, I felt goosebumps cover me from head to toe at the thought that I had left Canadian soil, maybe for the last time.

During the long flight to Afghanistan, the plane droned on monotonously, save for a refuelling break in Zagreb, Croatia. As we landed at the airport, I thought of the Canadian peace-keepers who had come to Croatia in 1993 to uphold a shaky ceasefire between the Serbian and Croatian armies. The Canadians had come under heavy fire but held the line against the Croatian army. The battle, which Canadians called the Medak Pocket, was denied by the Croatians and went largely unnoticed in Canada. I couldn't fathom the horror those soldiers must have felt when they patrolled behind Croatian lines the day after the ceasefire and came across mutilated Serbian civilians in still-smoking burned-out buildings. That massacre had been planned by a Croatian general in Zagreb.

In the bright sun, the nondescript airport held no more menace for Canadian soldiers. We were given a few moments to take in some much-needed fresh air and stretch our legs. When I went into the terminal, I saw a horseshoe-shaped coffee counter that was packed with people chugging espresso and chain-smoking pungent cigarettes. A fog of smoke hung heavily near the ceiling, despite the whirring ceiling fans. I wandered into a bookstore looking for a magazine to help pass the time. There weren't any, so I browsed the books and came across a Serbo-Croat version of St. Exupery's *Little Prince,* one of my favourites. I had been planning to give my dog-eared copy to Grace one day and figured everyone should have their very own copy in an obscure European language, so I picked it up.

Forty-five hundred kilometres later, at exactly 0946, we were wheels-down on the tarmac of Kandahar Airfield. As I stepped out of the plane, I could feel the midday heat wrap around me like a blanket. It didn't take long for my pores to open up and explode in hot, oily beads of sweat. This was the first step in the desert for me. The base at the airfield was the size of a small town. It sprawled outward for kilometres in every direction and was the home of untold thousands of multinational troops and civilians. I felt a shudder when I thought about how Osama bin Laden had lived and planned the 9/11 attacks from this very spot.

We were shown to a large corrugated metal hangar for our briefing. The whine of aircraft engines on the airfield combined with the constant grind of trucks on the dusty road outside was deafening. My eyes were drawn to the hangar roof and locked on round patches of blue sky. We were told the large, gaping holes were caused by rocket-propelled grenades (RPGs). At that very instant, it really hit home that I was in a war zone.

After the briefing, we left the hangar by a back door. I felt my boots sink deeply into a fine dust like brown talcum powder—a dust that would work itself into every square inch of my body and kit. We climbed into a truck for the short drive to the provincial reconstruction team barracks, which were housed in a huge white tent the size of a hockey rink and aptly nicknamed the Big-Ass Tent, or the BAT. The nucleus of the team was a company of regular force soldiers—in this case, Alpha Company, 1st Battalion Princess Patricia's Canadian Light Infantry. Rows of bunk beds lined the BAT. I was given a bottom bunk with army-issue sheet and blanket. No pillow. I stowed my kit on the floor at the foot of the bed with my rifle on top. We were told that, in the event of a rocket attack, we were to slip into our boots firefighter-style, grab our rifles and hustle into the bunker outside the BAT.

Showers were as short as humanly possible. Lather, rinse, get out. The water was usually chilly. Most of us had brought our own towels, perhaps to remind us of the comfort of home and the niceties we'd left behind for our mission. I always showered the morning of a long patrol because I knew it would be days before I'd get another chance.

The mess building was the size of a large community centre, with row upon row of tables. Beside one of the exits was a huge freezer filled with popsicles and ice cream. Seafood, steaks and all the salad you could eat were served cafeteria-style. In Canada weapons are never allowed into a mess, but here you couldn't get in the door without a loaded weapon. The building was hot, so some of us sat outside at picnic tables like we were camping at some nature park in the desert—a park behind a guarded chain-link fence topped with razor wire. Not far away was the twenty-four-hour, well-equipped gym, where the fittest soldiers in NATO worked out with drive and determination.

First Battalion formed the heart of Task Force Orion. CIMIC officers were attached to a platoon for information gathering and protection. Partly because of my advanced infantry training, I was assigned to A Company. A Company was the spear of 1st Battalion. One Platoon was the tip of that spear. The platoon was commanded by Capt. Kevin Schamuhn, a competent, compassionate, superbly trained Royal Military College graduate with no pretensions. We shared the same world views and hit it off instantly.

My first experience outside the wire was a familiarization ride with One Platoon. All platoons travel in light armoured vehicles, which are lighter than a tank and so move on eight wheels instead of two tracks. Eight soldiers with full battle array can squeeze into the belly of the vehicle on benches on either side. Our vehicle snorted and belched smoke as we loaded up. When I walked through the rear hatch, I felt comfort in knowing there was a foot of armour between me and the bad guys. My first sight of bandit country was not exciting—a flat tableau of grapefruit-sized rocks with hundreds of tattered white plastic bags swirling around. The landscape was festooned with smooth, brown car-sized boulders that looked exactly like they had oozed as molten lava from the slowly cooling earth millions of years ago. Everything seemed to be coated in a layer of light brown dust. This wasteland was a stark contrast to the rich greens of Canada.

One eerie dusk, as I took my turn as traffic sentry, standing in the back hatch to warn off cars that got too close, it struck me that the wedge-shaped rocks that lined the rubble-strewn, potholed roads looked like gravestones. The roads of Afghanistan have been deadly for foreign armies for generations. One of the most famous disasters was the British retreat from Kabul in 1842. After tensions with their Afghan hosts reached the breaking point, forty-five hundred British troops and the twelve thousand civilians who had followed them to Kabul exited the city gates on foot or horseback to find safe haven in Jalalabad—a 140-kilometre trek in the brutal cold of winter. Many died from exposure in the first days. Despite a treaty guaranteeing safe passage, the doomed column was picked off at leisure by Pashtun tribesmen from behind the rocks, perhaps the same rocks that would be used more than 150 years later by the Taliban to aim their roadside bombs. Of the thousands of souls who fled Kabul, amazingly only one man, Dr. William Brydon, a British Army surgeon, made it through to Jalalabad. He rode through the freezing desert on a horse more dead than alive. I thought of the sheer desperation and misery of the civilians and the frustrating impotence of the soldiers, who were being annihilated by an unseen enemy—the same frustration that would be felt by coalition troops far in the future.

Almost 170 years later, Afghanistan remains a perilous, frustrating battlefield riven by internecine rivalries between sworn enemies that is extremely difficult to navigate. It requires extensive preparation and discipline to conduct successful military operations there.

Capt. Kevin Schamuhn and I had discussed at length how we would conduct the *shuras*. Through our interpreter, he would talk with the elders to ascertain where their loyalties lay and the status of their security situation. He would then hand the meeting over to me. I would ask how the village was managing in terms of health care, food and water, and how we could help out. One subject I was particularly passionate about was education for girls. During workup training, I had read a UN report that laid out the crucial importance of educating girls in developing nations. One line from that report still resonates with me to this day: "Teach a boy, you educate an individual; teach a girl, you enlighten a whole community." A UN program develops this theme by providing funds and the guidance needed to, for example, buy a cow. Women are taught to use the funds from milk sales to buy a herd, generating greater profits. Village elders tend to notice their success and give them a voice in council. Women use their newfound influence to guide other girls and change the minds of men. This touched me profoundly because Afghanistan was not only a developing nation but also a developing nation at war. I knew that the education of girls would be a huge challenge in a country dominated by the Taliban, a group that violently opposes the very thought of educating women.

As we drove through the villages, I rarely saw women. They were hidden behind their veils and in their homes. I would constantly ask at *shuras* if the elders would allow the girls to go to a school if we built one for them. They roared with laughter at the very idea. Every time I saw a group of scrawny, ragged girls confined to the back of the group at a *shura* or playing by the side of the road as we drove by, I thought of my own daughter, Grace, who had all the advantages in the world: nutritious food, clean water, education and, most important, equal status. Grace would always be loved and encouraged and never denied anything because of her gender. Tragically, in Afghanistan—as in all Muslim countries that continue to follow archaic, feudalistic ways—girls hold the lowest status of all in the household.

I was eager to visit the villages and see how these strange customs played out in real life. But first I had to get off the base at Kandahar Airfield. Alpha Company's area of operations was five hundred thousand square kilometres in the foothills of the Hindu Kush mountain range. One Platoon was responsible for the area around the town of Gonbad. We were in the BAT for about two weeks, waiting to take over from an American artillery unit that was stationed at a forward operating base (FOB) near the town. We chafed at the endless situation briefings we had to attend before the handover was made. As there was no

CIMIC representative in the American unit to give me a subject handover briefing, I worked out in the gym or shot my weapons on the range. Occasionally, the Taliban would make life interesting by firing a grenade over the wire. Finally, we were told to get ready to move.

After the first few weeks at the Red Devil Inn, we started hearing about roadside bomb attacks. The strikes would crumple the vulnerable underbelly of the light armoured vehicles and kill or severely wound our soldiers. In my naivete, I was convinced that I was bomb-proof. This hubris painted an indelible target on any light armoured vehicle I was in. So perhaps it was inevitable that on the first patrol, as I swayed and sweated on the benches with the rest of the soldiers, a monstrous WHUMP slammed my helmet back against the steel side armour. As I jackknifed forward, my head felt like it was being crushed in a massive vise. I saw a wall of dust streaming down from the roof. Everything was moving in slow motion. Through my double vision, I could see the section commander, Rob Dolson, knocking knees as he scrabbled up and down checking that everyone was okay. When he swam into my vision, he sounded like he was shouting from the bottom of a deep well. I gave him a thumbs-up, and at the same time wafted a silent prayer of thanks to God and the assembly-line workers who had crafted this behemoth that had saved Grace's daddy today. I felt a strong kinship with the other troops. We had survived the Taliban's deadliest weapon—an improvised explosive device or IED.

To really interact with the locals, we would go on long foot patrols. The FOB was about seventy kilometres north of Kandahar City and right in the middle of traditional Taliban territory. There always seemed to be at least two rivers between where One Platoon was and where we wanted to be, so we usually ended up with sodden pants and wet boots. We were constantly wringing out our socks and changing into dry ones. Foot powder became an essential piece of kit. The rivers flowed between sloping slate-coloured hills strewn with small round rocks we called ankle-breakers. There always seemed to be a massive boulder on the top of the hills. One day we drove over a gravelly road that snaked up to a mesa, where our cannon gunners calibrated their weapons. Immediately after the shooting stopped, Afghan civilians in white robes appeared out of nowhere and started scooping the valuable brass shell casings into bags. Dusk was falling and the Taliban owned the night, so we had to make ourselves scarce. As the CIMIC officer, I was sent out with an interpreter to convince the brass hunters of the danger of getting run over by our vehicles and persuade them to leave.

On long patrols, we would often spend nights in the field. One morning I rolled out of my bivouac and gazed out at the sun-bathed but lifeless terrain of the Red Sands Desert. My eyes were drawn to something green and circular near my boots on the dusty ground. It stood out because the terrain was all brown and sharp edges. I was curious, since I hadn't seen much of anything round or green on our patrols. There were very few trees, shrubs, bushes or even grass—just a lot of rocks and dust. I raked my fingers through the sand to find a child's dull, pitted green marble. As I held it in my hand, I looked around at the barren desert and wondered how it could have possibly arrived on this lonely plateau and how long it had been here. I thought that people who could cling to life on this blasted heath could never be subjugated. We were literally kilometres away from human habitation of any kind. I slipped the marble into the pocket of my combats. When we got back to the compound, I put it in an envelope and wrote a letter to Grace in my notebook.

5 FEB 06, Kandahar Province, Afghanistan

Hi Little Wabbit,
This marble is the start of your "exotic little stuff from around the world" collection. Daddy found it in a place far from home, on a windy plateau on the edge of a beautiful desert called the Red Sands Desert. When you get old enough to not want to eat it, Mummy will wash it thoroughly and you can play with it. I will show you where I found it, and you will be able to see on the map where Afghanistan is. I will tell you stories about this extraordinary, sad land, and explain why I had to go away from you and Mummy for eight long months.

Daddy had to come here as a soldier. Hopefully you will visit Afghanistan as a pretty young lady, in peace.

Daddy loves you and holds you precious.

Hugs 'n' kisses, Daddy

When our vehicles needed servicing and our rations grew scarce, One Platoon would roll back to Kandahar Airfield. In that time, we would grab showers, eat fresh meals and connect with family back home. There was usually a lineup of soldiers impatiently waiting for each phone, so calls had to be short. When I spoke to Debbie, she would want to know—in excruciating detail—everything about my life in Afghanistan. For security reasons, I could talk only in generalities. I craved hearing the news from back home—in equally excruciating detail. I was disappointed one day to speak to the answering machine before we left for the FOB. "Hi Bee, I really wanted to talk to you. We're heading back out on patrol soon, so I'll be out of contact for a while. I'll phone again when we get back to base. Love and kisses for you and the Wabbit."

66

CHAPTER 5:
THE AXE FALLS

On March 4, 2006, the sun was already high in the sky as I prepared for another day of *shuras*. I picked up my notebook, making sure that the picture of Debbie and Grace was still neatly tucked away inside. "Miss you both and can't wait to see you in two weeks in Hawaii," I said as I kissed the picture and thought about my upcoming leave time. It was early in the tour, which would leave a long stretch once I returned, but I couldn't wait to hold them both. For now, though, I had to keep my mind on the challenges ahead.

"Hey, sir, will you be needing a medic today?" Shaun Marshall, the platoon medic, said as he poked his head into my room.

"I don't think so, Shaun," I replied.

I rechecked my rucksack and made sure I had enough food and water for the day. Equally important were the dry socks and foot powder I'd packed the previous night. I knew we would be sloshing through several small streams of icy Himalayan glacier water on patrol. Finally, I grabbed my rifle, double-checking the bolt, and headed out to meet Kevin. While the rest of the soldiers got their kits together, we talked about the plan for the day and the villages we would hit.

I heard the growls of the LAVs starting up in front of the compound and walked to the back of my vehicle to board with the rest of the guys. I heard the hydraulic whine of the rear hatch lowering and buckled my helmet. I walked up the ramp, ducking my head as I entered the narrow space, and sat on a bench along the side. Shaun came in last, saying that Kevin had said he might as well come along for the day. I positioned my rucksack and rifle between my legs as the other soldiers loaded up, then felt the familiar lurch forward as we headed out on the bumpy, dusty road. I was already hot in my desert combats in the tight compartment and was glad that the fan circulated fresh air where we sat. After about thirty minutes of bouncing and swaying, we arrived at our first village of the day. We parked the vehicle and filed out through the rear hatch, rifles held loosely in our hands. We met with the elders, sharing tea and communicating through our interpreter. After about forty-five minutes of genial talking, we said our ceremonial goodbyes and loaded back up for the second village.

The second *shura* was also successful, so we were optimistic about the third, at the tiny village of Shinkay. We received a typically warm reception and were once again invited to join the village elders for tea. We congregated on a peaceful, grassy spot in the shade of trees by a gently flowing river. After taking off our helmets and laying down our weapons, we sat facing the elders on either side of our interpreter to achieve the best eye contact. A young boy brought the tea for the meeting. The *shura* was quite typical, except that at one point a man from the village came out and took the children away. I listened intently as Kevin explained in simple terms where we were from and the purpose of our visit. He then asked about the Taliban and their presence in the area. This was exactly the mission I wanted—on the ground, interacting with the people I was there to help. I watched as the men from the village scratched their beards and fondled their prayer beads, and I wondered what they were thinking. I hoped we would gather enough information to guide reconstruction planning. At least in the short term, they would know coalition forces were in their area, watching their backs.

Kevin wrapped up his questions and turned the meeting over to me. I focused squarely on the chief elder. "Thank you for meeting with us," I began. I allowed time for the interpreter to speak, and as I formulated my first questions about health care and education, I listened idly to the desultory murmurs of the young people behind me. I put my glass of tea carefully in front of me and picked up my notepad and pen to make notes as I spoke. "I'm here to learn what your village needs . . ." I could sense movement behind me as I launched into my first question.

PART 2: THE WARRIOR PATH

Difficulties are meant to rouse, not discourage. The human spirit is to grow strong by conflict.

—*William Ellery Channing*

Dear Madam,

My name is Major Kirk Gallinger, Officer Commanding A Company Group, the "Red Devils." As our senior Civil-Military Co-operation (CIMIC) Officer, Trevor was a key member of my company command team.

On behalf of all "Red Devils," I would like to express our deepest sympathy over Trevor's grievous injury. We are reassured by the reports of his continued progress.

Although I do not wish to contradict any information that has been provided to you so far, I feel it my duty to explain to you the circumstances surrounding the attack on Trevor to the best of my knowledge. The majority of the information that follows comes directly from the soldiers that were present during the attack.

During the period 25 February until the attack on 4 March, Trevor was attached to 1 Platoon Group. This force was tasked by me to conduct security operations in the Gumbad Valley of Shah Wali Kot District, an area that has a long history of instability and has been the focus of our operations since the tour began. From its base of operations at the Gumbad Platoon House, security operations typically involved leader engagements, village assessments, mounted and dismounted patrolling and route reconnaissance.

The term "leader engagement" refers to the process of meeting with local leaders, normally at the village level, to discuss the topics of governance, security and stability, and reconstruction. We use this process to collect information, and more importantly to help empower Afghans. The term "village assessment" relates to the process by which our CIMIC officers conduct an assessment of a village's needs in terms of education, health and infrastructure.

On 4 March, a patrol consisting of three Canadian vehicles and three Afghan National Army vehicles set out to conduct leader engagements and village assessments south of Platoon House. The patrol was led by Captain Kevin Schamuhn, 1 Platoon Commander.

Trevor accompanied the patrol as the CIMIC representative.

At approximately 1330 hours local, the patrol drove into the town of Shinkay, which is also known by the locals as Nari Wala. The patrol established security with the Canadian vehicles pointing south and the Afghan National Army soldiers facing north. A group of Canadian soldiers were tasked to provide close protection in support of the leader engagement.

It took approximately 15 minutes for the village elders to gather at the meeting location on the bank of a wadi. The key coalition members in the meeting were, from left to right: Trevor; an interpreter; Captain Schamuhn; and Sergeant Rob Dolson, an infantry section commander.

A crowd of approximately 30 men and children gathered around the key speakers, forming a circle. Captain Schamuhn began the conversation with an opening address and then passed the conversation over to Trevor, who began asking questions related to the village assessment. Unnoticed until after the incident, the children at the meeting were escorted away by a young man and moved to an Afghan National Army soldier who was approximately 20 metres to the right of the Canadians.

During Trevor's conversation with the elders, a local male, whose age is estimated to be less than 20 years old, came from behind Trevor and pulled a homemade axe from under his clothing. Very quickly, he lifted the axe above his head, cried "Allah Akbar" (God is Great), and then struck Trevor in the head. He removed the axe and lifted it again, but was engaged multiple times by three soldiers before he could attack. The assailant dropped the weapon and fell dead into the wadi.

Trevor was knocked unconscious by the blow, and did not feel any pain. Throughout the entire medical evacuation, his vital signs remained stable, which is testament to his fine physical condition and strong will to live. A military medic in the patrol provided continuous care for Trevor.

Immediately following the attack on Trevor, a heavy volume of small arms and rocket-propelled grenade fire erupted from the north and south. It is now clear that the attack on Trevor was the trigger for a full-fledged ambush against the coalition forces. The Canadian and Afghan National Army soldiers returned fire. The Afghan soldiers then swept into the village to gather all of the villagers for questioning while the Canadians continued to secure the scene in preparation for casualty evacuations.

Additional ground reinforcements were quickly dispatched from the Platoon House. We also surged fighter aircraft overhead of the village, but they were not needed.

The casualty evacuation helicopter landed approximately one hour after the attack. Although this seems terribly long, I can assure you that the evacuation was executed as quickly as possible and the helicopter response time was very quick given the distances involved. Trevor was loaded into the helicopter by a stretcher party and evacuated to the military hospital at Kandahar Airfield. His vital signs remained stable and he did not regain consciousness during the evacuation.

The search of the village yielded two old rifles. Unfortunately, all males of fighting age had disappeared into the surrounding mountains. Captain Schamuhn spoke to the villagers and highlighted the extreme cowardice of the Taliban fighters. He also emphasized the fact that assistance would not reach the village as long as hostilities continued. The patrol then returned to the Platoon House, where it conducted a debrief. The platoon was extremely upset and angered over the attack on Trevor.

During the attack, I was on patrol in a neighbouring district located to the south. I monitored the incident on the radio and then returned to Kandahar Airfield that evening. My Sergeant Major and I visited with Trevor in the hospital that night. He was in stable condition and the level of care provided by the hospital staff was simply outstanding. At the time of our visit, no less than two nurses were caring for Trevor. The following morning, I departed for the Platoon House to meet with 1 Platoon Group.

I believe Trevor was attacked simply because, at the time, he was the one speaking.

To the best of my knowledge, this is the first occasion that coalition forces have been attacked during a village shura (Pashtun for "meeting"). This cowardly act is completely against their code of Pashtunwali, *which stresses honour, hospitality and a host's obligation to protect his guests. We have conducted shuras in this manner many times prior to the 4 March attack on Trevor. We always make the shuras as inclusive as possible in order to convey our messages to as many persons as we can. In order to speak to the locals, it is necessary to remove our helmets and sunglasses. To do otherwise would be an affront to their honour. It is also important in their culture to identify us as individuals and not merely as faceless soldiers of the coalition. We will continue to conduct* shuras *in this manner, although we have implemented additional procedures to help prevent a similar attack.*

After having discussed the circumstances of the attack with the soldiers and leaders of 1 Platoon Group, I am extremely proud of the actions they took. They did everything within their power to protect Trevor. Once he was injured, they were quick to provide first aid and expedite his evacuation.

Trevor remains foremost in the minds of all "Red Devils." He was a valued member of the team who made a significant contribution to our mission. He truly set the example for all of us with his compassion for the locals. We have a void within the company that cannot be filled.

To conclude, I am at your service should you require any additional information or assistance. My thoughts and prayers are with you and Trevor during this difficult time.

Yours truly,

K.A. Gallinger

CHAPTER 6:
OUR LIVES DERAILED

Debbie

I was lying in bed on a Saturday morning between sleep and wakefulness, listening for the sounds of Grace waking up. The house was still and peaceful. I was looking forward to taking her to visit my parents that day. I realized with a pang of longing that if my fiancé were here, Trevor would be holding me in his arms right now. The only sounds I could hear from the comfort of my warm bed were the birds and the faint sound of the odd car on the road.

A knock at the door disturbed my reverie and made the hair on my neck stand at attention. It was 6:30 a.m. Trevor was at war in Afghanistan. Friends don't come knocking that early.

Two army officers stood at my door. One was the deputy commanding officer of the Seaforth Highlanders, Maj. Paul Ursich. The other introduced himself as the brigade padre, Jim

Short. They looked solemn but entirely focused. Two officers had been at my door a couple of weeks earlier to tell me about an IED blast Trevor had been in. I had asked then if he would be coming home. I thought if it was serious and he was unable to complete his mission, he would be sent home. As it turned out, he'd had only a mild concussion and whiplash and would be continuing.

"Ms. Lepore?" the officer said now.

"Yes," I replied.

"Trevor has been seriously injured."

"Will he be coming home?" I asked.

They looked at each other sombrely. My heart froze at their next words.

"Yes," Jim replied. "May we come in?"

A jumble of thoughts swirled in my head. The first was how devastated Trevor would be at having his tour cut short. He wanted this field experience so badly so he could achieve his ultimate goal of working for the United Nations. He had always thought big. He wanted to make change in a big way. He had always dreamed of bringing peace and stability to Afghanistan, and of helping end the oppression of Afghan women and children. He knew they needed education to make that happen.

We hadn't discussed what we would do if he was ever wounded, but I'd always believed that we could manage any injury. Injuries from war zones are mostly bullet holes, broken bones, burns and lost limbs, or so I thought. Our family and our love could cope, because for the most part, those things can be repaired. Broken bones heal, burned skin repairs itself, lost limbs can be replaced with prosthetics. A few months of rehab would be no problem for us.

It didn't take long for Paul to tell me what little information he had: "Trevor was wounded a few hours ago in a remote village in Kandahar Province. Initial reports are that his platoon was at a meeting with village elders when he was hit." Paul went on to say that they believed he had been hit from behind, but they didn't know where on his body—or they weren't telling me. They had no idea how bad it was, only that surgeons were trying to stabilize him in a Kandahar hospital as we were speaking. "If he makes it," Paul said, "he will be flown to a much larger and more advanced medical facility in Germany." He told me delicately that reporters in Kandahar were eager to release the story but were waiting until the next of kin had been notified. I asked them to hold off until I could reach his tight-knit family. Trevor's parents, Dick and Bess, were avid news watchers and would be shattered to hear about it on television.

I first called his parents in Florida, but there was no answer and they didn't have an answering machine. In any case, I couldn't imagine leaving such a message on a machine without causing complete chaos. "Please pick up," I begged. I then called Trevor's sister, Suzanne, in Toronto. She picked up after two rings.

"Suzanne! It's Debbie calling. Trevor's been injured. It's really, really bad. I can't get a hold of your mum and dad." She screamed and called her husband, Andy, to take the line. I told him as much as I knew, which was only that Trevor had been attacked and doctors were trying to stabilize him. Calmly and rationally, Andy said that he would contact Dick and Bess, and that I should try to keep the line free.

I remembered that I was supposed to be on a ferry soon to visit my parents. I called my mother from my cellphone to tell her that Trevor had been badly injured and Grace and I wouldn't be coming over. She said she would be on the next ferry to us in Vancouver. I realized I was going to need more immediate emotional support, since my mother wouldn't arrive for a few hours, so I called my sisters Toni and Deanna, who were less than an hour away. Toni said she would head over immediately. My next call was to one of my closest friends,

Sam, who arrived within minutes with hugs and a latte.

When the phone rang, I knew I was about to have an acutely emotional conversation with Trev's parents. I dreaded the call because I knew how my parents would take the news if I were severely injured and clinging to life. Like any parents, they would be devastated. It had been about an hour since the officers arrived. Dick's voice cracked as he asked what Trevor's condition was and if there was any more information on the injury. I told him that we were still waiting to hear from the doctors in Kandahar, and that there were two army officers sitting in my living room, phones ready for updates.

My stomach churned when I turned on the TV and saw that the lead story was about the attacked soldier. At that moment, I realized this was not a bad dream.

On the other side of the continent, Trev's parents were making calls to their friends and family to pray for him. It was reassuring to know that we weren't alone in our small living room, and that the prayer circle was rapidly growing around the nation.

When my sister Toni arrived, she took command of the phone, relaying information to us as it came in. More friends and family arrived to provide what support they could. At one point during the day, it seemed that everyone was talking on their cellphones and all were saying the same thing: "We are waiting for more information." A few hours later, Trevor's commanding officer, Col. Rob Roy Mackenzie, arrived to relieve Paul.

As the story started to piece together in our living room, it was also gaining strength in the media. The video of Trevor being rushed off the helicopter on a stretcher with his heavily bandaged head tilted backwards at a grotesque angle seared itself into my brain. Just then, I heard Major Ursich finish a conversation and click off his phone. He looked at me with a perplexed expression on his face and said in a tight voice that Trevor had been hit in the head . . . with an axe. Silence filled the room. I felt the wind literally being taken out of me. Trev had told me repeatedly that he was going to war and not to a peacekeeping mission. I had been prepared for bullets or shrapnel, but an axe? I wondered how he could have been taken down by a Stone Age tool. I felt myself start to shake. Then the television reported that Trevor had been hit in the back of the neck. To me, there is a big difference between being hit in the head and being hit in the neck. Being hit in the neck means complete paralysis. Life in a wheelchair. Feeding tubes. Controlling a wheelchair though a breathing tube. Trevor was a very physical guy. He walked and biked everywhere. I didn't know the implications of being hit in the head, nor did I make the connection that the brain was *the* central processing area for the body.

I heard Grace wake up in her crib upstairs. I didn't want her to come downstairs and sense sadness and grief. I had to remain positive for her. I didn't want emotional trauma to affect her life forever. At fourteen months, she couldn't communicate verbally yet, so her cues were emotional and physical. She was young, but I believed she could sense my emotions. There would be many people around that day to keep her entertained. I hoped they could fight back the tears for her sake.

By now, my mother had arrived with all the necessary comforts: food, hugs and another cellphone. Later, more people dropped by with food and reassurances. The prosaic task of feeding a houseful of people took my mind off the drama and stress of the day. Trev's rugby mate Mike and his wife, Julie, turned up with a large tray of sushi. By the afternoon, we were watching foot-age of Trevor being hustled on a stretcher from the Black Hawk helicopter to the Kandahar hospital. That scene played over and over again at every news update on every channel. His head was contorted oddly back from his body. We knew it was Trevor from the sight of his large, protruding Adam's apple. Each time I saw the video I got the same reaction from the hair on my body.

It was like first stepping in the shower on a cool day—whether the water is hot or cold, the hair just stands on end.

I felt that Trevor needed more than the skilled hands of the surgeons to pull through. He would need the intervention of a higher power, so I started calling anyone I knew who was religious or spiritual. The first person I spoke to was a woman I had met a few years earlier, when I was working on my own personal spiritual journey. Anita Lawrence had invited me to attend her classes to expand my mind and become more in tune with myself.

Anita's advice to me was loud and clear: "The worst thing you can do is send Trevor worry energy. You must keep your thoughts positive." Her words brought to mind a piece of advice my wise grandmother once gave me. "Why worry about it now?" she said. "Worry about it when it happens."

Late in the afternoon, Colonel Mackenzie put his phone down to say that Trev had slipped to critical unstable. I hadn't been on my own at all that day to really concentrate on sending my prayers. I had been on the phone, watching the news, talking to the officers, looking after Grace and greeting people at the door. I immediately felt guilty for not making the time for Trevor, and I convinced myself that if I lost him, it would be partially my fault.

By evening, a stunned silence had fallen over the living room. I asked everyone to either pray or send Trevor positive thoughts, whichever they preferred. Personally, I was a firm believer in the power of prayer and had been ever since I went on a trip to Vietnam. My friend and I had missed a crucial flight; this threatened to derail our journey unless an unlikely chain of events happened. We sat down off to the side of the airport and prayed to get on the next flight, which we had been told was already overbooked. To our surprise, luck was on our side and we both made the next flight that day.

Soon after everyone in the living room started praying and sending positive thoughts, one of the officers relayed a message that Trevor had stabilized and would be flown to Germany, likely by morning. Colonel Mackenzie was on the phone immediately to have someone arrange flights to Germany for the following day. It was one less detail I had to worry about. He said Grace and I would be accompanied by Jim Short and an assisting officer from the Seaforths, Mike Larose.

That night I bathed Grace and pressed her tightly to my chest as I rocked her to sleep. Her room was peaceful and comforting, with just the sound of the rocking chair and her breathing. But my mind kept returning to the image of Trevor lying on a hospital cot somewhere in Kandahar, dirty and bloody with tubes keeping him alive. Tears welled up in my eyes as I sang to Grace, "Hush, little baby, don't say a word, Daddy's going to buy you a mockingbird." What was in store for us for the future? Would she ever know her father? "I can't think like this," I told myself. "I have to stay positive for all of us." Grace was already asleep when I put her in her crib.

When I came downstairs, I thought of the practicalities of leaving for Europe the following day, especially at work, since we were on a deadline to report the February financial results to the executive and the annual report to shareholders. My first priority was to let my boss, Khairun, know the situation, and to tell her that I didn't know how long I would be gone. Fortunately, we had the kind of relationship where I could call her at home if necessary. She said to take as much time as I needed. My sister and mother both offered to go with Grace and me to Germany. I decided my sister would be more of an asset, since she spoke fluent German. I realized as I packed that I was being flown to Trevor's side in case he didn't make it.

The second person I needed to contact was Regina, the wonderful live-in nanny we had been fortunate to find to help us for the eight months Trevor was overseas. She had moved in the same day he left, and had become a second mother to Grace and a solid source of support and friendship to me. Grace shared a very special bond with "Gina" and lit up when she saw her after her weekends off. Regina had left her husband and three children in the Philippines in search of a better life for them in Canada. When we met, she had already been away from them for five years. It would be another three years before they would live together as a family again. We were so blessed to have found each other. We were two women helping each other through the most challenging times of our lives.

After the practicalities were handled and everyone had departed for the night, there was nothing left to do but go to bed. Thankfully, my mum and sister were spending the night. In the middle of the night, I heard Grace's toy piano playing in the empty living room. Ordinarily something like that would have given me the shivers, but I sensed it was Trevor reaching out to tell me he was alive and not to give up on him.

The next morning I got a call from Trevor's best friend, Barb, whose son, Victor, was like a nephew to Trevor, and even called him Uncle Bubba. I had spoken to Barb on the phone the day before, shortly after the news was released to the media. She told me that Victor wanted to know why his uncle Bubba had been attacked on his ninth birthday. She told him that she wasn't sure, and that night, she asked Victor to join her in prayer. After kneeling and saying the rosary with his mother, Victor went to his room and fell asleep. A few hours later, he woke up and came to Barb's room. "Uncle Bubba just spoke to me in a dream," he said.

"What did he say to you?" Barb asked.

He told her what he heard: "Heyyy, Victor, it's your uncle Bubba. Everything's going to be okay. I'm coming home."

She told me the words Victor used were exactly the way Trevor would have spoken to him. I was hopelessly optimistic that his soul was sending these signs for us to continue to believe in him.

CHAPTER 7:

IGNORANCE IS BLISS

I was thankful to hear that Trevor had survived the night in Kandahar and was expected to arrive at the medical centre in Germany roughly thirty-six hours after the attack. We left for the airport the next evening with two military escorts: Mike Larose, our assisting officer from Trev's regiment, and the padre, Jim Short. After checking our bags and making our way through security, we found out the flight had been cancelled and there were no other flights until the next day. I was devastated. This meant we wouldn't reach Trevor until four days after he had been hit. On the one hand, the delay would give his body a few extra days to gain strength before we arrived. On the other hand, without the love of family encouraging him, he could succumb to his wounds. But I knew there was nothing I could do but send him my positive thoughts until I could be there in person to tell him how much we loved him and needed him. Fortunately, because of the delay, we were able to make the connections to meet up with Trevor's mum, dad and sister and fly to Frankfurt together the following night.

After a long, restless flight and drive, we all arrived at the enormous Landstuhl Regional Medical Center. We passed through two sets of sliding doors to a desk with soldiers in uniform sitting behind it. After our passports were checked, we were shown to a small room where we waited for Trevor's doctors. This was the first of several small rooms where I would wait with pounding heart for an update on Trevor's condition. The hallways flowed with people in civilian clothes, military uniforms and hospital scrubs and gowns. We hadn't heard any information since leaving home the day before. By then, Trevor had been at the medical centre for nearly two days.

The stale beige lounge room where we waited had a number of chairs, a couch, a desk and a bathroom. This would become our locus at the hospital, as it had for many families before us. Eventually, three doctors entered the room. One was Dr. Pete Sorini, a U.S. Army colonel and top neurosurgeon. Fortunately for us, he was on attachment at the Landstuhl Center and was working on Trevor. With him were two other American surgeons also working at Landstuhl. Dr. Catherine Gray, a Canadian military physician, was the liaison between our family and the medical team.

There was a hush in the room as Dr. Sorini spoke carefully. What he said sounded otherworldly, like a script from a TV hospital drama. "Trevor's lost a lot of blood and brain matter from the attack. There is a twelve-centimetre fracture in his skull from the right to the left. The axe sank about two centimetres into his brain and flipped the bone inside out." He went on to say that Trevor had been induced into a coma in an attempt to reduce the pressure on the brain from swelling. "He is not breathing on his own, his right lung has collapsed and he is fighting pneumonia from a bacteria he picked up from the soil in Afghanistan." Dr. Sorini said they would know what strain it was and how to treat it within forty-eight hours. The most shocking news was that Trevor's initial intracranial pressure was in the thirties, twice the normal range, which had forced them to remove two large pieces of his skull. This would allow his brain to swell without causing further damage. There was a stunned silence laced with sniffles as we heard the gruesome news. The doctor urged us to stagger our visits to reduce the amount of stimulation to Trevor's brain.

We decided that my sister Toni and I would go in first. Grace would stay behind for now, until I knew how Trevor looked. I was nervous about seeing him. Up to this point, I had been trying hard to be positive. I was worried I would lose control at the sight of him. I had probably been living in complete ignorance and denial, and it had worked well for me. As we were led into the unit, we walked past various rooms, some entirely enclosed in glass. I passed the occupied rooms and wondered if I would recognize Trevor. Finally, Dr. Gray pointed to the room at the end of the hall. I gasped when I saw Trevor's inert body through the glass.

I took a deep breath as we entered. Trevor lay partially upright on the hospital bed with no blankets and only a small covering over his groin area. A tightly wrapped white bandage was wound around his severely swollen head, which was tilted back on the pillow. A large brace encircled his neck. Plastic tubes, electrodes and hoses jutted from all over his upper body and arms, and a large breathing tube filled his mouth. White-and-orange air-filled stockings forced the blood to keep circulating in his legs. His face and arms were deeply tanned. Apart from the bandage on his head, there were no other visible signs of injury. He looked formidable on the small hospital bed. Since he had gone overseas in peak physical condition, I hoped his body would be strong enough to fight this injury.

I was afraid to speak to him. I was afraid of how I would feel when he didn't respond. I was even more afraid to touch him. He looked so strong and yet so fragile at the same time. I wanted to touch his arm and have him open his eyes and say to me, "Hi, little Bee," and tell me everything was going to be okay. I asked the nurse if it was okay to touch him. She indicated yes. I touched his hand and was relieved to find it warm. His body was on a cooling blanket because his temperature was rising from an infection. Toni and I looked at each other across his tube-infested body, as if to say, "We have to be strong here."

I hadn't thought about what this initial meeting would be like, but I knew I had to be stoic. I took a deep breath and spoke. "Trev, it's Bee," I said. "I'm here with you and Toni is here. I love you. Gracie is here, and your mum and dad and Suzanne. You've been injured, but everything is going to be okay." I expected monitors to start going off when he sensed that I was with him, but there was nothing, just the same rhythms as before. I desperately searched for words that would pierce the fog of the coma and reach his tortured brain. Knowing he had a keen appreciation for the absurd, I shared the trials and tribulations of our flight with him. I told him about how the first flight was cancelled and how Grace wouldn't sleep on the plane, so I had to lie on the floor with her. I held his hand tightly the entire time I spoke. Toni held the other and sent positive healing energy into his body. We stayed for only five or ten minutes. I knew that Dick and Bess would be waiting anxiously to see him. I squeezed his hand and leaned in and told him that I loved him dearly and needed him to come home to us. I thought that, with his strong sense of duty, the call to action as a partner and father would compel him to fight as hard as he could to overcome this challenge.

In the waiting room, I lied to Dick and Bess—and myself— when I said that Trevor didn't look that bad. After a few minutes, they came back to the waiting room visibly shaken. I could tell they were trying to be brave. Bess was wiping her eyes. Dick was looking down at the floor. I couldn't imagine what it would be like seeing your child in this state.

By then it was late in the day. We had slept very little the past few days, so we went back to the hotel to rest and eat. We felt confident in the specialists and nurses working with Trevor and were reassured to learn that a nurse would be with him 24/7. At suppertime, we digested our food and all that we had seen and heard that day. Later that night, Dick and I went back up to the hospital to see Trevor and check on his condition. No change.

After a sleepless night, we all went to the hospital in the morning. The nurse told us that Trevor had been taken off the breathing apparatus in the night for about an hour and was breathing on his own. I gasped when I saw that the tight bandages covering his head had been removed. Hundreds of staples crusted with dried blood circled his head and a small tube in the back drained a reddish fluid like watery tomato juice. The doctors had taken him off two of the medications that were keeping him in the coma, but he hadn't yet opened his eyes. A tube had been inserted into his stomach to provide nutrients to keep him alive.

After the first few days, I started to learn what the different monitors indicated so I could check them myself when I visited. Luckily the pressure in his skull and brain tissue had stopped rising, but his temperature had shot up to 40.6 degrees Celsius.

According to the standard Glasgow Coma Scale, Trevor registered between three and five, indicating deep unconsciousness. The scale ranges from three (deeply unconscious) to fifteen (fully conscious), based on the eye, verbal and motor responses.

Trevor registered the lowest level on the first two. The doctors found atypical movements in the motor responses.

A few days after we arrived, I took Grace in to see Trevor for the first time. Her schedule had been totally thrown off since we left home. She had spent the first couple of nights awake while Toni, Suzanne and I desperately tried to get some sleep in our shared room. Grace hadn't seen Trevor for eight weeks but had constantly watched the videos of him reading storybooks, feeding her and carrying on. I wanted her memory of him to be very much alive. I was afraid for her to see him in this condition but thought she wouldn't understand what was happening anyway. I was determined not to let her sense any sadness, so we opened his door and greeted him with a joyous "Hi Daddy!" I was hopeful that the sensors would start beeping from his awareness of her in the room. But again, nothing. He didn't even open his eyes. I wanted his longing to hug and hold his daughter to help him survive.

After the first couple of days, we started to explore the huge Landstuhl facility. We were beginning to develop a routine, and we would navigate our way around the various cafes and restaurants, shops and, our most important link to the outside world, the Internet room. We spent so much time pacing the miles of hospital hallways that Grace ironically began walking completely independently just as Trevor had lost his ability to do so.

Each evening we would meet with Dr. Gray at the hotel for a medical update. In her thirties, Dr. Gray had a critical role in our understanding of Trevor's condition, since the neurosurgeons were busy treating the daily casualties that arrived. We would discuss Trevor's intracranial pressure, oxygen levels and body temperature like we were discussing the weather. We didn't talk about the seriousness of his head injury. We knew the assault to his brain was a concern, but we didn't think it was as grave an issue as the bacterial infection in his lungs.

The bacteria that Trevor had picked up in Afghanistan was eventually identified as acinetobacter. Normally it is not harmful, but it can wreak havoc on a debilitated hospital patient. The good news was that Trevor's doctors believed it was not the severe strain that had killed other soldiers. Still, Trevor was on massive doses of antibiotics to treat this infection in his lungs, and he lived on the cooling blanket.

Back home, word had spread quickly. Some good friends arranged a gathering of positive thoughts at one of the local beaches. Despite one of the worst storms anyone could remember, forty people turned up that evening to burn candles and pray for Trevor.

We spent most of those days at the hospital, with the exception of a few hours in the afternoon or early evening, when we went back to the hotel to rest and eat. Each day was marginally better than the last. Dick read the newspaper to Trevor every day, as well as the many emails that poured in from friends and family. I would tell him what was happening back home and stress how much we desperately needed him to pull through this.

After a few days, the medical team started to remove some of the tubes from around Trevor's face and body. His eyelids began to open to speech, but his eyes were entirely vacant and clearly not transmitting messages to his brain. When an X-ray found no damage to his neck or spine, doctors removed the tight neck brace, which had left a seven-centimetre open wound that would take weeks to heal.

Ten days after being attacked, Trevor was medically stable enough for the flight back home to Vancouver. I was looking forward to getting home but was nervous about Trevor's still-fragile condition and his ability to make the long flight. I was also nervous to be leaving such a world-renowned facility and moving into the unknown. Trevor would be flown home by air ambulance, while we would be flying on a government jet. The evening before our departure, we ate dinner with the flight crew—two pilots, a military doctor and two nurses. It seemed like overkill to have so many specialists on board Trevor's plane, but at least he would be well taken care of.

After supper, Dick and I went back to the hospital to say our last goodbyes and thank-yous to the incredible staff. The hardest part was saying goodbye to Trevor. Since we were travelling on separate flights early the next morning, we wouldn't see him until we arrived back home nine time zones later. We likely wouldn't even get any information on his condition during the flight. Dick and I gave each other time alone to say our goodbyes. I took Trevor's hand in mine and could feel tears welling up in my eyes as I spoke in his ear. "Honey, we're all leaving tomorrow for home. Be strong for the flight. You have an excellent team with you. We love you and need you to come home to us. Please stay strong and fight this injury. You can do it. You are the strongest, bravest person I know. We need you. I love you. I can't wait until you can come home with us and start our life together." Then I said to him what he always said to me: "*Au revoir, mon cherie.*"

I left the room with the sick feeling that this could be the last time I saw him alive.

CHAPTER 8:
HARSH REALITY

It was 4:30 a.m. on a cold and rainy morning when we left the hotel. From the van I could see Trevor's tiny white Learjet warming up on the tarmac. We were all completely exhausted from the last few days and looking forward to moving on. I dismissed my worries as a feeling of peace and calm came over me. I felt as if everything would be okay. I had always considered myself to be spiritual minded, but how could I know everything was going to be okay? Trevor was lying on a stretcher with a large part of his skull missing after his head had been bashed in.

En route, we made a quick refuelling stop in Iceland. During the stop, we received word that Trevor wasn't having any problems on his flight. So far, so good. I was too tired to get off the plane to see what Iceland looked like. I wanted to stay with Grace, who had finally fallen asleep after being awake for hours, so we waited on board while everyone else got off to get a breath of fresh air. The flight home was long, but at least we were able to move around, eat decent food, not wait in line for the washroom and recline in the seats enough to actually sleep.

Hours later, we were setting down on the Vancouver tarmac. I looked down on the familiar airport and spotted a throng of media and army personnel waiting for us. It was daunting to have cameras thrust into our faces as we exited the plane and walked across the wet concrete to a smaller two-story building away from the main terminal. Trevor had become a public figure back home, and these images would help to complete the picture of our ordeal. It felt as if we'd had our privacy stolen.

We were greeted warmly inside the airport building by General Tim Grant and his contingent. After a few words with the family, General Grant turned to me and unexpectedly said, "I would like to present you with Trevor's Afghanistan service medal," or something to that effect. He handed me a small box. Inside was Trevor's Southwest Asia service medal. I tried to be strong as I accepted it and said, "Thank you, General Grant. It's an honour to receive this medal for Trevor." I looked over toward Dick and Bess, who were also holding their emotions in, and handed the box to them. Dick looked proud to be holding Trevor's medal but sad that it had had to be presented under these circumstances.

Trevor's plane touched down about ninety minutes later. Dick, Bess and I ran out in the pouring rain while he was transferred to an ambulance. He was resting comfortably and would be taken to Vancouver General Hospital. I felt a weight lift off my shoulders when I saw him alive on the stretcher. I wanted to go in the ambulance with him and hold his hand, but it wasn't practical. I was tired, Grace was cranky and Trevor would be examined over the next few hours. We went home for a few hours to rest.

When we met the neurosurgeon for the first time at the hospital later that day, he explained just how serious Trevor's head injury was. I was sure that after the doctors thoroughly examined the test results, they would realize the injury wasn't as bad as they had thought. Since a battery of tests were being performed, we wouldn't be able to see Trevor again that day, so we went home to unpack and sleep. We didn't know it at the time, but we had many sleepless nights ahead of us.

The following morning at the hospital, we found Trevor alone in a glass-enclosed room. He was under isolation because of the bacteria, so we had to wear masks, gloves and gowns and pass through two sets of doors to see him. His eyes were open, but there had been no change in his condition overnight. We were taken to yet another beige meeting room to see the attending physician, who would, I figured, tell us that Trevor's condition was not as bad as had been thought. At the end of the table was an ICU nurse and the spiritual services counsellor, Ray Mac-Donald. Dick and Bess sat on one side of the table and Toni and I on the other. The nurse appeared very serious and offered a greeting devoid of the customary pleasantries. The physician entered the room. He was short and wore round glasses. He had a discontented, serious look on his face.

He slowly gathered his thoughts and said with a Spanish accent, "I am very disappointed about the papers today." I knew *The Globe and Mail* had reported that Trevor was able to move his eyes and legs on command, and they quoted Dick as saying, "The family is confident that he will recover completely. He opened his eyes. He wasn't conscious or talking to us, but he's showing improvement every day. Even today, I could see it." I thought the article was accurate, except for the part about Trevor moving his legs on command.

He voiced his concern about the deadly pneumonia in Trevor's right lung and said he had pneumothorax, a buildup of air out-side the lung. "The bacteria is a very aggressive strain, resistant to most antibiotics."

The doctor continued, "Trevor has a diffused brain injury, and basically the whole cortex of the brain is damaged. He has a severe neurological deficit. He is in a vegetative state and will not regain consciousness."Across the table, Dick's eyes were wide in shock and Bess was wiping away tears. Toni's face was ashen, and a horrified silence filled the room. I couldn't believe what I was hearing. *This can't be happening*, my mind screamed. The situation hadn't seemed this bad in Germany. I was getting light-headed and was glad I was sitting down. I'd never expected to hear this from the doctor. I'd expected him to say that Trevor would wake up soon.

His next words were hollow: "I understand how you're feel-ing."

Before leaving, the doctor asked if we had any more ques-tions. Now I understood why the counsellor was at the meet-ing—he was there to pick up the pieces after we had been told that Trevor was never coming back. As we prepared to leave, the nurse said that the doctor understood what we were going through, and that one day we would be thankful. I never quite understood what she meant by that. I still don't.

That afternoon, we met with our military case manager for the first time. The four of us were still reeling from the doc-tor's words. As I struggled to hold back tears, the case man-ager blabbed on about our benefits and the forms we had to fill out. I don't remember one word of the conversation. My mind was buzzing with the news that my fiancé would *not* regain consciousness. The words kept running through my mind as I patted away tears. I had been surrounded by people from the moment I was given the news, and now all I wanted was to be alone. I was frustrated that there didn't appear to be anything the medical professionals could do to help Trevor.

"I've got to do something," I thought. "Trevor doesn't have a hope in hell here." The doctor's prognosis was decisive: Trevor would not come out of his coma. Just then, I remembered an email Anita had sent to me in Germany about a local young man who was rumoured to have miraculous healing abilities. This was just the hope I needed. I couldn't get out of that meeting fast enough. I didn't care about the tangled bureaucratic trails our case manager had navigated—I had to get to my computer and send this healer a message.

After the meeting Toni and I went home, while Dick and Bess went to their suite at the base headquarters. We all needed space to take in the awful news. On the way home, I told Toni about the healer and said that we needed to send him a message. We sat down together at the computer. I found his email address and typed in the subject line "Canadian Solider Injured in Axe Attack . . . PLEASE HELP!!" In the body of the message, I wrote:

March 18, 2006

Hi Adam,

I'm the wife of Trevor Greene, the Canadian soldier injured by an axe attack to the head in Afghanistan on March 4, 2006. He is currently in serious condition in Vancouver General Hospital. Today the doctors and neurosurgeons delivered their news that he has a "severe neurological deficit" and is in a "persistent vegetative state." They don't expect him to regain consciousness. He has large pneumonia in the right lung and continues to have a high temperature (40.6 Celsius today). His brain has swollen and they had to remove large parts of his skull to allow it to swell. Blood flow throughout the brain is limited and there was a transection of a large vein in the brain. He has opened his eyes on command

and tried to blink. We have people all over the world praying for him, but it's going to take more than that. We're hoping for a miracle now. If you're able to help us, please contact me at the number below. Our family would be greatly appreciative of any guidance you can provide.

Kind regards, Debbie Lepore and family

After sending the email, I called Anita and explained what the doctor had told us. We arranged to meet at the hospital later that evening. When she entered Trevor's room, she seemed to be able to "connect" with him on some level. Afterward, she told me that Trevor wasn't sure he could deal with the enormity of the injury, but that he was unable to let go because of Grace and me. She said I needed to tell him that we would be okay if he had to go. This would help him make the choice.

As Anita was leaving, she gave me a long hug and said she would continue to work on him on an energetic level every day. I walked her out and then went back in to see Trevor. It would be the hardest one-sided conversation I would ever have.

I held his hand in silence for a long time before I spoke. "Trev, I love you with all my heart. I need you to know that Grace and I will be okay if you decide you can't do this. We will go on and we will be okay. You have to do what is best for you. We want you with us more than anything, but we will be okay if this is too much for you." My voice cracked and tears streamed down my face as I said goodbye with *"Je t'aime, mon cherie."*

I went home that night with the heaviest of hearts. I didn't know how I would explain to Grace that I had told her father it would be okay to die. When I got home, I trudged up the stairs and stood looking down at Grace sleeping soundly in her crib. I asked myself what I had done to her. What did our future have in store for us? I was hit hard with the realization that I could end up as a single mother. As a stroked her fine baby hair, I mourned the fact that Grace might never know her father again.

I crept downstairs to the shower and let the warm water wash away the misery of the day. The sense of loss was too strong for me to hold back the tears. I couldn't get the events of the day out of my mind, and I let the tears flow out with the warm water. I had never felt more emotionally exhausted in my life. As I turned off the shower and wrapped myself in a robe, I thought about something I had read once. It is said that our souls make the choice to live or die when we are in mortal peril, depending on the difficulty of the healing journey. If the soul senses that there is a higher purpose in life and enough love as an anchor, it will fight against passing on.

When I crawled into bed that night, I remembered the letter Trev had mailed to me before leaving for Afghanistan. It was his "final letter" should something happen to him. I pulled it out of the drawer and opened it. On the front it read, "Stick this in a drawer and forget about it. You will never need to read it. Only read it if something happens to me. I love you, Maqua."

I felt compelled to know his final words, so I gently opened the envelope, sat down and began reading.

January 18, 2006

My darling little Bee,
If you are reading this, I have been killed in action in Afghanistan. We probably zigged when we should have zagged.

I know that you are in a great deal of pain right now. I hope that with these, my final words to you, there may be some way for you to gain some sort of comfort. If not necessarily now, then hopefully soon.

We are both believers in karma, or destiny. It appears that it was my destiny to die serving our country.

Know that I died proud and strong, without fear and without pain. The enemy took my life, but in so doing they had the fight of their lives. Do not turn your thoughts to revenge or restitution or justice. My brothers will make the enemy pay for my death. They will seek justice. That is their job now. Events that happen on the battlefield are best left there for warriors to deal with. I went to Afghanistan as a soldier from a foreign country bearing arms. I went there to defend Canada, but it was the duty of the people who killed me, frankly, to kill me.

Please do not view my death as a sacrifice. I took a soldier's chance and I lost. But understand that I died defending you and Grace as surely as if I had died defending you both from an intruder in our home.

A lecturer once spoke very movingly to us of what he called the warrior path. He applied it to armies and fighting but also more specifically to the police officers and firefighters who responded to the 9/11 attacks. We were shown two astonishing photos—one of a policeman and one of a firefighter, both re-entering one of the World Trade Center towers after having gotten people out. Their faces are white with shock and they look to be literally sick with fear. They were fearful because they knew that they stood a very good chance of dying that day. But they kept going back into the tower until they died because they were warriors. They understood that there were people they could save in there. People who believed in their courage and strength. People who knew that these guys, and guys like them, were their best chance to survive the day. People who believed in warriors.

I like to think that I was a warrior in my day, in my war. My duty was very clear to me: to defend my family and my country. I understand now that the policeman and the firefighter couldn't have lived with themselves if they didn't go back in. Every fibre of their being, every cell in their body was telling them to run away, just like everyone else was running away. But they went in that one last fatal time because they knew inherently that once they started on the warrior path, they were committed. Once you are a warrior, you never really are anything else. You may hand in your uniform and move on and call yourself by a different title and think of yourself as doing something else, but in your heart of hearts you know that you will always answer the call to duty. You will always brave the smoke and the flames, the danger and the darkness. You will always do the things that ordinary people—the people you have sworn to protect—are deathly frightened to do.

I would like you to be proud of me while you mourn. Be proud of me because I fought for you and I fought for life. Precious, fabulous life.

And that brings me to the most important part of this letter. If you read anything in here more than once, let it be this part. I need you to mourn for me, to cry for me and to grieve for me. That is healthy and that is right.

Then I need you to move on.

I need you to seize a precious and fabulous life and move on without me. Hold Grace tightly, cherish her, breathe new life into her and yourself and move on. You will love again. I know it. You will find someone who will make you a wonderful husband and Grace a wonderful daddy. Let your love for that man take its course. Let it flourish and bloom. Let him love Grace and let Grace love him. Tell her to call him Daddy. Tell him to consider Grace to be his daughter.

Let my memory fade. Let the army honour its dead. Stick my medals in a drawer somewhere. I am one more name on a roll call at Remembrance Day now, and that is enough for me. Let me go.

My purpose in life, and death, wasn't to become your ghost. If you cling to my memory to the exclusion of all else, you will dishonour me and all that I lived for. My death gives you a new lease on life. It puts you on a different kind of warrior path. It challenges you to see that I fought for life. I fought for my life, for *your life and for Grace's life. You must embrace the richest, most rewarding and utterly fabulous life that has ever been lived. Life filled with love and joy. And you must pass that on to Grace. That is your challenge and it is my gift to you.*

I love you, my darling, and I love our daughter. We went through some bumps and got some bruises, but I always knew that my love was solid ground for you to stand on. Use it now to stand on and launch into the next phase of a gloriously fun, cool, happy life. That is my final wish for you. That you choose to embrace life. Crack the bones of life and suck out the marrow every day. Every single day.

Tell Grace about me if she asks. Tell her that I loved her and that I thought she was the best little wabbit in the woods. But tell her that I am gone forever. Tell her that I am just a nice memory now. When you are alone sometimes, smile a fond smile as you recall what a bag of hammers I was. Love the Wabbit and feel the embrace of her love for you. Bounce our grandkids on your knee. Have a fabulous life. I love you with all my heart and soul.

Maqua

Reading the letter left me with a feeling of anger and abandonment. I was angry that he had given up and accepted his fate so readily. I wanted to hear more about how much he loved us and how dearly he would miss us and how sorry he was for leaving us behind.

When I left the hospital, I had given him the choice of living or dying. After reading the letter, I was determined not to let him give up so easily. I knew that he had the warrior spirit, and that giving up was not in his nature. Reading the letter convinced me that he was going to fight and I was going to help him. I felt my mind begin to take control of the situation. I decided to start writing a journal to preserve my sanity and to chronicle how I would prove the doctor wrong. I was proud of how I had handled myself so far. I had pretty much kept myself together and kept my mind strong. I felt grounded going into this nightmare. I believed that having a strong mind meant having a strong body, and I couldn't allow my body to break down. I had too much to give to both Trevor and Grace. After reading the letter, I had no tears left to cry and finally fell asleep.

CHAPTER 9:
RENEWED HOPE

The next morning I felt completely drained. I called the hospital to check in on Trevor and booted up the computer in the faint hope that there was an email from Adam. His father, Frank, had replied an hour after I sent my message.

> Hi Debbie,
> Please send us a clear close-up face picture in colour ASAP of him. It doesn't have to be a recent picture. Please send it over the Internet. No guarantees but Adam will take a look.
>
> Frank

I sent a clear picture of Trevor smiling into the camera. I figured that Adam would be better able to connect if he could look into Trevor's eyes. Adam was planning to make his first "remote connection" to Trevor at 12:30 p.m. that day. Frank asked that Trevor be undisturbed during the session, and that I observe his actions, so Grace and I went to the hospital early. Trevor was awake, but his face wore the same glazed-over look it had in Germany. The nurse told me there had been no change during the night. He was still on the ventilator, since he was coughing up pus from his lungs. His temperature had finally broken from a high of 40.6 degrees Celsius the day before. The nurse said that a doctor would be inserting a tube to drain fluid from the infected right lung at 1 p.m. I hoped this would give Adam enough time.

At 12:30 I put a note on the door asking that we not be disturbed and started to watch Trevor closely for any changes. I noticed a slight blink a few times and saw some movement in his left eye, but not any more than usual. At around 12:49, he drew in two very quick breaths and his heart rate took a couple of big jumps on the monitor, then he was quiet. This would be the first of many "distant energy" treatments by Adam. I later got an email from Adam explaining what he'd noticed: "I saw light sparking along the neural pathways in his brain. I have seen this before in brain injury cases I have worked with and it shows that a significant connection to healing energy has been achieved. It showed me that Trevor's brain had the capacity to heal and reconnect, so I bombarded his sparking neurons with light. Neurons were regenerating and reactivating rapidly. I was very encouraged by what I saw energetically." I was heartened by Adam's email, but I still had to juggle alternative energetic healing with the realities of conventional medicine.

Trev spent much of day sleeping after the tube went in to his lung. His commanding officer, Rob Roy Mackenzie, came to visit and stood silently by his side for hours. I went home to have supper with Grace, Dick and Bess. After Grace's bath, we rocked in the big rocking chair in her room. We said a prayer for Trevor and quietly sang songs until she fell asleep. When I went back to the hospital later that evening, the nurse said Trev was tracking with his eyes to the left but was more sluggish to the right. He was also flexing his foot to pain. I held up photos of Grace in front of him to see if there was any recognition there. His eyes moved toward the pictures, but the vacant look remained. I read a little of the newspaper to him and then turned it around to show him a picture. He seemed to look right at it, but again his face was impassive. On the way home, I thought about what the doctors had said about him being in a persistent vegetative state. At home I turned on the desk lamp and computer. I took my steaming cup of tea to the bedroom, typed in "vegetative state" and found out that after one month, a vegetative state is considered persistent. Patients can open their eyes and yawn, but they have no awareness of themselves or their environment. The only movements they are capable of are primitive, like a baby who instinctively grabs something that is put in her hand. My blood chilled when I read at the end that the prognosis is bleak, and the family may need to discuss withdrawal of care.

I couldn't stop thinking about the way Trevor's eyes looked at the newspaper and Grace's picture. It didn't seem consistent with what I'd read. When I finished my research, there was an email from Adam saying he would do a follow-up treatment.

The next morning at the hospital, Trevor looked about the same as he had the day before. Then I noticed that he wasn't in the air-filled plastic boots he had been wearing since Germany to protect his feet. The nurses had no idea where they were and said they didn't have anything like them in the hospital. I assumed they weren't necessary, since the nurses weren't concerned about them. But months later, when Trevor's feet became horribly contracted, I learned that the boots might have helped to prevent that.

...

Eventually, Dick and Bess had to go back home for medical appointments. I would dearly miss their company, and their help with Trevor and Grace. I wanted to be at the hospital all the time, but it wasn't possible with Grace so young. Thankfully, Trevor's favourite cousin and Grace's godfather, Mickey, was in town to see Dick and Bess off, and he spent the day with Grace so I could be at the hospital. When I arrived, Trevor's eyes were blank and his face was waxy and expressionless, very different from the animated man I knew. But I was excited to hear he had been taken off the ventilator for three hours that morning and had been breathing on his own.

One doctor told me that Trev had moved up to an eight on the Glasgow Coma Scale. I asked him to describe the coma scale to me and explain how they determined Trevor's score. I figured I could make my own daily assessment of him. I knew that when he'd left Kandahar for Germany, he was a four on the scale, scoring one for both eye and verbal (since he wasn't responding to either), and two for motor functions (since his brain was responding to pain). In Germany, he was between three and five. I calculated that he registered eight on the scale when he started opening his eyes spontaneously.

At night I kept friends and family up to date by email. Most of the return emails ended with the phrase "My thoughts and prayers are with you." Some said that their whole church was praying for us. Others said that their relatives, their friends' relatives and their friends' relatives' friends were praying for Trevor. I felt that we weren't alone on this journey. One email was from Trevor's friend from his Japan days, Greg Kelly, saying that C.W. Nicol would be in town for a short time and wanted to visit. I knew that C.W. was an iconic figure to Trevor, as both a close friend and a mentor, and that a visit from him would be powerful.

After meeting C.W., I knew why Trevor had spoken so highly of him. He was kind, gentle and eloquent. He spoke directly to Trevor, as if he could hear and understand him. Before leaving, C.W. leaned over the bed with tears in his eyes and said, "Hang in there."

Later that night, I received an email from Adam recommending that I help Trevor heal by visualizing the synapses in his brain firing off. I didn't know if I could affect anything, but if it would potentially help Trevor, I would do it. I picked up his picture from the desk and imagined miniature electrical flashes arcing along his neurons.

The next email I read was from Trevor's best friend, Barb. She was suggesting that I start saying a Catholic prayer called a novena, which is prayed over nine days. It is said that on the ninth day, the prayer will be answered. Trevor was a Catholic, so I figured there was a chance it would work for him. I committed myself to saying the prayer six times a day for the nine days. My intention was that Trevor would speak his first words on the ninth day. Unfortunately, nine days later, he was still silent.

Gradually, Trevor's sleep-wake cycles became more normal and he started to sleep less during the day and more at night. Because he was in such a sterile environment, I thought his sense of smell would need activating. I wasn't worried about damaging his brain with overstimulation because I knew that smell is our most primitive sense. I brought in coffee beans, lemon, chocolate and his cologne. I couldn't tell if he was smelling them or not, but I stuck them under his nose and told him to take a good whiff. On the twentieth day since his injury, Trevor marked two milestones: he was finally weaned off the ventilator at night, and he was lifted out of bed into a special wheelchair. I was also told that once his oxygen level stabilized, he'd be able to leave the ICU. Late that night, I called the hospital and learned that Trevor had been moved to Neuro ICU. Every move to a new level, where the nurse-to-patient ratio is lower, was a good one. I was relieved to hear that he was finally making tangible progress.

Trev's new room was much brighter and more uplifting than his isolation room had been. The large windows let in plenty of natural light, and I hung pictures on big, colourful paper around the room. He still looked glazed, but when I told him the date and time, he looked up at the clock. I was so excited to see a normal response and was convinced that it couldn't have been pure coincidence. It had to mean that his cognitive functions were intact. Just to be sure, I asked him a few minutes later if he knew where the clock was, and he looked right at it again.

A chest tube had been draining pus from inside his exhausted right lung for several weeks. But his doctor found that the buildup of fluid outside the lung was becoming more severe, increasing the risk of oxygen starvation. An incision was made under his right armpit, and yet another tube was slid down the outside of his lung.

Despite the bright new room, Trev was still kept in isolation because he continued to test positive for acinetobacter and E. coli. His white blood cell count was up, indicating that his body was trying to fight off the infection.

In the afternoon he became sleepy, so I headed out to find a book on reflexology. A friend had sent me the story of a woman who brought her father out of a coma using reflexology. Reflexology is based on the premise that different areas of the feet correspond to different areas of the body and can correct imbalances in the life-force energy, known as Qi. I bought an illustrated reflexology book and went home to have dinner with Grace. After she was asleep, I left her with Regina and headed back to the hospital with the book, excited to get started.

A diagram showed that the tops of the first three toes corresponded to the brain and the balls of the foot to the lungs. Even though Trevor still had the same unresponsive gaze, I greeted him with a kiss, showed him my book and told him I would be doing reflexology on him regularly to help speed up his healing. I thought about how he used to love rubbing my feet but hated the feeling of lotion on his hands. He would run to the bathroom immediately after to wash off the slimy cream. After warming my hands at the sink, I pulled back the sheets at the foot of the bed and positioned the book on the end. I placed my hands firmly on the top of Trevor's warm feet to get him used to my touch, then slowly moved my fingers to the top of his big toe and firmly held it with my fingertips. Following the intricate techniques in the book, I thumb-walked up the inside of the toe and then switched hands to thumb-walk across the top. I followed the instructions precisely for the areas that correspond to the lungs and gave his rough, dry heels a rub for good measure. I was pleased that after my first efforts, he seemed to relax and fall asleep.

When I walked into the sunlit room the next day, the head of the bed was raised, and for the first time, Trevor turned to look at me. I'd brought dark chocolate, banana and orange for him to taste. He still wasn't allowed to eat any food, but I thought a little sampling on the tongue would help activate different parts of his brain. When I brought the chocolate to his lips, he tried to take a bite of it. This again didn't seem to be consistent with someone in a vegetative state.

I also played one of his favourite movies, *Sideways,* and a few of Grace's Baby Einstein videos, which had colourful pictures set to classical music. He seemed to really pay close attention to the Baby Bach video.

At noon I watched another session by Adam, and this time I noticed slight movements in Trevor's body. His right leg bent up at the knee and his lower jaw moved from side to side. After Adam's session, I used reflexology to focus on Trevor's brain and lungs. He nodded off toward the end, so I said goodnight and left him to sleep. I came home to find that a girlfriend had left a beautiful basket of food and a music CD for Grace on my doorstep.

Now that Trevor's family had all gone home, I thought it was time he had more stimulation from friends. They had all been supportive and wanted to see him, but I had to be careful not to overstimulate his brain. I first invited Barb and Clare, two of Trevor's close, long-time friends from university. Although Trevor's face was entirely inexpressive during their visit, they said they could tell through his eyes that he remembered them and the stories they told.

One night, I found a handwritten letter that one of Trevor's army buddies had dropped off. Later that evening at the hospital, I pulled out the letter and read it to him. I was impressed by his friend's meticulously neat handwriting. Holding the letter up for Trevor, I said, "Look at how neat Rad's handwriting is. It's almost like he typed it." As I always did, I watched Trevor's eyes for any sign of recognition. I was stunned to see his vacant eyes follow the lines across the page and down to the bottom, as if he were reading. Still not quite believing what I was seeing, I flipped the page over and watched again as his eyes tracked the lines of the letter. When I got home, I turned again to the Internet and was shocked to learn that reading is impossible for someone in a vegetative state.

When I told the doctor the next day that I had witnessed what I thought was Trevor reading, he responded casually that he "wasn't in a coma anymore," as if he had known this for quite some time. His matter-of-fact attitude appalled me because I had expected to be told of such a major step forward. For the first time, I realized that I wasn't going to get the answers I needed unless I was more proactive.

...

Now that Trevor was officially out of his coma, the real work could finally begin. The problem was that he still had little or no active movement. The only things he could do were open his mouth and hold his head up for a few seconds. His arms and legs were so rigid it was if he were encased in an iceberg or steel rods, and his arms reacted abnormally to pain, which I later learned indicated severe brain damage.

The neurosurgeon's visits always began with him commanding loudly, "TREVOR, STICK OUT YOUR TONGUE." I hated the demeaning tone of his voice but knew it was necessary to pierce Trevor's post-coma stupor. On one particular visit, the doctor explained that Trevor's ability to follow commands to open his mouth and stick out his tongue indicated that he was doing better neurologically. The best Trevor could do was open his mouth slightly and squeeze his tongue just past his teeth. Still, I was hopelessly optimistic about his recovery, even though he was inconsistent and slow to respond to even this simple command.

I was in constant communication with Trevor's family, and together we were trying to think about his physical rehabilitation, but there were still medical issues to deal with. A recent CT scan had found a blood clot in Trevor's left lung, so he had to be put on a blood thinner. The neurosurgeon told us that the surgery to rebuild Trevor's skull wouldn't happen until the fall, or even the following year, since they "didn't want to be poking around the brain too much." On a positive note, the doctor planned to do trials to remove the tracheal tube in Trevor's throat. I was happy but concerned, since he was still on oxygenated air and thick secretions were still being sucked out of his lungs.

Because of the blood thinner medication, blood had to be drawn from Trevor daily and tested to ensure it was clotting properly. To avoid having to prick him every day, doctors inserted a line near his collarbone into a vein directly into his heart to get quick access his blood.

We also weren't receiving good news about Trevor's right lung. Despite heavy doses of antibiotics, the infection was still raging and the doctors talked about removing the lung. I could have given into despair, but with all the other issues Trevor was facing, losing a lung was the least of my concerns. Regardless, that night I sent an email to Adam and Anita about the potential surgery, and they both committed to focusing their intentions on the right lung.

It worked—or something did—and Trevor kept his lung. The doctor decided instead to remove the fluid that was building up outside the lung through a procedure called decortication. Two tubes would also be inserted to allow the infectious fluid to drain. Since Trevor would have to go off the blood thinners for surgery, a blood clot filter was inserted into his lung through his jugular vein. It seemed that every step forward was followed by two steps back. It was impossible to think beyond the here and now. That night, I went over in my mind all we had endured and wondered why this had happened to him. I thought about how he had been taken down at the peak of his life. I thought about how he had always had a gift for words and now could barely speak. I wanted our old life back.

CHAPTER 10:
ONE MONTH LATER . . .

I couldn't help thinking that exactly one month ago, Trevor was lying in a puddle of his own blood and brains in a dusty Kandahar village. Three weeks ago, I was told he wouldn't come out of his coma. A few days ago, I was told he might have to lose a lung. Today, I was watching his face grimace, as if in pain, while a healer treated his lung from a distance.

Having dealt on my own with all the medical drama and doctors over the past couple of weeks, I was ecstatic to see Trevor's mum, dad and sister, Suzanne, on my doorstep. Early the next morning, Suzanne and I went to the hospital while Dick and Bess reconnected with Grace. Trevor's nurse Kim rushed up to us in the hallway and excitedly said that Trevor had talked that morning. Kim said she had plugged his open trach tube with her finger and asked him if he knew where he was.

"Japan," he whispered.

I was desperate to hear him say my name, but part of me was worried that he wouldn't remember me. Suzanne, Kim and I scurried in and clustered at the side of his bed. Kim plugged Trevor's tube again and asked him to speak.

"Hi Suzanne," I heard him say faintly.

"Trevor, what's my name?" I blurted out.

I was overjoyed when I heard him whisper, "Debbie."

Kim asked if he was in any pain.

"Yes. Head. Chest," he murmured quietly.

To avoid infection, Kim cautioned us against plugging the trach too often, so we worked out a simple code with tongue out for yes and silence for no. But we soon found the system too rudimentary and inconsistent, so the speech therapist brought in a Plexiglas board with the words "yes" and "no" visible underneath. The idea was for Trevor to look at the proper word in response to questions, since he wasn't able to motion with his head. This system worked better, but still he wasn't always consistent.

The next morning, Suzanne and I found Trevor in his room, leaning backward at a sixty-degree angle, strapped to a padded table with a footboard. This was his first time on a tilt table, which was meant to reintroduce his body to a vertical position and put weight on his feet. Trevor looked frightened and indicated by open/closed mouth signals that he was in pain. After five minutes, his blood pressure dropped and his heart rate increased. When he tried to speak, his heart rate skyrocketed, so the physiotherapist cranked him down to forty-five degrees for another fifteen minutes.

After Trevor was comfortably back in bed, I asked him if he knew why he was in the hospital. He indicated no. We still hadn't told him that his tour had been cut short by an axe to the head. I was afraid of what that news would do to his mental state. He had been doing progressively better, and I didn't want to send him into a complete depression for fear his recovery would spiral downward.

Over time, Trevor's face slowly became more expressive and we started to see his pain. One day I pulled up a chair next to his wheelchair and held up the newspaper. It was something we always enjoyed doing together, especially on the weekends. I put my hand on his leg and gave it a slight squeeze, which triggered a spasm throughout his body. His face contorted in pain as if he had just been electrocuted.

Despite the pain, I believed his mind was healing. Trevor's orientation was tested every day—he knew he was at Vancouver General Hospital and not in Japan, and was pretty accurate on the year most of the time. The amount of pus in his lung had fallen significantly, and a chest X-ray would soon determine if the chest tubes could come out. Once the trach tube had been removed, an occupational therapist would assess his ability to swallow.

By early April, the swelling in Trevor's head had receded. His scalp was draped over the thin remnant of skull that the doctors in Germany had left down the middle of his head, creating grapefruit-sized depressions on either side. A little hair covered his head, but the depressions were still startling, as if the sides of his head had been smashed in with a hammer.

The neurosurgeon came by to discuss the reconstruction of Trevor's skull. He explained that his skull would be scanned into a computer and polyethylene bone flaps would be built from that image. When the doctor tapped his own head to demonstrate, I shuddered—Trevor wasn't aware that two large parts of his skull were missing and his head was severely deformed. I hoped he didn't understand what the doctor was talking about.

After the neurosurgeon left, Trevor looked at me and breathlessly mouthed, "I love you." It was the first I'd heard him say it since the day he left for Afghanistan four months earlier.

"I love you, too," I said through my tears.

I was eager to learn as much as I could about brain injuries, so I signed up for an afternoon seminar at the local rehabilitation facility. About ten people attended the seminar, all of them family members of survivors of car accidents and strokes. Unsurprisingly, my fiancé was the only axe-attack victim. Most people talked about how their loved one's personality had changed radically after the injury. The doctor talked about what changes to expect. This was what I was hoping to hear, because Trevor really hadn't completely woken up out of this fog he was in. As the doctor spoke, I scanned the "What to Expect" handout:

- Decreased level of consciousness
- Disoriented and confused, short-tempered
- Any memory around the accident will be gone permanently
- Confabulation: the brain makes up stories for loss of memory
- Impaired insight and judgment: the person may act inappropriately or may act on feelings immediately as if they were a child
- They can become angry when they realize their deficiencies

The only item on the list I'd noticed in Trevor was the decreased level of consciousness. I'd have to wait and see about the others, since at that moment, communication was limited. I was relieved to hear, however, that it's considered a good sign if there is continued recovery in the first two weeks. More than four weeks had passed and Trevor was progressing, albeit slowly. The doctor explained that recovery can still be happening up to two years after injury. After that, she said, "The patient has to find strategies to compensate."

After the seminar, I brought Grace to the hospital for a visit. On the drive in, we had been singing "If You're Happy and

You Know It." Grace had no problems clapping her hands and stomping her feet, but when it came to blinking her eyes, she comically scrunched up her face. When we arrived at the hospital, Trevor was in the wheelchair with his head sloped so far forward that his chin rested on his chest. He struggled to lift his head to look at us. I wanted to show him how funny Grace looked, so I began the song again. He managed to raise his head just enough to catch a glimpse of her while she was trying to blink. He started to laugh, but the movement only caused him to grimace in pain. I was shocked that he couldn't raise his head and saddened that laughing would cause him pain. I gently lifted up Trevor's head so he could see his daughter.

One of our favourite comedians, Dan Aykroyd, was in town on a charity motorcycle ride and had heard about Trevor on the news. He arranged to drop by his hospital room to visit on a Sunday afternoon. I didn't tell Trevor who was coming, only that someone special would be visiting that afternoon.

After lunch, I went down to the lobby to meet Dan, but I could see only a couple of large guys dressed in bike leathers with hats and dark glasses. One of the guys came over and asked if I was Debbie. He introduced himself as the manager, and then I realized that Dan was the other guy in the biker jacket. I took them upstairs to Trevor's room. I could tell by the look in his eyes that he recognized Dan immediately. Unfazed by Trevor's noticeably dented head, Dan put us all at ease with his wit and charm. He was kind and down to earth and had even brought Trevor an autographed bottle of tequila.

After Dan left, Trev turned to me and whispered, "I love you." It made me cry. The little he was saying to me was all I needed to hear. He hadn't been able to say very much to this point. The speech therapist thought it was because of problems with motor planning, a condition called apraxia. Seeing me teary-eyed,

Trevor said, "Made you cry," just like the old days—which made me laugh. Finding humour together again felt so good after all the stress and sorrow of the last month.

The following Monday morning, two physiotherapists came in to sit Trevor on the side of the bed. They had to support his entire body, for it was immediately evident that he had no control. The weight and muscle mass he had lost made him look like a frail old man in a thin blue hospital gown. That afternoon, an occupational therapist and a speech pathologist came by to do a swallowing assessment. They fed him pureed fruit and thickened fluid dyed with blue food colouring. After he ate they opened his trach and slid a long hose down to see if he had aspirated any of the blue dye into his lungs. Seeing no dye, they approved a diet of pureed food and thick fluids to supplement his tube feeds.

When I visited again in the evening, I was looking forward to having some time alone with Trevor and hoped he might be able to talk a little more. But his eyes scanned my face like he didn't know who I was. I quickly shrugged the bizarre episode off because I knew things like that might happen from time to time. Then I noticed that his trach had been removed. A tight bandage covered the hole, known as a stoma, where the tube had been. I asked the nurse about the trach site, and she said they didn't stitch it up because the hole closed over on its own quite quickly. She also said that the trach had been removed because his chest tubes weren't draining any more fluid and his cough was strong enough to clear his own throat. I was both excited and disappointed that the tube had been removed—excited because it meant progress, but disappointed because the nurse said it would be impossible for him to talk until the hole closed over.

At least he could finally eat. Grace and I were there the next day to witness his first meal in five weeks—plain oatmeal, custard and apple sauce, topped off with a glass of thickened apple juice. Not the most sumptuous of banquets, but he wolfed down every last bite. He wasn't allowed to sip water yet, but he could suck on small pink sponges glued to the end of a stick. At the same time, he tried to follow fifteen-month-old Grace around the room with his eyes while she blissfully pasted heart-shaped Post-it Notes to the walls. After breakfast, we left him to rest and allow his body to digest the meal while I took Grace home for a nap. Before we left, the nurse said that his chest tubes would be removed that day, and that because he required less nursing care, he would likely be moved to the next unit, the "neuro step-down" ward.

When I returned later, the chest tubes were gone and Trevor had already been moved to the new unit. The new room overlooked the city, the mountains and the landing pad for the hospital's helicopter. There was a lot of hustle and bustle in his new room, and I could tell from the look on his face that he was uncomfortable and anxious about all the change and stimulation. When I asked if he needed anything, with a sad face he mouthed, "You." I had been away for only a few hours, and yet I felt like I had abandoned him when he needed me to help him adjust to the new surroundings. I reassured him that this move was positive because it meant that he was progressing, and I told him that the next move would be to the general ward and then home.

After only a few days of mush, Trevor graduated to minced meals. I was hoping that sinking his teeth into his food instead of slurping it would put more meat on his bones. He was down to 169 pounds, thirty-six less than he'd weighed when he went overseas. After feeding him his first semi-solid dinner, I told him I'd be back in the morning to help with breakfast. I was heartened to know that his sense of humour was still intact when I heard him whisper, "You don't want to miss that." It seemed that the upgrade to minced food had made him feel more like himself again. But I sensed that this newfound confidence—and the fact that he still wasn't aware how badly he was hurt—had made him impatient to get back in the field.

Dr. Pankaj Dhawan, a physiatrist, came by the room the following afternoon to meet us and assess Trevor's rehab potential. I had never heard of a physiatrist, but Dr. Dhawan explained that he specialized in physical medicine and rehabilitation. Physiatrists treat injuries that don't require surgery. When he turned to Trevor and asked what had happened to him, he whispered that he was wounded in Afghanistan. But when Dr. Dhawan asked Trevor where he was, I was shocked when he answered, "Tokyo."

After his examination, Dr. Dhawan recommended that I activate different parts of Trevor's brain by showing him nostalgic photos, playing videos and posing questions about his environment. He voiced his concern about the tightness and contraction in Trevor's ankles. He and his colleague, Dr. Rajiv Reebye, wanted to try Botox and serial casting (a series of casts) to gradually reposition Trevor's ankles and prevent them from locking straight down. I mentioned to the doctor that I felt Trevor's arms were also becoming very tight. No matter how many stretching and range-of-motion exercises we did, they still remained rigid. He explained that Trevor's body was wracked with spasticity because his damaged brain had made the muscles overactive without the ability to turn off. He said that he hoped to reduce the tightness by increasing the dosage of the anti-spasmodic drug Trevor was already on and was also considering adding another new drug to the mix.

Once the hole in Trevor's throat closed over, he began to speak more, but I noticed it was only ever in response to a question. He never initiated conversation, even with Grace. Also, most of his replies were only a few short words, and those were a great effort for him. Because of this, I had to look for moments to connect father and daughter again. Most weekends, I brought Grace in for a visit, but every time the glass doors slid shut behind us, I was concerned that her young immune system would succumb to the aggressive bacteria of a large city hospital. Still, it was the only way we could all be together as a family.

One Saturday, not long after Trevor was moved to the neuro step-down unit, Grace was sleeping in the stroller when we arrived. When she woke up, she pointed to Trevor and said, "Dadda." I put her on the Plexiglas lap tray on the wheelchair facing him, then turned her to face the window when I heard the muffled whine of a helicopter. They sat there together and watched it take off. The peaceful image of the two of them watching the helicopter was endearing, and they could have been any father and daughter, anywhere in the world. But every time I saw the hospital helicopter, I thought of the people whose lives had been irrevocably changed by a horrific tragedy, just as ours had.

Around week seven, I found Trevor towering over his physiotherapist, Cynthia, on the tilt table as she pulled at his stiff arms and adjusted his feet. On the table, he was over seven feet tall and made her look like a small child. But we'd lucked out when we were assigned the athletic, spunky little redhead, even if she was half his size and weight. She walked double-time around the hospital, always with a big smile on her face, and she and Trevor seemed to hit it off instantly, probably because she challenged him to the extreme. On this day, she was excited to tell me that Trevor's range of motion wasn't getting any worse, and that she was even able to get his ankles to ninety degrees.

A few days later, the physiatrists injected Botox into Trev's gastrocnemius, the large muscle at the back of his calf, to temporarily paralyze it and prevent it from pulling the foot down during serial casting. That day, Trevor surprised me when he asked out of the blue, "How am I doing medically?"

"You are defying all the odds and impressing all the doctors and nurses," I told him with a big smile on my face.

After six days of gumming minced food, Trev was again upgraded to a diet he could finally sink his teeth into. I'd expected him to be excited, but I had to coax him to tell me what he wanted on his first day of normal food. "Sushi and latte," he finally said. I watched him roll his food around in his mouth and blithely thought that with this milestone, Trevor would be home with us in a matter of weeks. I naively ignored the fact that he couldn't feed himself, and that nothing south of his head worked very well.

Three days after the Botox injection, Trevor sat upright in the wheelchair for the three hours it took for the occupational therapist to cast both calves down to his feet. It was the longest he had sat upright, and his legs were in spasm and his face contorted in agony when he was finally lifted back to bed. He wouldn't eat and wasn't able to communicate. Immediately after the casting the nurses gave him hydromorphine and Tylenol, but neither seemed to work. Around dinnertime they gave him a sleeping pill, and by eight o'clock he was finally starting to relax and doze. It killed me to see him in pain, but there wasn't much I could do other than be there for him.

Trevor slept most of the next day. He was despondent and wouldn't eat any breakfast or lunch and had only a little of his supper. He looked me in the eyes and said very clearly, "I've beaten the infections, but the convalescence is killing me."

I took his hand in mine. "You are the strongest man I know," I said. "You will get through this. The pain is only temporary. You can bear it. We need the casts to help get you on your feet again so you can come home." I was astonished by the next words to come out of my mouth: "I promise you'll walk again." I couldn't believe what I just blurted out. I didn't even form the words in my mind—they just seemed to come through me.

Trevor slowly closed his eyes, as if in affirmation.

Four days after the casts engulfed Trevor's feet, they were removed to give his skin a break. If the skin broke down, the casts could not be put back on. He stoically endured another three hours in the wheelchair while his casts were removed and cut in half lengthwise. Once cut, the casts would be fastened on and off at four-hour intervals to help keep his feet flat. Later that night, I checked over his feet and found a dark circle the size of a small orange on the pad of his right foot and a sore on the outside of the left. Even with the Botox, the casts had been left on too long. With his strong muscle tone, he was pushing against the casts and causing bruising and other problems. I was concerned and asked the nurse to have a look and to contact the occupational therapist first thing in the morning.

After examining his feet the next morning, the OT said that because of the skin breakdown, casting was no longer a viable option for Trevor. Unfortunately, the sores on his feet also ruled out tilt table sessions, which were the only means of bearing weight in order to keep Trevor's ankles at ninety degrees.

Eight weeks after the axe fell, Cynthia finally got Trevor back in a gym. I was looking forward to the gym session for the change of scenery and the mental shift it would bring. Trevor loved to work out and had always felt at home in a gym. Cynthia started by stretching his arms and asked him to pull them back in so she could see how much active movement he had. She was very excited when he was able to squeeze both arms slightly to his sides. After physio, Trevor said he just wanted "peace and quiet," so I took him back to his room for a rest.

A couple of days after the gym session, we got the good news that the bacteria that had been breeding in Trevor's lungs since Afghanistan had finally been conquered. As a result, the doctors lifted the order requiring gowns and gloves—another move forward.

Early physiotherapy sessions focused on range-of-motion exercises to loosen Trevor's tight arm muscles. For me, they made the week pass quickly. I had come to dread the weekend doldrums, when there were no therapies scheduled and little to do. I would often find Trevor propped in front of some mundane TV program that he was forced to watch until Grace and I arrived. He still wouldn't speak to anyone except me, so he couldn't articulate which program, if any, he wanted to watch. When we walked in, the look in his eyes implored "Save me."

One bad Saturday, I heard on the radio that another soldier had been killed in Afghanistan. And it wasn't just any soldier. Bill Turner was a good friend of Trevor's and had replaced him after he was wounded. When Trevor's kit bag returned from Afghanistan, I found tucked inside a note from Bill that read, "Trevor, Sorry you were wounded, big guy. Hope it all goes well for you. I will carry on your good work. Bill." I said a prayer for Bill's family as we drove to the hospital. I didn't want Trevor to hear the news because I knew he would feel responsible. I was on tenterhooks as Grace and I walked into his room, and when I saw that the news wasn't on, I felt immense relief. I decided I would share the tragic news with him when he could handle it.

Every evening after Grace went to sleep, I would race back to the hospital. One evening, I asked Trevor how it felt to be there. "Like a prison," he replied. He said the nurses came into his room in the middle of the night and turned on the bright overhead lights to reposition him.

"I'll talk to the nurses about it. I wish you could come home with me. I wouldn't turn on the lights in the middle of the night," I quipped. "I miss having you at home. The house feels empty without you."

"I miss you, too," he replied.

When I arrived the next day, Trevor wasn't in his room. I

panicked and my mind immediately raced to the worst-case scenario: he's in emergency surgery—or worse, he's dead. My mind screamed: "Why didn't anybody call me?" But I quickly learned that he had been moved during the night to the ward because he needed even less nursing care now that he was medically stable. The nurse-to-patient ratio on the ward is about one to seven. I was disappointed that nobody had mentioned it the previous night, especially after I asked the nurses not to wake Trevor. But on a positive note, his room was bright, had its own bathroom and was close to the nurses' station. And I was excited that the bone flap surgery was the only hurdle left before his discharge to a rehab centre.

Just after lunch that day, the military doctor teaching trauma care at the hospital dropped in. Trevor hadn't been speaking very much to anyone, but I asked him if there was anything he wanted to know from the doctor. In an unusually clear voice, he asked, "How is the deployment going?" The doctor gave him an update on the mission. Then Trevor asked about his buddies and if there had been any casualties. The doctor said that it had been a tough mission and there had been some casualties, many from improvised explosive devices. Then Trevor asked, "What happened to me? When will I be going back to Afghanistan?"

His parents walked into the room right as he asked the question. They stood just inside the doorway and knew by the look on my face that Trevor was being given *the* news. We hadn't told him about the attack because his doctors had advised us to wait until he started asking questions. I had hoped he would ask me one evening when we were alone so I could tell him in my own way, sparing him some of the gruesome details. I knew the conversation would be difficult when the time came, but I would be there for him. I'd guessed that Trevor thought he was taking a little downtime to rest and recover before going back into the field. I don't think he realized that everyone was doing everything for him, and that he was being moved from bed to chair by a sling-and-lift system.

This was the most Trevor had spoken to anyone in some time. Clearly his mind was engaged with the mission, and he didn't want to make small talk. I cringed when I heard the doctor casually say, "A young man came up behind you and hit you in the head with an axe." Hearing it so matter-of-factly was devastating. The words hung in the room like a ticking time bomb. Trevor stared at the doctor in shocked disbelief. It seemed as if his heart stopped pumping with the doctor's words, suspended by the stark reality of life. I was furious at the doctor for blurting out the gory truth about the axe. I thought he would spare him that detail.

I broke the silence by asking Trevor if he had any other questions for the doctor or if he just wanted to take it all in. "Take it in," he muttered and then was silent. After the doctor left, Trevor's mum came up to him and said, "You'll get back there, Trevie. Every day you get stronger." His dad chimed in, "Just keep it up, bud. We're behind you."

I met with the rehab doctors later that day. I couldn't focus on the conversation because my mind was on Trevor and what he was dealing with emotionally. He had just been told that his mission to help the Afghans was over. Full stop. I listened dispassionately as the doctors warned me against giving too much stimulation to Trevor. "It's best to keep his environment calm," one said, "with only one or two people at a time speaking in low voices and low lighting." They were considering drugs to reduce spasticity, increase his alertness and improve his mood. They explained that the rigidity in his body was caused by the muscles not being able to turn off. The doctors wanted to be aggressive with Trevor's medications, since his brain was active but his body was not. They wanted to get the right "concoction" of drugs and planned to give him more Botox to increase the range of movement in his elbows. I had no idea what the effects of prolonged inactivity were on the body. It was like rigor mortis had set in on a living person. It was frightening.

Meanwhile, Trevor continued to shed flesh and now weighed about 165 pounds. His Afghanistan tan had long since faded, and his once muscled body had withered and shrunk. At least his sense of humour was intact and his frame of mind upbeat— or it had been before he was told he wasn't going back to his mission. Now he was grim and withdrawn and wasn't talking even to me. The speech therapist couldn't get a word out of him after he learned about the attack. She told me that he was avoiding eye contact with her and said he didn't want to participate in speech therapy.

It became harder and harder to keep Trevor positive and motivated. We had been expecting the lung filter to be removed, but when the doctors checked it, more clots were found and it had to remain. It was yet another blow. But it wasn't all bad news. Anita was still doing daily energy treatments, and Adam, who had been working on Trevor at a distance, was due at the hospital that day for his first in-person treatment. It was a surprise when I finally met him. I'd expected him to look somewhat mystical, but instead he was a typical twenty-year-old guy in a button-down shirt and jeans. He introduced himself to me and Trevor and asked me to close the door and curtains so he wouldn't be disturbed and could focus. I watched Adam slip into a trance-like state and move his hands purposefully, as if he were manipulating Trevor's body. He said that he could see the brain was making new connections, and that Trevor needed to visualize himself being active so the intentions of his thoughts would help heal him. After the session, he said that Trevor needed to visualize a lightning bolt hitting the top of his head and jump-starting his system. I asked how often he could work on Trevor, and if more frequent treatments would make a difference. "The power of your own intentions can make a huge difference," Adam said. "You don't need me." He left us his CD with specific visualizations to follow and said he would continue to follow Trevor.

After the session with Adam, Cynthia put Trevor through an intense stretching routine. He was clearly in pain, but his eyes showed me he was laughing like he enjoyed it. He always enjoyed things that pushed him beyond his limits, and this was no different. He hadn't been able to show much emotion since the attack, but I could usually tell by the look in his eyes what he was thinking. One day, I heard Trevor say something when my back was turned. When I asked him what he'd said, he replied, "You have a nice ass." That absolutely made my day—not so much the comment but the fact that he was able to process the thought.

That same day, Trevor savoured his first breath of fresh air in nearly two months. The large cement patio outside the hospital's fourth floor had a few skinny trees and a view of the mountains. As Trevor fell asleep basking under the glow of the sun, my mind turned to all the things we wouldn't be able to do that coming summer. There would be no running, rollerblading or walking hand in hand along the seawall with Grace in the stroller. I told myself we would have missed the summer anyway with him overseas, so the only difference was that I was spending my summer largely indoors at the hospital. Still, I enjoyed the time outside immensely. I had been off work since the attack and would be going back full time soon.

CHAPTER 11:
A DELICATE BALANCING ACT

On the way to work my first day back, thoughts of Trevor consumed me. I was worried about his care because the nurses seemed to be horribly overworked. I kept hearing the same thing from each different nurse: "I'm new with Trevor. How does he take his medications?" I went in after work to see how he was after this first day without me. He looked at me blankly, as if he didn't know who I was. His arms were so tight they were hard to move, and he didn't want to work them. I also noticed that he was losing more range in his ankles. On the drive home, I started to worry that my absence would cause him to regress. I consoled myself with the only good news of the day: Trevor's PEG feeding tube—the final tube infesting his body—had been removed.

When I went to see him after my second day at work, I

noticed that Trevor was slumped in the wheelchair with his feet dangling. I spoke to the nurse about proper positioning in the wheelchair—something I had been taught by the occupational therapist. I had the nurses put him in bed and I turned on a rugby video a friend had brought by. Trevor seemed to tense up even more watching it. When I tried to do range of motion on his body, his legs were so rigid I could barely move them. It felt like his muscles were attacking his body. Cynthia had told me that his muscles would shorten and become tight very quickly if they didn't get moved. But there weren't enough physiotherapists or nurses to do range of motion, so this fell to me.

To fight the spasticity wracking his body, Trevor was on the highest dose of a medication meant to hinder the nerve signals that cause spasms. The downside was drowsiness and muscle weakness. The rehab doctors wanted to try drugs that are typically used to treat Parkinson's disease to stimulate Trevor's mind and get him talking more. They wanted to try another drug to counteract the drowsiness. I didn't know whether to laugh or cry at this ridiculous game of pharmaceutical pinball. Besides the immediate side effects, this toxic drug stew could wreak havoc on Trevor's liver and kidneys, not to mention his bowels. The entire concoction was often too much for him to stay awake during the physio session.

I managed to get to the hospital by about eight o'clock every night after having supper with Grace and Regina and hearing about their day. I cherished the last part of my day with Grace: dinner, bath, stories in the rocking chair, a prayer for Daddy and bed. It was the only time in my week that I could give her my full attention. Ever since I went back to work, it had become harder to juggle my time between home and the hospital. I tried to bring Grace in to have supper with Trevor as often as I could. It was a nice break for both of us because she brought such happiness and light to the dreary hospital. One night when I asked

Trevor if he wanted Grace to sit with him on the bed, he said no. I was sad to hear it but felt that being in the hospital was finally starting to take a toll on him.

The next evening, I noticed that Trevor's feet were jammed into the footboard of the bed when I arrived. I brought the nurse in to show her and told her that I was concerned about the constant pressure causing sores. I stressed the importance of raising the foot of the bed when raising the head of the bed so Trevor wouldn't slide down and damage his feet. She said she would put a note in his file, but with so many different nurses and care aides cycling in, it didn't seem to do much good. I eventually put up a sign reading "To protect feet, raise foot of bed when raising head of bed." When I asked Trevor what else I could do to make it better for him, he said impassively, "Get me out of here."

Trevor had been talking less and less since he was told about the attack. "Just be here" is all he would say whenever I asked him what he needed. I felt it was because he wasn't getting the daily attention and stimulation from me that he wasn't able to be grounded and present. I voiced my concerns to our military case manager. She was sympathetic, and within a few weeks, a private nurse came to be with Trevor for a few hours a day. I also called the physiatrist and told him my concerns about Trevor regressing. He told me that Trevor couldn't transfer to a rehab facility until after the bone flap surgery in a few weeks, and he said he hoped to see a change after the surgery.

The next day, Trevor had his first shower in two months. "Wonderful," he moaned as the nurse and I towelled him off and covered him in warmed blankets. We weren't able to give his head a good scrub because there was only a thin layer of skin covering his brain where the bone flaps were missing. Seeing him naked in the wheelchair was demoralizing. He was down to 160 pounds, just pasty white skin and bone.

I sat on the bed next to him and inhaled his baby-fresh scent, then we cozied up under the blanket to watch basketball. It was the first time I'd ever sat still for a game. We dined on home-made spaghetti I had brought in. The uncertainty of our future was forgotten and we just enjoyed being curled up in bed like teenagers. After the first half, I asked him if he was ready to start working his arms. "I was born ready," he said. "Bring it on."

The next morning, Trevor was scheduled for a procedure to insert a new line to allow blood to be taken without constant pricking. Since the procedure required surgery, Trevor had to fast until afterward. By the end of the day, he still hadn't gone for surgery and hadn't eaten. When I asked the nurse what was going on, she told me he had been bumped by higher-priority cases and would likely go later that evening.

When I called the next morning to see if he had gone for surgery yet, the nurse said he would be going any time. He still hadn't gone when I called from work later that day, and he hadn't eaten since I fed him spaghetti a day earlier. I checked in again when I got home from work at around six o'clock. I expected the nurse to be aware of the situation, but she rudely told me that she didn't know what was going on because she was new and didn't have time to "deal with me." In my opinion, the most important things for Trevor were nutrition and rest—neither of which he was getting. I lost my patience and threatened to go higher up if she didn't find out what was going on immediately. Five minutes later I got a call from the charge nurse, who told me that Trevor would have surgery the following morning and they would make sure he got food as soon as possible.

Nine weeks into his injury, Trevor became distant and gloomy and stopped responding, even to me. To prevent contractures, his arms were now being casted. With his muscles struggling against each other in the casts, it was a challenge to keep his mood up.

The following weekend wasn't great for either communication or meals. Trevor hadn't spoken to anyone in a few days, and he said only one word to me all weekend: "Later," when I asked if he wanted spaghetti. He had eaten only a small lunch the day before. He seemed very depressed, and I was concerned that he was losing his motivation. He fell asleep for about an hour when we went outside.

With his feeding tube removed, Trevor wasn't getting any nutrition at all. It seemed that he was quietly giving up. I was desperate to keep him alert and aware, but I didn't know what to do. That night, I thought about whether I could afford to work less so I could be at the hospital more. The Canadian Forces were still paying Trevor's full salary and would continue to do so until he was discharged from the hospital. With my reduced salary and Trevor's benefits, we could still afford to keep Regina to look after Grace, and I could spend more time at the hospital to help rehabilitate Trevor. It felt like the weight was all on me to keep our family together until we could get Trevor to rehab. I couldn't believe such a cruel twist of fate would happen to a guy who had set out only to do good.

By Monday, things were worse. Trevor hadn't eaten since lunch on Saturday, and he was being cajoled to eat soup through a syringe. He hadn't spoken for five days, except for that one word on the weekend. The cast was removed from his left arm, and as I suspected, we found a bright red pressure sore with a black centre, so casting was discontinued. Medications were now the only option. Trevor looked tired and worn out, and the psychiatrist suggested starting him on an antidepressant. The downside was that it would take about four weeks to take effect. And then yet another antibiotic was added to the stew after a chest X-ray revealed pneumonia in Trev's right lung. I'm sure that even Mother Theresa would have been a little depressed about now.

Thankfully, on Friday afternoon Trevor's friends Barb and Clare brought in music and food. He ate well at lunch for the first time in nearly a week, but didn't eat any supper. He didn't even talk with his friends. So, just before the May long weekend, I asked for a feeding tube to be reinserted to help forestall his weight loss.

Meanwhile, the bone flap surgery had been scheduled for Thursday, May 25. I desperately hoped the surgery would reverse the funk that Trevor was in. I brought in a poem he had written before he left for Afghanistan to help remind him why he went there. If he felt his mission had been all in vain, I knew he would sink lower and lower. I put the poem in a prominent place on the wall so he wouldn't forget what he was fighting for.

I was relieved to see Mud, Trevor's best friend from his Japan days, arrive three days before the surgery. His timing couldn't have been better. Trevor always spoke so highly of Mud, so I was hopeful this visit would cheer him up. I explained to Mud that although Trevor hadn't been talking lately, he still understood everything. I asked Mud to treat Trevor just as he would have in the old days.

That week, the neurosurgeon explained that while the bone flap surgery was a relatively simple routine procedure, it would be the largest bilateral cranioplasty the surgeon and the hospital had ever performed. The porous polyethylene plates that replace the missing skull pieces are custom-made in the U.S. and shipped in sterile packages ready for implant. The implant flaps are designed to integrate seamlessly and allow the existing skull to grow into them. Curious to know more, I searched the Internet and was amused to find that the product is marketed online like anything else: "Off-the-Shelf Implants for Complex Procedures," the website boasts.

The doctor explained that the surgery itself should take only about two hours. This surgery carried the usual risks, like infection and loss of blood, but an added complication could arise if Trevor's scalp had shrunk since his bone flaps had been removed two and a half months ago. This would make it difficult to close up his scalp after the surgery. But I had read that the procedure had been around since the time of the Incas, so I felt confident that the advancements in modern medicine would guarantee a successful surgery.

On the day of the surgery I was eager to see Trevor. When I entered his room that Thursday morning, I could sense he had trepidations. I shared with him with what I'd read about the Incas and joked that what he was about to go through wouldn't even come close to giving birth. Mud came by and we all shared a few jokes at Trevor's expense to lighten the sombre mood in the room. The porters came around at eleven o'clock to take Trevor to the operating room. Before he left, I leaned in and kissed his lips. "I love you," I said. "Everything will be fine. I will be here later today after the surgery. Mud will be waiting here for you in your room. After this surgery is over, you will go to rehab and then come home. I look forward to that day." Our eyes locked as he was being wheeled away, and I mouthed the words "I love you" as he disappeared around the corner.

I got nervous when I spoke to Mud from the office at around four o'clock. He told me that Trevor wasn't back yet and he hadn't heard anything. I told him I would go home after work to see Grace, since she had contracted a virus and had been vomiting during the day. I would be up at the hospital as soon as she was asleep.

Trevor got back to his room at around seven o'clock I was happy that Mud was there, so he wouldn't be alone when he came out of surgery. When I walked into his room at 8:30, he was still out of it. I was completely overwhelmed by what I saw.

Trevor's face was swollen and there was a tight bandage wound around his head—it was like my first sight of him in Germany. Jutting out of the back of his dressing were two small hoses draining fluid that looked like watery tomato juice. A wave of nausea came over me, so I rushed out of the room to catch my breath.

When I went back in, Trevor was trying to open his eyes as if he was fighting to wake up. Mud was sitting next to the bed. Despite his calm demeanour and quiet air, I could tell he was concerned. He left so we could have some time alone. I put my hand on Trevor's arm and spoke softly. "Honey, it's all over. The surgery was a success. You look good," I lied. "I want you to get some rest so your body can heal. Grace is sick, so I have to go home now. But I will see you first thing in the morning. Mud will be here with you. I love you." The more I talked, the more nauseous I became. With bile rising in my throat, I left the room abruptly. I was starting to feel quite ill but chalked it up to the emotional cost of the day. I came back in to say goodbye for the night, kissed Trevor's cheek before leaving and asked Mud to call me if there was any change.

When I got home I checked on Grace, who was sleeping soundly in her crib, then went to the bathroom to get ready for bed. I looked in the mirror and pondered our bleak future, then turned on the shower and climbed in. It felt good to have the water streaming down my achy body. After a long shower, I crawled into bed. Not long after that, I went to the kitchen for a glass of water and vomited all over the floor. And it wouldn't be the last time. I was up most of the night. By the time morning came, my head ached and I had nothing left in my stomach.

I couldn't even go to the hospital that day. It felt like I had been hit by a bus. When I called the hospital later in the day, the nurses said that Trevor was resting comfortably and the neurosurgeon had removed the drains from his head.

When Grace and I went to the hospital the following morning, we found Trevor in his wheelchair vomiting milky liquid all over himself and the floor. The nurses said he'd started vomiting at 5:30 a.m. He was being fed through an NG tube down his nose and was retching up the liquid. It was a horrible sight, with his grotesquely swollen face and bandaged head. One of the care aides had accidentally ripped the tube from his nose, so another had to be inserted. With each vomit, Grace would get scared and start crying. I stood there helplessly holding her out of the way. We had to leave the room because vomit was literally spewing everywhere. I was torn between the need to stay and look after Trevor and the urge to take Grace, at only sixteen months, from this bacteria-infested ward. My concern for Grace won out and we left. Trevor vomited intermittently all day until 10 p.m. Despite all the vomiting, the tube feeds were continued through the day and into the evening.

At 4:30 the next morning, a nurse found Trevor breathing shallowly and in apparent discomfort. By 8:15 he was breathing laboriously, his oxygen saturation had dropped to 85 percent and the nurses could hear congestion in his lungs. Trevor wasn't opening his eyes, and he had a fixed and dilated right pupil and a sluggish left. At 8:45 the doctor ordered an urgent CT scan.

Oblivious to the drama unfolding at the hospital, I called to check on Trevor's condition. When the unit clerk picked up the phone, I asked to speak with Trevor's nurse. She first said she would transfer me and then said, "Um, actually she's on a break." There was something in the tone of her voice that struck me as odd. I hung up the phone and planned to race to the hospital as soon as I could get Grace and myself out the door.

A few minutes later, an unfamiliar doctor called. "Ms. Lepore?"

"Yes," I replied nervously.

"There was pressure indicated on Trevor's brain during the night," he began. He informed me that the bone flaps would have to be removed because of blood clots and asked for my consent. With my heart in my throat, I told him to go ahead.

CHAPTER 12:
ONE STEP FORWARD,
TWO STEPS BACK

Trevor was rushed to surgery, where the two-day-old staples were pried apart and removed. Once the surgeon extracted the tiny screws holding the plates in place, he took the bone flaps off Trevor's skull. The thick, solid blood clots seen on the CT scan were removed. After irrigating the area, the surgeon inserted drains and closed up Trevor's scalp once again, without the bone flaps this time. He was taken back to the ICU, masked with a ventilator to help him breathe and kept on constant watch.

When I saw the doctor, he told me it had been a risky procedure because of the blood thinner medication. There was still some pressure on Trevor's brain, but they weren't sure if there was additional damage from the swelling. He went on to say

141

that they expected him to eventually return to the condition he was in before the surgery, but it would take a while to know for sure. The consolation was that there was no bleeding in his brain and his pupils were reacting normally.

When I reached Trevor's bedside, I was astounded by his appearance. His face looked like he had just come out of a boxing ring, and his head was horribly swollen and wrapped in a tight bandage. A tube as thick as a garden hose was wedged down his throat and held tightly in place by a thin piece of cloth tied around his head. It looked like he was being gagged to death, bondage-style. He looked dazed and couldn't speak because of the contraption in his mouth and throat.

This was a huge step back. It meant that rehab was out of the question for the foreseeable future. It would be very difficult for me to keep Trevor motivated after this, I realized, if he was even able to recover. I was totally exhausted—mentally, emotionally and physically. So far I'd been running on belief, trust and will, and all three were steadily waning. I wasn't sure how much Trevor knew about the failed surgery. I picked up his cold hand from the bed as I desperately searched for the right words to say.

"Trev, it's Bee. I'm here with you. Everything is okay. There was a complication, and they had to remove the plates. Once you're strong enough, they will be put back in. Don't worry. It's just a minor setback. We'll get through this. You are the strongest man I know." I hoped my words were sinking in on some level.

Trevor's friends Barb and John arrived and were shocked by the sight of him. Barb held me for a long time, gathering her strength and thoughts for Trevor. "Bubba, it's Babs. Johnnie's here, too. Know that God gives a person only as much as he can handle. You can handle this. We will move heaven and earth to get you well again."

I met with the doctor the following day. He told me the scans of Trevor's head showed that the swelling was a little worse, but his pneumonia was better and was likely just a common bug. He'd saved the worst news for last, however: "The next attempt at surgery won't be for a minimum of four to six weeks." This was a hard blow to take, given that we had counted on a successful surgery to move Trevor to rehab. I was desperately hoping that with his brain fully protected and at a normal atmospheric pressure, he would eventually make a complete turnaround.

When I saw Trevor after speaking with the doctor, he tried to open his eyes, but they were too badly swollen. I was so grateful that he was alive, but I wondered whether he was grateful, too. I tried to inspire him by talking about all the things we had to look forward to in the future: our wedding, Grace's first day of kindergarten, her graduation and our grandchildren. This would be a massive, daunting disability to overcome, and I was just starting to realize the magnitude of it.

The next day, the bandages came off and the swelling had already started to go down in Trevor's face. I was told he might be taken off the ventilator in the next day or two. There were also fewer IV bags hanging from poles around him—down to two from about six to eight. I couldn't imagine what condition his blood was in, given all the medications being pumped into him.

There was another patient, an older man, in a bed just a few steps away. I spoke to his wife and found out that they had just retired when he had had a blackout and fell. He had the same awful tube in his throat gagging him. After his wife left for the evening, I could see him struggling in the bed. He was obviously scared, desperately alone and unable to speak.

Two nurses sat at a nearby table monitoring Trevor and this other fellow. I overheard the man's nurse bark angrily, "You better stop moving around or I'll give you something to stop you!" Only a thin curtain separated Trevor from this brutal nurse. My heart ached for the man.

The following day, I called the charge nurse to complain about the lack of compassion and emphasized that this woman shouldn't be working with patients who are unable to speak. I asked her to ensure that this problem nurse wasn't assigned to Trevor. She thanked me and indicated that she was already aware of the problem, and that I didn't need to worry. We never saw the nurse again.

I called Dick, Bess and Suzanne and told them about the botched bone flap surgery. Suzanne flew out within a couple of days. I picked her up in the morning and we headed straight for the hospital. We found Trev much more alert and able to track us with his eyes. On the Glasgow Coma Scale, he was back to a nine, meaning that he was not fully conscious.

When we saw Trevor after lunch, he was sweating profusely, his body was rigid and he looked distressed, so the nurse gave him a sedative to settle him. Despite my efforts to stretch his ankles, his toes were inexorably starting to curl. This was the beginning of the end for his feet. Over the next few weeks, Trevor's ankles lost all their mobility and his feet became so badly contracted that they locked straight down like a ballet dancer's.

My mood went further downhill at our meeting with the infectious diseases doctor. She gravely told us that Trevor's pneumonia could be fatal because the bacteria was very resistant to antibiotics.

After six days, the ventilator was finally pulled from Trevor's throat and the swelling in his head was coming down. He appeared to be wide awake but not fully conscious, like someone sleepwalking. Despite being able to track with his eyes, he couldn't follow even simple eye commands, like looking up.

The nurses weren't able to do any oral care because he kept biting down on anything put in his mouth. The medical team was concerned with his oxygen saturation, which was at only 87 percent, so they gave him an oxygen mask. He was finally moved out of the ICU, but the team was concerned with his inability to clear his throat, and he wouldn't open his mouth to allow the nurses to clear it with suction.

Ten days after surgery, Trevor had only two tubes snaking out of him: a feeding tube and an oxygen mask. I'd been stretching his limbs but was fighting a losing battle against the tightness. He'd lost thirty degrees of mobility in his left arm, and there was talk about casting the arm again and possibly his leg. I dreaded the thought of it, since the huge sore on his foot was just starting to heal. I tried to keep his motivation alive by reminding him of his promise to come home to us. Most days, it seems like an insurmountable task.

Trevor's parents also flew out to give me a break and some much-needed quality time with Grace. When I visited the hospital one evening, the nurse told me an X-ray had confirmed a large infection in Trevor's right lung from an aspiration of his tube feeds during the day. A lump formed in my throat when I noticed a tear running out of his right eye. At times like this, I wished I could do more. I felt like I had the power to make changes, but I wasn't sure what to do.

On top of all the medical problems, we had to deal with equipment issues. Trevor slept on an air-filled bed mattress, which helped prevent pressure sores. When Dick visited early one morning, most of the air was out of the mattress and Trevor was flat on the bed frame. The nurses told Dick that they hadn't been able to get it working properly. He insisted they get a new bed ASAP.

At 9:06 a.m. on Friday, June 9, a Code Blue was called. Trevor's oxygen saturation levels had dropped to the dangerously low seventies and didn't improve with extra oxygen. By 9:27 a.m. the team had him out of danger. He was transferred back to the ICU and put back on the ghastly ventilator. I was at work, oblivious to the traumatic events once more unfolding at the hospital.

I saw another tear running from Trevor's eye when I came in later that day. I started to question how much more he could take. My fear was that either his body or his soul wouldn't be able to withstand this abuse and would give up. I resigned myself to accept whatever fate was in store for us because I couldn't bear to see him go through this any longer.

I was also nearing my limits, both physically and emotionally, and I realized that in order to stay strong for us all, I had to pace myself. My sister Toni and I got up early one Saturday morning and took Grace and my niece, Olivia, for a walk on the beach. I usually felt guilty taking any time for myself, but this day I didn't. I knew Trevor wanted me at the hospital all the time, but he would also want me to take time for myself and for Grace.

I brought Grace in to see Trevor on the Sunday. I hoped it would cheer him up to see her, especially after the Code Blue. When we got out of the car to walk into the hospital, Grace started saying, "Dadda, Dadda, Dadda." Six months had passed since he had deployed to Afghanistan and she still had a connection to him from the videos I showed her every night. At the end of the videos, she would turn to me and say, "More Dadda." Yet as we approached Trevor's bedside that day, I felt her tense and pull away from him, frightened by the sight of the tube in his mouth.

Later that evening, I went up to the hospital on my own to try to communicate with Trevor using the Yes/No board. I had my doubts about the method because he would sometimes look to No on questions that clearly warranted a Yes, such as "Is your daughter's name Grace?"

I decided that we needed to work on clearing his lungs on our own, so I put on one of Adam's visualization DVDs. It showed a drawing of a man with a fire burning in his lungs. I told Trevor to picture the same fire burning up his lung infection. We watched the short clip over and over again and imagined his lung becoming clear.

Dick visited the hospital early every day during his and Bess's visit and stayed late every night. He would leave Trevor's bedside only to share a coffee or lunch with Bess. I recognized that Dick, like my own father, came from an era when men showed affection not with hugs but with hard work and by providing for their family. Being there was his way of showing he cared. He knew Trevor loved to read newspapers and books, and he wanted to provide the one gift his son could enjoy. To see Dick stand and read to Trevor for hours on end was incredibly endearing and showed me how much love he had for his son.

Four days after the Code Blue, Trevor was moved out of ICU and back to the fifth-floor unit where he'd started—his third trip out of ICU. He was much more cognizant now and could communicate via eye blinks. One blink for yes, two blinks for no. He came off the ventilator only because the doctors reinserted the trach tube in his throat to help him clear the mucus. A few times a day, the nurses would slide a long suctioning tube down the trach and into his lungs. When the tube hit his lungs, it would cause his body to convulse wildly. I would often ask the nurses not to go so deep, as it was obviously agonizing for him, but sometimes they had no choice.

One night, I took a few hours away and met some friends, all relatively new mothers like me, for dinner. The conversation eventually moved to the father's role in parenting. It was nice to get out but difficult to relate to my friends' conversations, since my life was no longer just about everyday struggles. I knew that under different circumstances, Trev would have been on deployment, so I would have temporarily been a single parent regardless. I shared with them the irony of tracking the progress of both Trevor and Grace. She was learning to put on her shoes by herself and would say a strong "No" to any offers to help. Eventually she would get so frustrated that she'd give up. Meanwhile, Trevor had just learned how to communicate by blinking.

Three months after his injury, Trevor had his first seizure. Another setback. More frustration. It was a small seizure, fortunately, and the nurse was there the entire time, but it was frightening nonetheless. His face looked gaunt and his arms and legs were sticks and he was down to 153 pounds. Only a week earlier, the trach was out and we were talking about moving on from the hospital after the surgery. Our optimism was tested when the trach was put back in.

This latest crisis impelled me and Trevor's parents to meet with his medical team. The neurosurgeon told us that Trevor was neurologically unchanged since before the surgery and would be back in acute care for the next month. He told us that Trevor could die from something as simple as an infection if he remained at this low level of neurological recovery. The worst part of the conversation was hearing that the brain doesn't make new connections for a badly injured motor cortex like Trevor's. The neurosurgeon asked if we wanted to get aggressive with the treatment. This would mean attempting another bone flap surgery, trying different medications, more casting and more intense rehab. "Trevor challenged himself in everything he did. I believe he would want to go aggressive," I told him. "At this point, we have nothing to lose." Dick and Bess both agreed.

I then met with our new Veterans Affairs case manager to talk about disability benefits. She would become more involved once Trevor was, inevitably, medically discharged from the army. She wanted to know what activities he was no longer able to do, but it was easier to list what he could do: nothing but blink. In the past, the list was long: military operations, rugby, running, rowing, swimming, rollerblading, cycling, basketball, volleyball, surfing, rock climbing, writing, cooking and, most important, holding his baby daughter. Compiling the list made me realize what life could have been like for him, for all of us. This injury would affect his relationship with everyone, especially Grace. Instead of being defined by the strength of his character, he would forever be defined by his brain injury.

When I started to write my list, I remembered our friend Gregory saying Trevor was like a vortex that sucked everybody in. It was true. People were attracted to his passion for whatever he engaged in. A normal conversation with him would invariably be about something of substance. It was easy to share his passion, especially his social and environmental conscience. If he had the power to save the world, he would.

I always wondered what he saw in me. We were different in so many ways, but maybe that was what we liked in each other. He was confident, open and relaxed. I've always been more reserved. Drama swirled around him because of his passion for life. I'm grounded and don't court drama. He lived in the moment. I always thought about the future, planning trips for the following year, mapping out my career path and preparing for retirement. But we were similar in our views on religion, politics, health and children, and we were both close to our families.

Unfortunately, this injury would affect Grace most of all. The rest of us had known Trevor during the "good times." I was afraid that she would only know her father as a wheelchair-bound man, old before his time—a father who had trouble holding, comforting and protecting her. He would probably never coach her sports teams and pick her up from Brownies. We would likely never be able to have a second child or celebrate our dream wedding.

...

One day after work, Grace and I took the bus to the hospital. She loved being on the bus and said hello to everyone who walked by. When we entered Trevor's room Grace blew him kisses, but his face was frozen. I didn't know if he was even capable of forming thoughts. We couldn't stay long because it was close to Grace's bedtime. On the way out, she spotted her blanket on Trevor's bed and wanted it, but I convinced her that Daddy needed it to get better. I hoped her blanket would comfort him. I put music on for him and once again walked out of the hospital, leaving my heart behind. After Grace was asleep, I was filled with a renewed sense of purpose and went about making signs to hang in Trevor's room. Every one said "I will walk by Christmas."

At the hospital the next morning, I could sense that Trevor was mad at the world. Undeterred, I posted my homemade signs around his room. I thought it would be encouraging for him to have a goal to work toward. Everyone probably thought I was absolutely crazy to believe that he would walk at all, let alone by Christmas, but I wasn't going to give up on him.

Since his lungs were doing better, he was moved once again to the next level of nursing care. The neuro step-down unit is two stages removed from the intensive care unit and one step away from the general ward. I began running the stairs to the fifth floor as often as I could. If I was to remain resolute, I needed to stay in shape and this was one way to do it. I challenged myself to see how quickly I could get from the main level to the fifth floor.

I also decided to get a scooter so I could travel easily between home, work and the hospital. I'd always wanted to learn how to ride a motorcycle, so I thought this was a good start. I was excited to show Trevor a picture of my new purchase, since he'd ridden a motorcycle in his student days. I imagined myself flying through town with my scarf blowing in the wind. The scooter turned out not to be that glamorous, but it did give me a sense of adventure and freedom. It also helped me with my struggle to find balance between being at the hospital for Trevor and being at home with Grace as she progressed through this critical developmental stage of her life.

The next surgery date was fast approaching, and Trevor hadn't changed neurologically; he still wasn't speaking or following commands. He was also on a large concoction of drugs, so we decided as a family to delay the procedure. It would take about twenty days to get him off the drugs, which were preventing us from getting a cognitive baseline.

After work the following day, I tested the route by scooter to the hospital—twenty minutes door to door. Once I got there, Trevor and I worked on moving his left hand and thumb to activate the call button. On the fourth try, it rang. It would be a long shot to reach our goal of walking by Christmas, which was only six months away, but I felt we needed to have the goal to keep us focused and motivated.

I flipped the calendar to July and realized that Trevor's tour would've been almost over. The sun was barely filtering through the clouds as I prepared him to get some fresh air on the patio with me and Grace. I positioned a ball cap on him so people didn't stare at his misshapen head. I also took care to avoid mirrors and Plexiglas on the way down to the patio because I was worried that Trevor would catch sight of himself and be devastated by his appearance.

Grace toddled next to us as we made our way downstairs but ran around the minute she reached the large open patio. Trevor never took his eyes off her, not even for a second, as she climbed and scrambled around. I imagined that time had stood still for him, and that he found it bizarre to see his baby daughter six months older and walking.

CHAPTER 13:
MINIMALLY CONSCIOUS?

It was the twenty-first day since Trevor had been taken off the drugs, and we were starting to notice the effects. Dick was excited to tell me that when he left Trevor's room the previous night, he'd said, "I'll see you in the morning." And Trevor had uncharacteristically responded, "Wake me up."

When I left later that night, Trevor said the words I hadn't heard in weeks: "I love you." To celebrate, I unplugged his trach, sucked out a gob of thick mucus and said, "I love you, too."

Grace's love for Trevor was also growing. She was becoming more comfortable around him and less afraid when he coughed. She even mimicked him with a pretend cough—her way of saying she was less afraid.

My agenda now was to get Trevor's brain coordinated with

his hands and arms. I used the Yes/No board to ask him questions. He tried to move his hand toward the board but too often couldn't find the motor plan to make it happen. When I asked him one day if he would do anything to protect Grace, he moved his right arm immediately over to Yes.

I wanted to show Trevor the incredible healing power of the mind with a video a friend had recommended. One of the segments featured a pilot who had survived a near-fatal plane crash that had left him immobile. Simply by the power of intention, he'd willed himself off the ventilator and ultimately began walking again. The message was clear: anything can be achieved if the power of will is harnessed. The critical part is to believe the goal has already been attained so those positive vibes that you send out will eventually return to you. The idea is not to expect it to happen instantly. Trevor would have to be patient, and he wasn't very good at that.

One evening, I asked Trevor if he needed anything before I left. I thought I heard him say the words "engagement ring." When I asked him to repeat himself, he said it again: "Engagement ring." I could feel tears welling up in my eyes. It had been two years since he proposed, and I didn't know if he even remembered. I blinked back my tears and said, "Let's go shopping together when you get out of here."

The fact that Trevor was thinking about the future meant to me that he was getting stronger, so I figured the time was right for him to reconnect with more friends—his rugby team, in particular. They had been eagerly waiting to see him, but I'd held off for fear of overstimulating his fragile brain. I was also worried that they would be scared off by his appearance. But I knew how much their friendship meant to him. On a number of occasions, he had come home after a game and some post-match beers shouting, "I love those guys!"

153

Trevor asked to see his long-time scrum partner, Francis Szabo, first. The visit went well and paved the way for the rest of the boys. The next to visit was Mikey Cochrane, who had always shown a real interest in Trev's military service, and he was followed by Gregory Fitzpatrick. A Jamaican-born naturalized citizen, he and Trevor met at the rugby club shortly after Gregory first came to Canada. Their friendship was cemented when Trevor, in uniform, attended the ceremony at which Gregory and his wife became Canadians. Our daughters were born six months apart and became fast friends.

Gregory brought in a rugby ball signed by the team so Trev could have a visual and tactile reminder of the good old days. Even though Trevor wasn't responding, it felt good to see Gregory lean in and talk to him like a brother. When he left, he gave Trevor's hand a squeeze and said, "I love you, man." It was so endearing to see these incredibly masculine men showing their feelings. I knew Trevor was loving every minute of it.

These guys became a constant fixture at the hospital, providing humour to Trevor and emotional support to me. They transformed the atmosphere of Trev's room, boisterously cracking jokes, telling stories and reliving games. To keep Trevor from getting too tired out, I posted a sign on the wall with a few rules: No more than two people at a time. Firm touches only. Talk from one side of the bed only. And definitely try to make him laugh. I placed Gregory's ball right by the bed so Trevor would feel the game beckoning him back. It seemed to have an effect. He was up on the tilt table during one of the visits and showed off by staying up longer than he normally did.

Some people believe a damaged brain is devoid of thought and imagination. I often wondered if that was true for Trevor as he lay in bed staring at the ceiling. Did he think about his old life? Could he recall the many walks and talks we had had together? Did he remember his baby daughter sleeping on his chest?

At nearly eighteen months, Grace was already the size of a two-year-old. It was an adorable age that Trevor wouldn't get to enjoy. I tried to compensate by constantly telling him stories about her. I told him how she repeated almost every word said, and how she said "thank you" at random moments and "please" only when asked. I told him how she had become picky about the books she wanted read and the order in which they were read. I told him how she loved to dance . . . with the same unbridled enthusiasm as her father.

Trevor's battle group was coming home in three or four weeks. In less than a month, I would have welcomed him home safe and sound. I searched hard for the deeper meaning in this, but it eluded me. Instead, I continued to track Trevor's recovery, which I measured in baby steps. His speech was progressing at the same slow place as Grace's, but he was now able to squeeze very hard on command. The nurse even said he was able to wiggle his toes a little, although I hadn't seen it myself.

In August, I went to a health food store to ask about the effects of medications and antibiotics on the body. The staff told me that anyone in the hospital should be taking in probiotics, or friendly bacteria, especially if they were on antibiotics. The antibiotics destroy the friendly bacteria that guard our intestines, whereas the probiotics protect us against pathogens such as salmonella, yeast, cholera, and the bad E. coli. I bought a large bottle of probiotics and gave it to the nurse to approve and add to Trev's regular medication list. Then I asked the hospital dietician whether probiotics were in the cans of liquid nutrition being pumped into patients' stomachs. She agreed that they were necessary but said the "system" was years away from adopting such things.

That night I read about how taking course after course of antibiotics, as Trev had been doing, can help the growth of fungi that may lead to ailments like heart disease and diabetes. I eventually stumbled across several articles about how the animals we eat are given low doses of antimicrobials and growth hormones— drugs that have been linked to cancer. It's no surprise that cancer rates have jumped in the last twenty-five years. I thought about Trevor and the hospital full of sick people and couldn't help seeing a connection.

One day a friend asked if I would be interested in having someone do Reiki on Trevor. Reiki is a Japanese healing technique involving the transfer of energy. I had been introduced to the energy therapy years before when Trevor and I visited his cousin Kathy, a Reiki master on the East Coast. When she treated me, I felt an unbelievable amount of heat coming from her hands. I must have fallen into a deep sleep on the table, because two hours went by in the blink of an eye. I remember Kathy telling me that Reiki heals by flowing positive energy through the affected parts of the body's energy field. It also clears, straightens and heals the energy pathways, allowing the life force to flow in a healthy and natural way. At times the negative energy in the hospital hung heavy on us all, so I knew this was exactly what Trevor needed.

I met our new Reiki master, Eve, in the hospital cafe. She was a warm and friendly middle-aged woman who looked younger than her years. She spoke in a beautiful watered-down New Zealand accent. I invited her up to meet Trevor, warning her that although he could understand everything she said to him, he might not respond. She introduced herself to Trevor the minute we walked in the room and seemed to make an instant connection.

The day after Eve's first treatment, a nurse said she thought she saw Trevor singing along to a song, even though he had not spoken for weeks. He was also noticeably more alert and had begun to read the paper, another thing he hadn't done for weeks.

I couldn't help thinking how coincidental it was that "Adam and Eve" were working on Trevor. A new beginning. I chuckled as I thought about a comment Anita had made once in an email: "Coincidences are God's way of remaining anonymous."

After Eve's second treatment, Trev fell into a deep sleep, so I left him alone. When I came back, his good friend Shane was visiting with his martial arts instructor, who was also doing energy work on Trevor. Shane leaned over and whispered to me that Trevor was trying to ground the energy though his feet, and that's why they were pointing down like a ballerina's. The martial arts instructor said one way to get rid of negative energy is to bathe the feet in sea salt.

Of course, we hadn't given up on conventional medicine. After Trevor was assessed by the rehab doctor, I finally understood why he seemed to be in a fog all the time. The doctor told me that Trevor was in what is called a minimally conscious state; it was one step down from a vegetative state and two steps down from a coma. It wasn't good, but at least I had a name for it now. He told me there was little I could do to pull Trevor out of this state, beyond the things I was already doing: showing him pictures, talking to him and trying to work his brain. He then broke the news to me that Trevor wasn't a candidate for the local rehab facility because he wasn't able to actively participate. It seemed the only thing that would pull Trevor out of this nightmare was his own will.

When Trevor had been in the hospital for five and half months, the occupational therapist began testing him on some "assisted devices." Trevor could control a switch by the blink of an eye, the twitch of a brow or the movement of the mouth or a finger. He was most consistent with eye blinks, so we started with that, although this meant he had to wear ridiculous-looking glasses with a control box attached to them. Each time he blinked, a bell would go off. Apparently, a disabled person can independently work all kinds of equipment this way.

I wondered if this was what our future held for us—silly glasses and bells going off every time Trevor blinked or sneezed. I thought about Sean Penn's developmentally delayed character in the movie *I Am Sam*. As the daughter in that film grew older, she became more intelligent than her father, and everyone felt sorry for them. I didn't want people feeling sorry for Grace or laughing at Trevor, this kind, intelligent, strong man who'd been reduced to a shadow of his former self.

I thought back to all the times over the years when he'd come up with grand ideas to help people in Third World countries. Eager to help but always the practical one, I would ask the logical questions, like "How are you planning to get the used hotel mattresses to India?" He always dismissed my concerns as negativity and would retort, "Just have faith in me." He would tell me that the details would work themselves out, to which I would say, "Okay, but someone has to work out those details to make it happen, right?" In hindsight, I regret saying to a visionary that some details don't just work themselves out.

One morning in late August, we had a rare team meeting. I dreaded these meetings because nobody ever seemed to say anything positive. This one was no different. Trevor's neurosurgeon opened the meeting by saying that the complication with the first bone flap surgery was the worst he had ever seen. He said that the damage from the axe was major, and that the primary motor connections were not recovering. "It's a very unpleasant neurology for Trevor: he has consciousness but very little ability." He went on to say that Trevor didn't show the typical characteristics of brain injury. Three weeks earlier he could communicate, and now he couldn't. Sometimes he was conscious and other times not. Unlike the rehab doctor, the neurosurgeon said Trevor was in a conscious state. He said that along with the impaired brain function, the "overlying tone" in Trevor's face could be impeding his ability to talk. He said that he believed Trevor was fully conscious and suffering, but that I was the only one who could determine this for sure. Trevor was never one to talk about his feelings before this injury, but maybe that would change.

The neurosurgeon also said that he had seen minimal improvement in Trevor's ability to control his arms, and that while he'd hoped other areas of the brain would compensate, this hadn't happened yet. Large components of the motor area were injured so badly that Trevor would not regain control of his legs. The doctor had seen only modest neurological improvements, and he pointed out that Trevor had language ability but couldn't muster the motor planning to say what he wanted to. "What you see is what you've got," he concluded. The big question was how to determine the extent of Trevor's suffering, and what to do to make things better for him.

The doctor also explained that Trevor was likely feeling some delayed neurological effects of the brain injury, and this was why he seemed to have regressed. He wondered whether it was necessary to have the surgery to rebuild Trevor's skull. We would have to balance the risks of surgery against the benefits, he said. The reconstruction wouldn't make Trevor more mobile, so there was no medical reason to have it done, he reasoned. Besides, he went on, there were risks to every surgery, including infection and bleeding. On the other hand, he said he knew of similar cases where patients had claimed a greater quality of life after surgery.

I was trying my best to be stoic. I wanted to scream out that Trevor couldn't possibly be left with two gaping indentations in his head. What if a caregiver accidentally knocked his head with a tray or an elbow? These people were discussing *Trevor*, not some unthinking, unfeeling non-person. This was surreal.

If we decided to go ahead with the surgery, the neurosurgeon said it could take place in a matter of weeks, depending on when the new plates arrived. He made it clear that Trevor's respiratory status would be fragile as long as nothing changed neurologically, but he felt that we should get the surgery over with as soon as the plates arrived.

I asked the doctor if the plates could be blessed before surgery. Trevor's cousin, the Reiki master, had recommended they be blessed, and I wanted everyone religious or spiritual who knew Trevor to be involved. It seemed like a good idea, since his body had rejected the first set of plates. The doctor said it was no problem at all, as long as they remained in the sterile packaging.

It seemed logical to talk about where to put Trevor next, since he wasn't ready for rehab. There were many options, including public care facilities, private nursing homes and group homes. The problem was that most places didn't accept patients with trach tubes. The doctor said that we should think about quality of life and making the best of what Trevor had when deciding where he would go next.

I asked about transferring him to a specialized brain injury centre in another province. The doctor was against it, saying it was pointless to go to a rehab facility such a long way from home when there was limited possibility of recovery. Trevor was better off near loved ones, he rationalized. I saw it differently: transferring out of province was our only chance. Trevor was in the worst possible condition—trapped in his own hell—and I had to give him an opportunity to break free.

I thought about Trevor's final letter and what he had written about the warrior path. I knew I had to join him on that path. I had great faith in Trevor's will but very little faith in the medical system's ability to help get him where he needed to go. It felt as if it was up to me to get him beyond this seemingly endless loop of gains and setbacks.

After the meeting, I went back to Trevor's room to give his feet a warm salt bath. I didn't say anything about the meeting. I couldn't see the point. All I said was that the brain flap surgery would happen in the next few weeks and then he would be able to move on to rehab.

The rehab doctor came by later in the day and said the Ritalin he'd started giving Trevor was improving his concentration. Normally I would have felt pleased about this, but this day I was discouraged. Outside the room, the doctor told me he was very excited about Trevor's recent thumb movements because once quadriplegics can get a thumb moving, they can work a whole room full of equipment (computers, lights, DVD players, etc.).

I told him stonily that Trevor would never want to live like that. As much as I wanted Trevor around, I knew he wouldn't want to be here if he could move only a thumb. I knew he would rather be dead than simply observing life around him. His zest for life was what attracted people to him. It was infectious. I feared he would sink into a depression so great that he would die because his will to live would disappear.

The next day I asked Trevor how he felt. I gave him a few options: angry, frustrated or just focused on recovery. He said clearly, "Focused on recovery." I felt joy wash over my body. Hearing those words restored my belief that one day he would be back to the man he was before the attack.

My joy was tempered, however, by the realization that there were some unpleasant facts we had to face. Soon we would have to trade in the temporary hospital wheelchair for Trevor's permanent chair, which had been designed specifically for his large frame. This would be an improvement over the other chair, which ended halfway up the back of his thighs and left his feet dangling because of the contractures in his ankles, but it meant that Trevor would transition from visitor to permanent wheelchair resident. The chair also symbolized the unreality of our expectation that he would walk out of the hospital.

That night I was out with some girlfriends and ran into Adam. I hadn't seen him in quite some time, since he usually conducted his healing treatments from a distance. He told me that Trevor would recover, but it would take time. People might think it ludicrous that I believed in an energy healer more than an experienced neurosurgeon, but I guess Adam gave me the hope I desperately needed.

My stepfather, Bill, and I visited the only public long-term care facility in Vancouver that would accept patients with trachs. At first glance, the George Pearson Centre looked as if it hadn't changed since it was built as a tuberculosis hospital in the 1950s. One nurse we spoke to said it could take anywhere from six months to a year for a bed to come available, depending on how quickly people died. I felt sorry that the residents had to live in a place pervaded by failed hope and misery. It left me wishing that our public system provided more for people with severe disabilities.

That day we also checked out the highly regarded GF Strong Rehabilitation Centre. The contrast was startling. It was bright, modern and uplifting. Coincidentally, a couple of old war veterans were sitting in the main lobby when we arrived. They raved about the facility and said it was just the place for one of Canada's finest. Because of his total dependence on the trach tube, though, Trevor wasn't an eligible candidate. Still, the facility gave me a standard to which to compare others. If there was a comparable rehabilitation facility anywhere in the country that would accept him, I would get him there.

At times like this, I couldn't help thinking where we would have been at that moment if Trevor wasn't injured. I hated playing this game of "what if," but sometimes I couldn't help it. I imagined that we would have been planning our next career and family move, maybe to somewhere overseas. Trev had always wanted to complete a master's degree and work for the UN after his deployment, and we'd talked about moving abroad to give Grace a broader perspective on life. But all those dreams were over.

CHAPTER 14:
BLESSED SHALT THOU BE

The plates arrived on the five-year anniversary of the September 11 terrorist attacks in the U.S. Trevor's skull was to go under the knife again in ten days. I'd waited so long for this day, but now I feared it. I knew that if Trevor's body rejected these plates too, we would probably have no other option but to put a helmet on him and find a long-term care facility. And yet, there was no other choice but to do the surgery—Trevor just wasn't healing. If we didn't do anything, he could get much worse.

At lunch one day, I made a list of the people I wanted to have bless the plates. I knew for certain I wanted Jim, the military padre who went to Germany with us, and Jeremy, the padre from Trevor's home unit. I also wrote down the names of Sister Cecilia, a Catholic nun; Ray, the hospital's spiritual care representative; and Eve, our dedicated Reiki master.

Eve and I had become quite close over the course of just a few months. She came to the hospital two to three times a week to work on Trevor. Afterward, as he slept, we would gab over tea in the cafe. It was nice to have someone to talk to who understood what I was dealing with—someone who wasn't family, or from the military or the hospital.

On the day the plates arrived, I made a quick call to the hospital after my lunch break only to find that Trev was having spasms and had turned blue. An oxygen mask was immediately slapped onto his face, and the nurses hovered over him for forty minutes until the colour in his face returned. No one knew what had happened. I couldn't help thinking how coincidental it was that this was September 11, the date of the event that had put Trevor on the path to Afghanistan. What a cruel twist of fate it would have been if someone hadn't noticed him turning blue.

In the tense days leading up to the second surgery, a friend told me about another alternative therapy called Emotional Freedom Technique (EFT). It involved tapping on various points of the head and neck to reduce the intensity of a negative emotion—like the feelings surrounding being hit in the head with an axe, for example. I was sceptical but willing try to anything to get to the bottom of whatever was causing the block in Trevor's system. My friend said she knew an expert who wanted to volunteer his time with Trevor.

A few days later, Andy Bryce was standing next to Trevor's bed telling him that he deserved to heal and tapping gently on his chest and head. Once again, I was surprised to find that Andy was quite normal looking, even athletic. In a deep, gentle voice he told me that EFT releases emotional blockages so the life force, or Qi, can flow to help the body heal itself naturally. He said he was working to release the anger stored in Trevor's body. As Andy tapped away, he said he had to convince Trevor's body that it deserved to heal.

After what Trevor had been through, I couldn't fathom that he wouldn't think that he deserved to heal. I knew it was critical for the surgery to be a success because if Trevor's body rejected the plates a second time, we could be forced to give up hope for a normal life. I decided to have the plates blessed by everyone who believed in Trevor.

Eve and I were the first to bless the plates. I didn't know what to expect, so I was surprised to see that they looked like a dense Styrofoam. We gave each other a few minutes alone with the plates. I don't know what Eve did, but I took the plates and sat in a quiet area and had a talk with God. "Dear God," I said, "we need your help. Please watch over Trevor so that no complications occur with this surgery—no excess fluid buildup, no clotting, and no infection. Please ensure that Trevor's body accepts these plates as his own, and that there are no future complications. I thank you with all my heart." With that, I brought the plates back to Trevor's room for the rest of the group's blessing.

I started talking to God every night after I blessed the plates. It was therapeutic in a sense to think that someone might be listening and nodding as I spoke. I asked for help for Trevor and for me. I asked that I be given the strength and guidance to get through this and to know what to do for Trevor.

Five days before the surgery, Trevor's body was loaded up with healing energy by Adam, Eve, me and now Andy. My goal was to make Trevor's body as strong as it could be for the surgery and to have the plates practically glowing from all the blessings. Although I was still apprehensive, I felt confident that I had done all I could. The rest was up to fate.

A few days before the surgery, I took Trevor outside to feel the warm September rain on his face. Water droplets caught in his long, curly hair and scraggly goatee. I daydreamed about Trevor as he used to be. I pictured him with his feet up on the desk in our den, laughing out loud as I left for work and Grace went to school. I told myself this dream would come true one day.

Two days before the surgery, I received a call from Lynnette Nahirney, the wife of Justin, One Platoon's second-in-command. She told me that the platoon commander, Kevin Schamuhn, was in town and had asked to meet me the next night. The call caught me off guard. I had always hoped I would meet Kevin one day, but I thought I would have more time to prepare. It was emotional for me to know I would soon come face to face with the person who was sitting next to Trevor when he was attacked.

My voice cracked when I spoke to Lynnette. I apologized and said I definitely wanted to meet Kevin. The fact that he also wanted to meet me spoke of his character. I hung up the phone and thought about the irony that I was meeting the man who had saved Trevor's life just one day before Trevor would be having life-saving surgery.

The next night, I headed over to Lynette's house. I was nervous. I wanted to know the details of the attack—in particular, how it could have happened when Trevor was surrounded by so many soldiers—but at the same time, I was afraid to hear them. As soon as I saw Kevin, though, I felt more at ease. He was tall, clean cut and well spoken. He had an air of confidence about him, but he seemed nervous to be meeting me. He spoke carefully as he explained in his own words what had happened to Trevor.

"That day we hit four villages, and Shinkay was one of them," he began. "We hit the first two, stopped for lunch, then went to Shinkay. We had about thirty-two soldiers with us, twenty Canadian Forces and twelve Afghan National Army soldiers. We pulled up into a dry riverbed. We could see an open field and farmland, then about ten to twenty compounds. Six to eight men came out, a few boys and young men, and a couple of girls.

"We were motioned to sit down and were brought tea. We sat across from the elders, an interpreter between myself and Trevor. Rob Dolson, my best section commander, was on my other side. A few boys were behind us, with the security forces behind them [and] facing out in case of an attack. I opened the meeting and passed it over to Trevor. Not long after Trevor started to talk, this young guy with a deranged look on his face came from the group, started yelling, pulled a homemade axe from beneath his robe, and swung it into Trevor's head before we could even react. I saw Trevor's pen drop from his hand and blood spatter on his notebook. His eyes rolled into the back of his head, and he fell back instantly. I assumed he was dead.

"The attack was a signal for a carefully laid ambush. Villagers scattered in all directions as the platoon came under fire from across the river. Rob Dolson said he could feel the hiss of the bullets and could hear his troops screaming for him to put on his helmet. The attacker pulled the axe from Trevor's head and raised it up to take another swing. Rob said he struggled for what seemed like minutes to take off his rifle's safety, but the latch clicked instantly and Rob fired five rounds into [the man]. After fourteen rounds he slumped to the ground before he could take another swing at Trevor.

"It's hard to know how much time passed, but I think the medic, Shaun Marshall, got to Trevor in about four minutes. We were shocked when Shaun said his pulse was stable and he was breathing normally. Shaun reacted quickly, closing the wound and bandaging Trevor's head to prevent further blood loss. When I called it in, I had to stop after every sentence and catch my breath. They were having trouble understanding me, asking me again to repeat the nature of the wound. I repeated loudly, 'NATURE OF WOUND IS AXE TO THE HEAD.'

While we waited for the helicopter, the platoon kept talking to Trevor and telling him everything was okay, even though he was unconscious.

"We carefully moved Trevor onto a stretcher and waited for the helicopter to arrive. After the longest forty-five minutes of my life, the helicopter arrived, but [it] landed 150 metres away, kicking up a dust storm. When we hustled Trevor to the helicopter, he started to vomit, so the medic put a vent in his mouth to open his airway. I got intensely frustrated when we got to the helicopter and the stretcher wouldn't fit. We had to shoehorn it in. After Trevor left for the base hospital, a young Afghan threw a grenade at the Afghan [National Army] vehicle, then ran off. We shot at him and then were left with only the sound of the babbling brook."

As Kevin spoke, I broke in occasionally, asking about the whereabouts of the axe, who had attacked Trevor, and why he was targeted. Kevin said that no one wanted the axe around, so they took it back to the forward operating base and burned it. The villagers told them the boy was mentally deranged. He could have been threatened or coerced by the Taliban.

When Kevin asked if he could see Trevor, I told him about all the complications of the last surgery and said that I didn't want Trevor having an emotional response to his visit before going into surgery the next day. Kevin's eyes were half closed as he talked about his feelings of guilt over the decisions he had made that day, but I told him he had made the best decisions he could have at the time.

CHAPTER 15:
HEALING THE MERIDIANS

I woke up early and nervous on the day of the surgery. I wanted to get it over with but was worried about major complications, including death. So that Trevor wouldn't pick up on my anxiety, I faked excitement as I walked in the room. It was eight o'clock and he was just waking up. His eyes were red and watery, and I sensed he was nervous about the day ahead. I told him how positive I felt and explained that the plates had been blessed and couldn't wait to be part of his head. I said the doctors would probably make his skull look better than before.

"I want to read you an article from a magazine I picked up," I said. I cleared my throat and began to read. In the article, the author profiles Trevor as a character from an old adventure novel who travels the world having adventures and helping people. It ends by describing Trevor as a hero we can all learn from. My voice cracked as I read him the last line: "It would take more than an axe to take down Captain Trevor Greene."

I made a copy of the article and posted it on Trevor's door so the nurses would know a little more about him. Many of them said that they had thought he was "just a soldier," echoing a common misconception that soldiers lead one-dimensional lives. One of the nurses said, through tears, that she hoped Trevor would get better. She was touched by what she'd read, and her newfound knowledge of him had made him more human to her.

At 11:30, the porters came to get Trevor. This time I walked beside his gurney down the long hallways to the OR waiting room. I sat on the bed and stroked his hair as we waited in a curtained-off area. He leaned his head into mine as I told him all the joys that awaited us in the future. I reminded him again that his body was in good shape and the plates had been blessed, so he was not to worry. He didn't talk, but his eyes bore into mine as I spoke.

"I love you," I said. "Don't worry about the surgery. I have a very good feeling about it. I will stay with you until you leave, and I'll be here for you when you get back." I put two fingers on his lips and said, "This kiss is from Grace. She tells you to get better soon and come home."

At 12:17, I squeezed his hand and gave him a kiss before the porters wheeled him off to the OR. I knew the surgery would take about one and a half hours. I called the family to let them know when to expect to hear from me.

At 3:30, the neurosurgeon came into the waiting room to tell me that the surgery had been a success. "Aren't you getting discouraged?" he asked. I assumed he was talking about Trevor's long-term recovery. It had been six months since the attack and Trevor was not showing much progress, despite my efforts to rehabilitate him. "No," I responded, "this surgery could change Trevor's condition neurologically." I had chosen to disregard the fact that it was a long time since the attack and there had been no real change. But I knew Trevor inside and out, and I believed that he could pull off a miracle. The doctor told me that he felt Trevor would remain in his present neurologic condition forever, and that we had to think about his suffering.

After the surgeon left, I offered a thank-you to God for watching over Trev and then contacted family and friends with the happy news that the surgery had been a success. Next, I called Eve and Kathy to tell them that the surgery was finished so they could begin sending healing energy remotely. When I called post-op, the nurses said Trevor was already on the way back up to his room, so I bolted up the stairs to fulfil my promise to be there when he got back.

When I arrived, Trevor was sleeping with what looked like a big white turban on his head. I knew to expect the two small hoses that jutted out from the back of his dressing to allow the excess fluid to drain. I didn't see any swelling, and he looked as comfortable as could be expected. The neurosurgeon came in to check on him a few minutes after I got there. He asked Trevor to open his eyes, which he did. "That was a good sign," he said.

To my surprise, the surgeon would come by every day thereafter to check on Trevor, calling him "bud" most of the time. I felt he was starting to see that there was something special about Trevor—something I knew was worth fighting for. I thought that the man had probably seen so much tragedy over the course of his lengthy career that it was nearly impossible for him to remain optimistic about a case like Trevor's. But he seemed to be slowly coming around.

I knew that Trevor would need to rest after surgery, so I went home for my treasured nightly ritual with Grace of supper, bedtime stories and a prayer in the rocking chair. Trevor was more awake when I returned around eight. The nurses were checking his blood pressure, oxygen saturation and pupil dilation every hour. I was so happy to see his eyes open and no swelling in his head or face. At this point in the last surgery, he'd looked like he was on the verge of death. I leaned in and gave him a kiss and told him that he looked like a million bucks, even with the tight white dome on his head. I reminded him that with the surgery behind us, we could focus our efforts on rehab. This would be just a momentary blip in our lives.

The next day, I was amazed at how good Trevor looked. He was awake and very conscious. I held up the newspaper for us to read first thing. He didn't fatigue and didn't even fall asleep that day. I massaged him and did range-of-motion exercises on his limbs. When I left later in the day, he even mouthed "Bye." It had been such an effort for him to talk for so long that that one little word put me in high spirits and I could hardly contain my excitement. I wondered if these changes I was seeing could simply be the result of his brain being safely enclosed.

Over the next few days, the tight bandage around Trevor's head was taken off. The blood-encrusted staples tracking all over his skull made him look like Frankenstein's monster. His blood pressure was very low and he was put back on antibiotics because of a chest infection. He seemed dozier and less aware than he had immediately after surgery. He wasn't speaking, so we communicated with eyebrow raises. When Grace first saw him, she pointed at his head and said, "Owie."

A few days after the surgery, Dick and Bess arrived. Grace and I needed a little mother–daughter time, so we took the weekend to visit family in Nanaimo and work on the house we had built for our new life after Trev's tour. The living room had a beautiful view of the mountains, and the back overlooked a treed backyard. We'd planned for the house to be the next step for us while we awaited an international posting, but now the staircase to the main living room was an impassable barrier.

I called Trevor's parents that first night to find out how his day had been. I expected good news, but instead they told me that Trevor had been sitting in the wheelchair when they saw his eyes roll to the back of his head. At the same time, his left arm and his legs shot straight out and his head jerked sharply to the left. Bess grabbed Trevor's shoulders while Dick ran to get help. A nurse rushed in and checked his vitals. She said it was a seizure. It lasted one minute and should have been prevented by the medication Trevor was taking. When a CT scan didn't find any additional damage, they got him back in bed. Hearing this, I felt all the hope I'd had for his post-surgery recovery dissolving in my heart. The worst part was that I wasn't there for him.

Seeing Trevor after the weekend was a relief. He was no worse off and even appeared to be more conscious. Even the staples had been removed, leaving thin red lines where his scalp had been opened up and peeled back like an orange.

While Grace and I were in Nanaimo, my sister had introduced me to her friend Janet. Janet studied acupuncture in China and was mentoring under a doctor of traditional Chinese medicine in Vancouver. She said she would arrange a consultation with him for Trevor.

According to Chinese culture, the human body is a small universe made up of energy, or Qi. Complex systems of energy and matter work together to maintain a healthy human mind and body. These systems run through the body in twelve meridians. For two thousand years, the Chinese have studied these meridians and used them to cure illnesses. I was hoping that all these centuries of medical know-how would complement the modern Western medicine at work in the hospital.

Dr. Tran was a small man who spoke broken English. He walked purposefully into Trevor's room without saying a word and took pulses from each of his arms. "Uneven," he pronounced. He stepped back and motioned for Janet to check Trevor's pulses. When she was finished, they spoke quietly between themselves.

Janet then turned to me and said the doctor would write Trevor a "prescription," which I could pick up at his shop in Chinatown. The prescription, she said, was for a concoction of plants, roots, bark, ginger and earthworm. Soaking the feet in this mixture was meant to increase circulation all the way up to the brain. After Dr. Tran left, Janet said, "He thinks he can help. He's treated people worse off than Trevor."

So it was that on a crisp, sunny Saturday in early October, I drove down to Chinatown on my scooter. Dr. Tran's shop looked like the type of store you'd expect to find in a Third World country. Rows of glass jars containing weird and interesting bits of dried plants and ocean specimens stood behind a glass case festooned with labels in Chinese writing. The store was stocked with food items and packages of tea to cure every ailment.

I spotted Dr. Tran at a little desk at the back of the shop with a couple of patients standing around him. I didn't want to interrupt, so I wandered around the store, gazing at the fascinating displays. When Dr. Tran saw me, he motioned for me to join him. As I sat down at the desk, he reached into a file, pulled out a standard prescription and handed it to a guy behind the counter. He told me to bring the prescribed concoction to a boil, then hold Trevor's feet over the steam until the water was cool enough to submerge his feet. Dr. Tran then said, "Follow my instruction, I have your husband walking and talking again."

The fellow behind the counter asked me how many "buckets" of the prescription I wanted. I'd never dealt in buckets before. He said that each bucket could be used seven times, except in the case of infection. I ordered three buckets, which thankfully were only the size of a brown paper lunch bag. On the way back, I wondered how I was going to boil this pungent mixture in a busy hospital ward.

When I got back, Trev's friend Greg was visiting. Trevor and Greg had met years earlier in Japan and had climbed the local mountains together. Greg had dropped by the hospital to describe a vivid dream he had had. In the dream, he'd visited Trevor on the top of a castle. Under a dark and foreboding sky, Trevor had told him intricate details about his tour in Afghanistan. The dream was so stark that Greg had written down all the details. "I think it means that you are destined to reach great heights in your recovery," he said.

After Greg left, I asked Trev if he wanted to see himself for the first time in seven months. His hair had grown in a little, and the incisions had faded from the angry red they were after the surgery. Besides being much thinner and paler, he looked close to the pre-injury Trevor. He gave me an eyebrow raise to indicate that he wanted to see himself, so I wheeled him into the bathroom and moved out of the way of the mirror. He stared at himself in blank amazement, just as a woman does when she cuts off all her hair for the first time. I put my arms around him and kissed him on the top of his head. "Even with a few scars, you are still the most attractive man I've ever laid eyes on," I said.

A few days later, I had all my supplies for the herbal foot bath. I filled a large metal stockpot with water, added the herbs and set the pot to boil over a single electric burner on the floor in Trevor's room. The concoction smelled just as you would expect of a boiling pot of strange dead plants and marine life: putrid. After a few days, the nurses asked me to relocate the foot baths, saying that other patients were complaining about the stench. So I started to boil the herbs every day in the communal kitchen. I brought the tightly covered pot to Trevor's room, stuffed a towel under the closed door and steamed his feet. Friends eventually stopped asking, "What are you doing???"

...

A month after the surgery, it took five of us to sit Trevor on the side of the bed. His muscles were tight and his limbs rigid. Trying to bend his hips was like trying to bend a board. The struggle exhausted Trevor and discouraged me.

But the news wasn't all bad. Physiotherapy continued despite Trevor's badly contracted feet, and he could now at least watch himself in the large wall mirror in the gym. During Cynthia's session that week, she stressed how important it was for Trevor to watch his hands as he tried to move them. Trevor sat in the wheelchair, and Cynthia put his hand on a pole and asked him to push it forward and bring it back while watching his hand. No matter how much he tried, he just couldn't muster the coordination to complete the movement.

In the meantime, I had been struggling to convince Trev's neurosurgeon to take out his trach. I was talking to him one day that week while I was with Grace in Trevor's room. He insisted that Trevor needed a permanent trach to protect his airway long term and prevent chest infections. I understood how important it was for safety, but I felt that the doctor was condemning Trevor to a life with a tube stuck in his throat and no hope for rehab. He eventually relented and ordered the open hole in the trach to be plugged to test Trev's ability to clear his own throat. Trevor managed reasonably well, although the plug had to be opened on occasion to help him.

After the doctor left, a small figure came through the door so gently that she seemed to float. It was Sister Cecilia Cham, a Catholic nun appointed to visit patients. She stood next to Trevor, looking into his eyes, and said carefully and peacefully, "God has a plan for you." She then offered a quote from a book I had recently read by psychotherapist Viktor Frankl: "If there is meaning in life at all, then there must be a meaning in suffering." Trevor stared directly into her eyes the whole time she was speaking, as if she were channelling words directly from God. When she finished, I heard him say quietly, "Amen." She left as soundlessly as she had come in, leaving an air of godliness in the room behind her. Even Grace was quiet as she spoke.

After Sister Cecilia left, I gave Grace the only thing at the hospital that kept her entertained for longer than thirty minutes: ice chips. I put on a *Shrek* DVD for her and Trevor to watch while I stretched his muscles. They watched the video and sucked on their ice chips in blissful ignorance of my scheme to exercise Trevor's tongue and mouth muscles—even though he hadn't been approved to eat or drink. I watched Grace as she looked intently at Trevor crunching his ice chips. It was an oddly normal portrait of a father and daughter spending time together.

"Lonely," said Trev one night when I asked him how he was feeling. It was now September. I had gone back to work four months earlier and couldn't be at the hospital as much as I was before. "Quit work," he replied when I asked what I could do to make things better for him. I told him how horrible it felt to be at work when all I wanted to do was be at the hospital, but I also knew that in some ways it was better for me not to be there full time. Without me around, Trevor was forced to speak up for himself more often, which was an important step in his rehabilitation. I knew he couldn't do it all on his own, though, so I decided to drop down to three days a week at work.

Around the end of October, I noticed swelling in Trevor's right leg. When I mentioned it to his nurse she said she didn't know what could be causing it. When the left leg also started to balloon, I asked that a doctor assess it. The next day, an ultrasound indicated deep vein thrombosis (blood clots), despite the blood thinners Trevor was on. Thankfully the lung filter had been kept in, preventing a potentially fatal pulmonary embolism.

Trevor and C.W. Nicol in Nicol's kitchen in Kurohime, Japan, in 1990.

Trevor running a race up Mount Fuji in 1992.

Trevor in his formal white naval uniform in 1998, shortly after the voyage of the HMCS *Oriole*.

Early days in Vancouver, March 30, 2005.
(*Courtesy Lisa Petka*)

The Greene family on a Vancouver beach in 2005.

Trevor sleeping with Grace at Debbie's grandmother's home in 2005.

Trevor teaching English to a curious boy after a *shura*, using an extremely rare homemade Pashtun-English dictionary, in February 2006. (*Courtesy Rick Madonik/* Toronto Star)

Trevor (background) in a remote village in Afghanistan before a *shura*, in February 2006. (*Courtesy Rick Madonik/* Toronto Star)

Trevor shaking hands with village elders before a *shura*, in February 2006. (*Courtesy Rick Madonik/*Toronto Star)

Trevor having tea at a *shura* with platoon second-in-command Justin McKay (*far left*), in early 2006. (*Courtesy Rick Madonik/*Toronto Star)

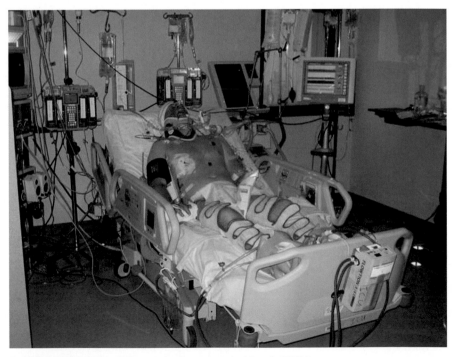

Debbie's first sight of Trevor in Germany, in March 2006.

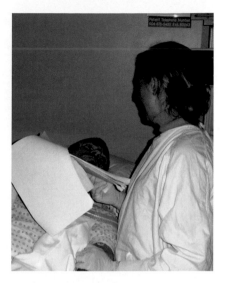

Doctors Pete Sorini (*left*) and J. Patrick Johnson, the American surgeons who operated on Trevor in Landstuhl, Germany, in March 2006.

Debbie at Vancouver General Hospital in early 2006, reading Trevor's manuscript about his voyage aboard the HMCS *Oriole*.

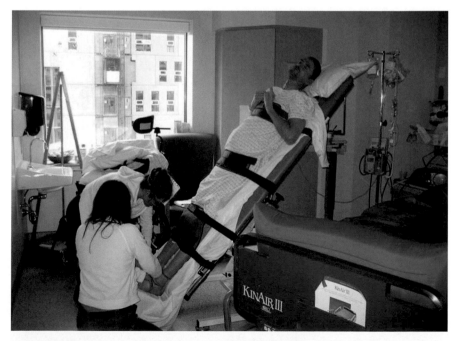

Trevor on the tilt table at Vancouver General Hospital in 2006, with physiotherapist Cynthia Wilson (*centre*) and her assistant working on his feet.

Debbie and Trevor in Ponoka, Alberta, in the summer of 2008.
(*Courtesy Shaughn Butts*)

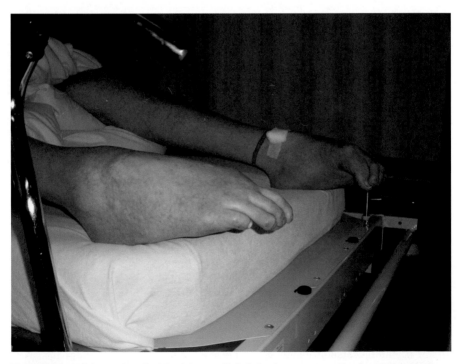

Trevor's horribly contracted feet immediately before surgery in January 2009.

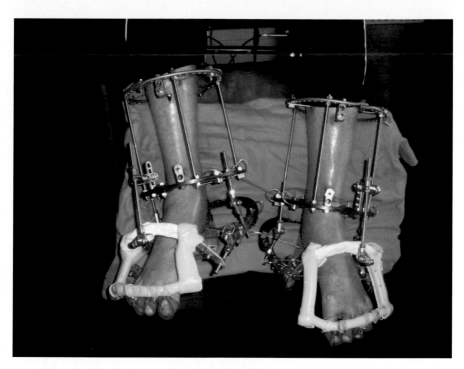

Trevor's feet post-surgery in January 2009, in Ilizarov frames.

Debbie and Trevor's wedding
ceremony on July 24, 2010.

Debbie and Trevor at a fundraiser in Victoria for the Boomer's Legacy foundation, in November 2010. (*Courtesy Rob Jirucha*)

Debbie and Trevor near the beach in Nanaimo in July 2011.

On Grace's second Halloween, we stayed home to greet trick-or-treaters. She had fun playing with the candy bowl and answering the door. Whenever she heard a knock, she screamed, "More kids! More kids!" Later that night, I went up to tell Trev about it. A couple of the guys had come by the hospital, complete with smuggled-in beer, to watch a hockey game. I felt that Trev was struggling a bit to clear the phlegm from his throat, and when the nurse unplugged the trach, a thick gob flew across the room. We all started laughing, Trevor included. Before I left, I dipped my finger in a beer for him and watched the smile spread across his face when I ran my finger across his lips. Unfortunately, he would get to enjoy only the guys' company, not their beer.

I had been monitoring Trevor's weight since I first noticed his muscles starting to wither. Recently I'd also started to watch his hemoglobin levels, an indicator of how much oxygen is being carried through the blood. Late one night as I left the hospital, I asked the nurse about Trevor's levels, as I typically did. He said they were at 82. I knew from my research that normal hemoglobin levels for a man are 138 to 182 grams per litre of blood, so I asked what level was considered dangerous. The nurse said, "Around 80." I asked what could have caused such a drop, since Trevor's levels were above 100 a few days earlier. He said it could indicate internal bleeding, but he didn't seem the least bit concerned about it. I insisted that a doctor check it out. It was about ten o'clock and no one would be around until morning, but the nurse said he'd request a blood test. Within a couple of days, Trevor's hemoglobin levels inexplicably climbed back up to a reasonable range.

On our days together, I would bring in exercises for Trevor to work on when his feet were submerged in the stinky Chinese herbal soup. One day I brought in a mirror so he could see his blank expression and start working on moving the muscles in his face. I got only slight twitches from them, but we kept at it daily. Another day I brought in flash cards and had him do addition and subtraction. Trevor did well, so we moved on to simple multiplication and division. I always kept the box of activities on the windowsill. After our daily hand and arm exercises, we would dip into the box to exercise his brain. The doctors had said that most healing happens in the first six months after an injury. This ceiling was always in the back of my mind, so I couldn't afford to waste a moment. When I went home each day, I needed to feel that I was leaving without any regrets.

CHAPTER 16:
FIRST REMEMBRANCE

With Remembrance Day looming, I was nervous about how Trevor would react. For years I had attended the local parade out of habit, but after meeting Trev, I felt the importance of the day in my heart. That year, on November 11, Grace and I dressed up and pinned poppies over our hearts. I had invited a few friends to watch the local ceremonies live on TV with us at the hospital.

The mood in the room that day was sombre. When the ceremony started, Trev sat with his eyes glued to the screen, waiting to see his regiment march in their traditional kilts. No one spoke. The only sound came from the TV. Trevor was stoic partly because he was able to show emotion only in his eyes. But it was difficult for everyone in the room to watch the ceremonies.

Our generation was now being affected by war, and our young soldiers were being honoured alongside those from their grand-fathers' generation.

At the end of the ceremony, I cringed as photographs of soldiers killed in action scrolled slowly down the screen. I was afraid of how Trev would react at seeing the face of his good friend Bill Turner—his replacement—on screen. When his picture rolled by, Trevor stared at it unflinchingly. I turned off the TV as the last picture faded, then felt compelled to break the silence. "We are all here for you today because we are proud of you and believe in you," I told Trevor. "The small improvements I see in you every day will all add up to big improvements one day. Your strength and will and the support of your family and friends will help pull you through." I paused and then said, "We're so glad that we're not watching your picture scroll down the screen."

With that, I couldn't maintain my composure any longer and started to cry. I was picturing the faces of the fallen and thinking how close Trevor had come to being one of them. His face started to grimace, too, as if he was sorry to have caused this pain for me. It was a good pain, though, because I didn't see his picture scroll down the screen. I was the lucky one. I got to visit Trevor every day and feel his warmth in my hand when so many other families were mourning their loved ones.

As I turned to thank everyone for coming, I noticed there wasn't a dry eye in the room. Throughout the day, more friends visited, a revolving door of love and honour for Trevor, Grace and me. Trevor was exhausted by the time Grace and I left, and so was I. It had been an emotional day for us all, and one that I would never forget.

Trevor turned forty-two in a hospital bed, dressed in a thin green gown. I brought in an oversized Canadian flag cake for a party in his room. The only parking spot that day was five long blocks from the hospital. As I struggled to balance the massive cake, my purse and umbrella, plates, forks, napkins and cups in a torrential downpour with high winds, I suddenly realized how crazy it was to be worried about dropping anything. Losing the cake was low on my worry scale compared to losing Trevor.

I had emailed family and friends to let them know we were having an "open house" in Trevor's room and to ask them to drop by anytime in the afternoon or evening. It seemed there was once again a steady stream of people through the door. One of the rugby guys, Alex, brought yet another of his wonderful giant casseroles. Even some of Trevor's former nurses stopped by. It was a fabulous day, and I believed Trevor loved every minute of. He was the perfect guest of honour because he stayed awake all day.

By late November, Trevor was participating in physiotherapy for up to twenty minutes a day. The emphasis was on holding up his head, which he could do for only five minutes at best. After fifteen or twenty minutes, he would close his eyes, forcing Cynthia and me to attempt to wake him by yelling, "TTTRRRREEEVVVVOOOORRRR, WWWWAAAAAAKKKE UUUUUPPPPP!" Half the time that didn't work, so we would have to lift his eyelids and try again. We might muster another few minutes out of him before he shut down again. But Cynthia never gave up on him. She got louder and continued to push him every week.

After Trevor had been at the hospital for eight months, we started to plan for discharge. Trevor wasn't eligible for the local rehab centre because he was still a long way from participating at the minimum required level. And he wasn't eligible for the brain injury rehab program in Alberta because he had a trach. So the only suitable placement was a public long-term care centre where no rehab was provided. Once the paperwork for the facility was complete, he'd be put on a waiting list. It could all add up to another dreary year in hospital.

Since it looked like Trevor wouldn't be leaving the hospital anytime soon, I decided, for his own self-esteem, to get him out of the faded hospital gowns and into regular clothes. It would give him a small sense of normalcy. I ordered tear-away pants online and got my mother, an excellent seamstress, to make several T-shirts with snaps down the back. The clothes would be easy for the nurses to get on and off, and Trevor could finally feel dignified in regular clothing.

I was still driving my scooter in early December. A bulky grey-and-red snowsuit covered my neatly tailored blue pinstriped suit and made me look like an overgrown toddler on the way to a snowball fight. The previous December I would have been sitting on a warm bus immersed in a fabulous book or planning my workday. This December day I was in traffic in the rain and cold, exposed to the elements and planning to meet after work with a reporter and a cameraman who had been embedded with Trevor's platoon. Sometimes it felt like I was watching a stranger play me in a movie; life was going on around me while I stood still, frozen in time. As friends and colleagues went out for comfortable lunches, I was weaving in and out of traffic, hungry and cold, trying to make it to the hospital and back within the hour.

The two journalists, Mitch and Rick, had invited me to meet them over coffee. They had spent ten days with the platoon, on assignment for the *Toronto Star*, in late February and early March 2006. On the day of the attack, they had uncharacteristically stayed back at the FOB to file a story. The two shared with me how well they had got to know Trev, especially when they were sitting around the bonfire at the FOB the evening before the attack. He had opened up to them then about his ambitions to return to Afghanistan as a civilian to establish an educational aid program and empower the Afghan people.

Mitch and Rick talked as well about the night after the attack, when they had sat down with Kevin, the platoon commander, and learned that he had upbraided the village elders for allowing the attack to happen during a *shura*. Kevin admitted to Mitch and Rick that he hadn't slept the night before because he feared seeing what his subconscious would reveal. Two days later, Mitch and Rick spoke to Dr. Homer Tien, the trauma surgeon who had resuscitated Trevor at the Kandahar hospital. Dr. Tien told them he'd seen a lot of brain injuries caused by motorcycle accidents and gun shots, but that Trevor's injury was particularly dire.

I enjoyed hearing this different side of Trevor's experiences in Afghanistan and being able to ask the journalists questions about their time together outside the wire. It filled in some of the details that Trevor hadn't been able to share with me. I sensed by the stories they told about their time together that the two men had established a real friendship with Trev. It all reminded me of why I had fallen in love with him.

When I arrived back at Trevor's room later that evening, the nurse was asking him the same orientation questions she always did. For the most part, Trevor knew who he was and where he was now, but often he didn't know the month. On this day, he thought it was April. When I told him it was December, he said, "That's embarrassing."

I'd been pushing to get Trevor eating again by Christmas. I had long since given up the impossible goal of his walking by Christmas, and the last time we had changed rooms, I left the "I will walk by Christmas" signs behind. Before Trevor could get on a more substantial diet, though, he had to pass the swallow test again with that awful thickened apple juice and blue food colouring. I was cleaning off his mouth after the test one night when I caught him staring at me the way he used to. With the same cheesy lilt as before, he said, "You're so pretty." I leaned in close and heard him say, "Will you marry me?"

The proposal caught me off guard, and I started thinking about the uncertainty of our future and what kind of married life we would have with him in a long-term care facility, unable to move. "On one condition," I said. "You must get yourself out of these hospitals."

"I promise," Trev replied.

CHAPTER 17:

THE HEART OF CHRISTMAS

I could tell that Grace was becoming more comfortable around Trevor. On our way out of town one Friday afternoon, we dropped in to say goodbye. She said "Love you, Daddy" without any coaching from me. In response, his eyes looked both sad and happy—sad because he wasn't coming with us for the weekend, but happy to hear his daughter say she loved him.

When I called in to check on him on the Saturday, the nurse said there had been a steady stream of visitors. A couple of the guys had made Trevor laugh so hard the nurse had to come in to check on him. I never would have guessed that this group of beer-drinking buddies would end up being one of the biggest support systems we had.

On the days I wasn't working, I was at the hospital by 8:30 a.m. for breakfast and then would spend the entire day there with Trevor. One day when I was getting ready to go home and have dinner with Grace, Trevor said, "You're always going." As a mother, I had to go home to Grace, who needed me as much as he did. I wanted to stay so many times, but my mother's guilt over not spending enough time with my daughter always overwhelmed me. "It kills me not to be able to be with you both all the time," I explained to Trevor. "It's important that Grace has a routine with me she can count on. Being there for dinner and staying until bedtime is part of that routine. During the day she has Regina and play groups. At night she has me. Please understand."

I knew that if I ever hoped to have the three of us together again, Trevor had to start making more progress. Step one was to get him back on solid food. I'd been pushing hard for a modified barium swallow test, and finally Trevor was scheduled to have one seven days before Christmas. The barium swallow test is a video X-ray exam showing how food moves from the mouth to the esophagus. Trev had been successful with all the dyed-food tests, so I was hopeful this next one would clear him for eating. In the test, various foods and liquids are covered with barium. This allows doctors to see what happens as the bolus—or as I like to say, ball of barium shite—passes into the esophagus from the mouth. If Trevor was able to choke down food coated in white goo that tasted like chalk, he might be eating by Christmas.

I went with Trevor to do the exam. It was fascinating to watch the bright white image as the food was broken down into smaller pieces and then re-formed as a ball prior to being swallowed. I had never thought before about all the mechanisms at work while I enjoyed a meal.

Next came the chalk-like fluid. A tiny bit did go into his lungs, but overall the doctor was pleased and Trevor was approved for soft foods and thick fluids. It meant he would be able to enjoy Christmas dinner.

Later in the afternoon, Trev's close CIMIC colleagues and his immediate superior, Maj. Ron Locke, flew in for a Christmas visit. Trevor had trained with Tony, Gwen, Jay and Julien, and the five became very close over that year. A huge smile played across Trevor's face when they walked in, and I could tell he was trying to say something to the major. I leaned in to translate.

"Major Locke, I want to go on the next deployment," he said with all his whispered force.

Trevor would have been absolutely devastated to hear that he would never be up for another tour. But Major Locke handled everything well. "I'll keep a spot open for you," he answered.

On Trevor's first full day of semi-solid food, he asked for more after eating a full breakfast. That same day, after ten months of waiting, his custom wheelchair arrived. I never thought I would get excited over a wheelchair, but the loaner was much too small for him, so this was something he desperately needed. I could tell he wasn't thrilled about having his very own wheelchair, so I reasoned with him: "Think of it as a temporary tool until you get the strength back to walk again."

That evening, I crawled into bed with him and we snuggled. I didn't want to open my eyes and see where we were. After I thought Trevor had fallen asleep, I snuck out of bed to get ready to head home. He opened his eyes as I was getting out, so I crawled back in for a few more minutes to say goodbye.

"Score! You came back," he said.

I could have stayed all night if I didn't have Grace to take care of as well. For just those few precious moments, I felt like we were a normal couple leading a normal life.

We took one more step toward normalcy when a resident doctor came in three days before Christmas and said it was time for the trach to come out. The trach had been mostly plugged for quite a few weeks by then, which demonstrated that Trevor had been breathing and clearing his throat all on his own. I'd wanted the trach out for so long, but now I was worried that something could happen over the holidays, when fewer staff would be around. The resident agreed to leave the trach in until after Christmas.

To celebrate this new milestone, Trevor and I had a candlelight dinner in his room. I had picked up some of his favourite foods, and we enjoyed each other's company while we ate. It wasn't quite like the old days, since I was feeding him, but it was lovely all the same. The next morning, however, I got a lecture about open flames near an oxygen source.

The right people always seemed to find us just when life at the hospital started to get a little routine. We met Kelly Johnson on a cold and clear Christmas Eve morning. Kelly was a registered massage therapist and craniosacral therapist, and she had heard about Trevor through a mutual friend. A craniosacral therapist attempts to manipulate the spinal fluid by lightly guiding her hands on the patient. Kelly rounded out my integrated approach to Trevor's recovery perfectly. The holistic team began with Adam's and Anita's sessions, then Eve's Reiki treatments, acupuncture, Dr. Tran's traditional Chinese herbs, and now Kelly. I disguised her as a massage therapist so the nursing staff didn't get alarmed that we were doing something bizarre with Trevor.

That afternoon, Grace sat on Trevor's bed trying to open Christmas presents on her own. I'd wrapped up a book I found for her in Trevor's kit bag and gave it to her to open with him, since he wouldn't be seeing her on Christmas Day. My sisters, Toni and Deanna, and their families also came to spend time with Trevor before taking Grace to Deanna's house, an hour's drive from the hospital, where we would spend the night. I stayed behind to help Trevor with his spaghetti supper. After dinner,

I told him that while it was hard for me to leave, Christmas should be special for Grace as well. We were building our family traditions, and her second Christmas shouldn't start with both her parents being away. He said he understood but would miss us. Trevor would spend Christmas Eve alone with $M*A*S*H$ reruns and I would spend it with my heart cut in two.

On Christmas Day, Grace and her cousins opened their presents and played with their new toys all morning. After a few hours Grace was exhausted, so I put her down for a nap and headed for the hospital. I made good time on the empty roads. When I arrived, I was relieved to see our good friends Gregory and Claire Kirkpatrick and their daughter, Elise, visiting. I gave Trevor a kiss and wished everyone a merry Christmas. Trevor wasn't as responsive as he had been, but the Kirkpatricks just ignored it and carried on as they always had.

After they left, I sat on the bed next to Trevor and put my arm over his shrunken waist and my head on his shoulder. He dipped his head to mine. I pulled a small box out from under the covers.

"Merry Christmas, my love," I said.

I opened the box and pulled out a ring with the words "love," "faith" and "courage" engraved on the outside and "100% recovery" engraved on the inside. I took the ring out of the box and placed it on his finger.

"I love it," he said. "But I didn't get you anything."

Then I pulled out another box, which held a gift I had bought for myself. The label on the box said, "To my darling Bee. Love, Maqua." In it nestled a circular pendant with two words: "I promise."

By the end of the year, there was less of a delay in Trevor's responses. Although he still spoke in a whisper, he could now put together short sentences. Grace was also starting to form longer sentences. When I told her I loved her, she would often respond with "I love Daddy." Hearing her say that made all my efforts for Trevor worthwhile.

On the last day of 2006, Grace brought in some of her books and we crawled on the bed to read them with Trevor. She sat next to him and turned to face him for the first time. He stared at her like he hadn't seen her in a year. For the first time that she would remember, Trevor said "Hi Wabbit" to her. It was also the first day she ever made an effort to touch him.

She wanted to put hand lotion on Trevor's face after seeing me do it. I watched him close his eyes and savour every second of her baby-soft touch. After hearing me call him honey, she mimicked me, with the same intonation. Trevor and I laughed, which egged her on, making for a wonderful family moment. We cherished it because for us these moments were few and far between.

In between videos and popcorn, Trevor and I rang in the new year at 7 o'clock with a toast: "To a glorious year of health, happiness and peace."

As I fell asleep that night, I couldn't help thinking what a wonderful way it was to end the year and what a harbinger for a new year of solid recovery.

CHAPTER 18:
IS IT REALLY 2007?

My New Year's euphoria ended abruptly at 10:45 the next morning when I called the hospital to check on Trevor. Breakfast usually arrived at around eight o'clock, so I had assumed he had already had fed. I was stunned to be told that the staff was too busy to give Trevor his breakfast. I was so disappointed for Trevor and so pissed off at the system for allowing this to happen, especially on the first day of a new year. Hospital food isn't fabulous, to say the least, but there is something satisfying about chewing, and for Trevor, even dry toast afforded a flavour explosion.

Grace and I quickly packed our bag of activities and food and headed in to see Trevor for the day. I sensed he was down when we arrived. His eyes were red and he said he was "tired of it all." I couldn't blame him. I was, too. "It's the start of a new year and the worst is behind us," I reminded him. "As soon as the trach comes out, we'll be going into intense rehab. You just need to hold on until then."

After we'd eaten some fresh fruit and yogurt, Trevor's mood seemed to improve and we finally got down to business. While Grace loaded up her new shopping cart and pushed it around the room, Trev and I started with stretching and then opening and closing his hands. He could easily grip a ball just by reflex, but he'd never been able to release it. On this day, the ball dropped out of his hand after a few tries and landed on the bed. "Grace, Daddy dropped the ball!" I yelled. She looked at me and smiled and then went back to her shopping.

After Christmas our everyday concerns crowded in again. Trevor's diet was woefully lacking in fresh greens and fruits, so I bought powdered greens for him. It wasn't so simple to give them to him, however. First, the dietician had to ensure there were no contraindications with his medications. If the food proved safe, she'd then request an order from the doctor. Once the doctor had put the order in, the container was sent to the pharmacy department to be identified (I guess so they could determine that it was in fact powdered greens and not marijuana). This process could take one or two weeks, depending on my persistence. One day the dietician commented that she'd never had a patient on so many supplements before.

The next day, I turned on *Oprah* while Trevor dozed. I'd never had the luxury of watching daytime TV, and I felt like indulging myself. The show that day happened to be about kids growing up without a father. Tears started to well up in my eyes as I listened to the kids talk about what they'd missed out on. I thought about Grace and how she might also grow up without a father in the house. I never wanted this for her. Trevor heard my sniffles and woke up, so I told him about the show. "Don't worry. I will be coming home," he said.

Before leaving that night, I asked the nurse behind the desk how much fluid Trevor was getting, because his lips seemed a little dry. He said nine hundred millilitres, which to me seemed low. I said I thought the average person needed eight glasses, or almost two litres, of water a day. "That's a medical myth and has never been proven," he snapped. He then leaned over from his seat, looked into Trevor's room from six metres away and said, "He's fine. His skin isn't sagging." At that point, I knew any further attempt at convincing him would be a wasted effort. When I spoke with the dietician the following day, she agreed that nine hundred millilitres was too low and said she would increase the amount being flushed through his feeding tube.

At the end of the first week of January, there was a lot of congestion in Trevor's throat that he didn't seem able to clear. I was thankful I'd resisted taking out the trach over Christmas. One night, the nurse came in to check vitals. Trevor thought it was February 2006, and the last thing he could remember was that he was about to fight the Taliban. A few days earlier, I'd heard him tell the nurse that it was February 2003 and he was thirty-one. When she told him the actual year, he said, "Is it really 2007? Seriously?"

I tried to bring in as many homemade meals as I could, but one evening our friend Greg Kelly came by with homemade salmon bisque. We had already had dinner, so I put it in the patient kitchen for later. I labelled it with the date and Trevor's room number so the cleaners wouldn't throw it out. The next day, despite Trevor's objections, I opened the trach three times to help him clear his throat before our supper. When I went to the fridge, however, the salmon bisque was gone. The cleaners told me that drug addicts in the hospital often go searching for food on all the floors. I was disappointed about it, but Trevor understood how drug addicts think and act, so he didn't particularly mind being stuck with hospital pork cutlets.

That evening, Trevor asked for my work phone number and said he was going to give me a call during the day. I found it interesting that he thought he could call me. There was no phone in the room, and I had never seen the nurses use a cordless phone. Then Trevor started talking about becoming a police officer. I was a little surprised, given that he was only able to move his thumbs up and down and had just started to hold his head up for fifteen minutes at a time, but thought it was good he was planning for the future.

Later as we sat in bed together, I took Trevor's hand in mine. He confessed that he felt guilty for the deaths of the Afghan boy who'd attacked him and his friend Bill Turner, who had replaced him. I told him that he had to let go of the guilt so his body could begin the healing process. Trev whispered, "The whole platoon was damaged. The soldiers who fired probably feel guilty about killing a young man who was not a soldier."

"We have to assume that fate played a role in the destiny of all our lives," I said. "Two people were killed and one seriously injured, but so many other families are mourning, too. We are mourning the loss of your life, even though you are still living. Your attacker's family is questioning the loss of their son and brother. And the soldiers who took him down will forever question their actions. We have to believe this happened for a reason."

I felt Trev squeeze my hand for the first time in a long, long time. I sensed that more than a gesture of affection, it was a deep-rooted gratitude for my being with him on this journey.

Eleven months after the attack, Trevor got to come home for the first time for a short visit. Before we left the hospital, he told me that he didn't need the wheelchair to get home. I was glad he was being positive, and I didn't have the heart to tell him that he did. We took a taxi for the fifteen-minute drive home. The taxi driver lifted a ramp down from the back of the minivan and wheeled Trevor in. He couldn't fit facing forward, so he had to face backwards. When I looked back during the ride, I saw Trevor's head bouncing like a bobblehead doll's against the headrest, no doubt scrambling his battered brain.

When we got home, Trevor looked around and seemed to show signs of recognizing the house, even though we had moved in only a few weeks before he left for Afghanistan. I hoped to have him home more, maybe even overnight, but I soon realized that would be impossible. There was no way to get his large, stiff body out of the wheelchair easily.

Trevor's chair took up practically the entire small kitchen, so he had to sit in the entranceway while we ate. I had prepared his favourite meal: spaghetti and chocolate cake. Grace faced Trevor in her highchair, and he faced her in his wheelchair. I stood between father and daughter, feeding Trevor while Grace fed herself with her pink spoon. It was glorious to all be eating together in our own home. But at the same time, I was overcome by the crushing realization that life would never be the same for us. Over a year ago, Trevor had walked out of this house under his own steam and I'd just wheeled him back in as a victim of war.

Trevor didn't eat much of his lunch. He said he didn't feel well because of the taxi ride and the unfamiliar smells and noises of home. He just wanted to rest. He and Grace both slept, but when he woke up he said he wanted to go back to the familiar ground of the hospital. I was disappointed that for him, our home had become an alien place.

By Monday, Trevor had recovered from the trip home and set a new record for holding up his head: twenty-one minutes. He was approved for thin fluids that day, so I was able to reward him with his first latte in months. And there was another first: the occupational therapist began testing Trevor's cognitive functions. She started by giving him problem scenarios to solve. What would he do first if he smelled a gas leak? Which of three things would he fix first—broken fridge, broken light or broken mug? How would he make a cup of tea? Judgment and abstraction problems came next, and then he was asked to count backwards from one hundred by sevens. I knew from our conversations that he had the appropriate answers, but he seemed to have difficulty initiating a response. He usually did quite well on everything except the math questions. He could respond in a louder whisper now, thanks to a voice amplification headset the speech therapist was testing.

The following weekend, I extended Trevor's second visit home to seven hours. Grace kept saying, "Watch, Daddy! Watch, Daddy!" while doing somersaults on the bed. By the end of the visit, his eyes were red and tired. He didn't even have the strength or the desire to do our regular exercises when Grace went for her nap. Over the past few weeks, I had started to challenge Trevor more, and I'd been looking forward to the opportunity to continue my efforts at home. When he said he wanted water, I put a cup with a straw in his hand and told him to try to bring it up to his mouth. The only way he could come close to connecting was by bringing his head down as far as it could go.

Two days before Valentine's Day, Trev began asking for his bank cards. He thought someone had stolen them from his hospital room and he needed to cancel them. I told him not to worry because I had them at home. I thought he was thinking about getting me something for Valentine's Day, so I reminded him of the pact we'd made in the early days of our relationship to boycott the "Hallmark holiday."

That first Valentine's Day, we had been seeing each other seriously for eight months, and I had high expectations. I waited for him to call and ask me to meet him at our favourite restaurant for dinner that night. When he didn't, I assumed he was planning to surprise me with a fabulous meal at home. He met me outside my office as usual after work, but never mentioned anything. On the walk home, I asked him if he knew what day it was. "February 14," he said. When I reminded him that it was Valentine's Day, he replied: "I don't need an official day to show how much I love you. I try to do it all the time, and not in lock-step with the rest of the world. Can we agree not to celebrate the day, since it is a scam conceived by companies that want to sell shit to men who are forced to show their love on one day when they should be showing it throughout the year?"

I couldn't help agreeing with him. He did show me—through his actions, if not necessarily his words—how much he loved me, and I realized that I didn't need a card or flowers to prove it. The weekly dinners and walks home from the office were more than enough proof. It was so liberating to let the sham die forever.

But this year, I couldn't resist bringing in one small chocolate heart and a rose. With a twinkle in his eye, Trev said, "You dickhead," like he used to in the old days whenever I did something sweet that I shouldn't have. As I walked out of the room that night, I looked back to see Trevor sleeping soundly in his bed. I had left a scented tealight burning safely in a jar and noticed that the flame cast a shadow on the ceiling from the rose. The simplicity of the image amidst its complex surroundings stopped me. It looked like an angel watching over Trevor. On my way home, I thought about both Trevor and Grace tucked in their beds and how reassuring it was to know that they were comfortable, safe and deeply loved.

A week after Valentine's Day, Trev's good friend Kevin "Relic" Ryan, in town from back east, paid a visit with some of the rugby guys, making for one of Trevor's best nights since his injury. An accomplished musician and songwriter, Relic brought his guitar and everyone sang along, including Trevor, who mouthed the lyrics. Years ago, Relic and Trevor had made an agreement that on the publication of Trev's first book, they would swap works of art: words for music. Now Relic was performing the song inspired by Trevor's book *Bad Date*. I could see the music sink into Trevor's bones and nourish his soul. The love in the room was palpable.

On the Saturday, Trevor was resting in the living room at home while I was around the corner in the kitchen. The house was quiet as Grace napped upstairs. As I cleaned up the lunch dishes, I heard what sounded like Trevor's chair rattling. I thought it was strange to be hearing noises from the chair, since Trevor couldn't move on his own. When I peeked around the corner, I saw his eyes rolled up into the back of his head, his mouth gaping open and his body convulsing as if he wasn't able to breathe.

Terrified, I grabbed the phone and dialled 911. With shaking hands, I quickly opened Trevor's plugged trach to allow air in. But that didn't seem to help him get his breath. While the 911 operator rattled off a series of questions, I screamed, "Is the ambulance on its way?" I didn't want Trevor to die here in our living room, under my hands. The woman told me to try to remain calm while she gathered information. I asked again if help was on the way. The attendant said calmly that the ambulance wasn't far away. By now, the convulsions had passed and Trevor was breathing raggedly. With a dazed look in his eyes, he whispered that he was okay.

The ambulance arrived within minutes, and two paramedics rushed into the room. As they took Trevor's vital signs, I explained that while this was his home, he had been living at the hospital since his injury in Afghanistan almost a year ago.

They slapped a breathing mask on him and lifted him out of the chair and onto a gurney. I walked out with them as they rolled Trevor into the back of the ambulance. I squeezed his hand and told him that Grace and I would see him soon at the hospital.

After they drove away, I walked back inside and saw the empty chair sitting like a coffin in the living room. As I sat shaking on the couch, I wondered if this was what our future would be like: constant 911 calls for near tragedies. Once I calmed down, I trudged up the stairs of our silent, empty house to wake Grace.

As we waited for a wheelchair taxi, Grace and I sat together in silence in the living room, where it had all happened. When the cab arrived, I packed her into her car seat and wheeled Trevor's empty chair up the ramp. At the hospital, I was relieved to see him resting in bed. He looked frail and haggard, but he was alive. I told the nurse what had happened and said that it was the first seizure I had ever experienced. She could tell I was still shaken and reassured me that no one had ever died from a seizure.

Five hours later, Trevor had another one.

CHAPTER 19:
HEALING THROUGH FORGIVENESS

After nearly a year of being tube-fed, changed and hoisted out of the bed, Trevor had shown no improvement in his functionality. I knew his mood was sliding downhill fast. On many nights, we talked about the anger he felt toward himself and his attacker for ending up a bonerack with a caved-in skull lying inert in a hospital bed. I could tell it was killing him to be a burden on me.

Now that he was medically stable and the trach trials were going well, we knew he could be discharged in as little as two months. I wanted and needed to leave the hospital clear of mental baggage. "You need to be able to forgive to move forward," I told him, "or you are holding yourself hostage."

For most of the previous two years, Trevor had defined himself as a soldier—a strong, principled force for good in a flawed world. He knew that his attacker's village was in the very heart of Taliban territory, and that the man had likely been under the Taliban's sway for most of his short life. Trevor often spoke about how he could have saved his attacker if only he had got to him before the Taliban—if only he had empowered him to find meaning in this life instead of the next one. Through our nightly conversations, Trevor and I searched for the significance of the violent assault to give us a handhold for the future. I reminded him that because of this injury, he could have a much greater impact on the world than he ever would have had as a soldier. I sensed this struck a chord in him.

I knew the first step would have to be forgiveness. I felt that unless Trevor's mind was clear, he wouldn't be totally free to focus on rehab. A while back, someone had given me a book about emotional and spiritual health called *Healing with the Angels*. In the back of the book, I found a number of visualization exercises to help become free of anger. Trevor agreed to give them a try. In the first exercise, you hold an image of the person who has wronged you in your mind and imagine yourself saying to them, "I forgive you and release you. I hold no unforgiveness back. My forgiveness for you is total. I am free and you are free."

Since Trevor didn't know what his attacker looked like, I told him to imagine himself speaking to a young Afghan man in a long robe. Night after night, we talked about forgiveness. I would ask Trevor to imagine himself standing under a waterfall, with the water running over his body and washing away any feelings of resentment.

In another exercise, the corral visualization, you imagine yourself standing in a country field. A road leads to you through a corral. The corral has two gates, one facing you and one facing the road. If both gates are open, all the material, emotional and spiritual support you need flow to you, and your gifts to the world flow from you. If you hold anger in, the corral gates are closed and nothing flows in or out.

Trevor would often close his eyes during the visualization exercises, but he'd snap them open whenever it came time to talk to his attacker in the corral. One night he looked at me and said he didn't want to continue. I didn't force the issue and left the subject for a few days.

Trevor surprised everyone at the end of February by performing his best in three successive therapy sessions that were filmed for his rehab application. The first was a thirty-minute OT session on comprehension. This was followed by a thirty-minute speech therapy session and a forty-five-minute physiotherapy session. By the end, he was utterly exhausted. We wouldn't hear for another month whether he would be accepted into rehab.

Seven days shy of the one-year anniversary of the attack, Gary Adams, the U.S. Black Hawk helicopter flight medic, flew in to see Trevor. Our good friend Julie had emailed him on Remembrance Day to thank him after he posted the following message to a blog about Trevor: "My name is SGT Gary Adams. I was the flight medic that picked up and treated CPT Greene on the day he was injured. I am writing this to let CPT Greene, his family and his friends know that I have been tracking his progress as best I can from Afghanistan and I am glad to hear that he is improving daily. My thoughts and prayers are with you, CPT Greene, and with your family. I look forward to hearing about a full recovery in the near future. GARY A. ADAMS SGT, USA, Flight Medic."

When I first met the stocky young medic, I gave this total stranger a big hug and thanked him for saving Trevor's life. He told me that the last time he saw Trevor was when he was being hustled out of his Black Hawk into the base hospital. He had been following Trevor's story ever since, and was impressed by what he'd read of Trevor's life and the amount of support he had. "His life is not typical of a soldier," he said.

That afternoon, Gary saw Trevor at the hospital. I wasn't able to go with him, but Gary later told me that Trevor didn't talk during the visit. He also said that he looked a lot better than he'd expected. The rugby gang took me and Gary out to a pub that night to say thanks to him in their own special way. They dropped him at his hotel in the wee hours, with just enough time to grab his bags and head to the airport for his six o'clock flight.

CHAPTER 20:
THE FIRST LOST YEAR

On the first anniversary of the attack, the last thing I wanted to do was remind Trevor that he had lost a year of his life. I decided to treat it like any other day, going with him to physio and bringing Grace in for a suppertime visit. She was in the room when I changed Trevor out of his day clothes and into his lovely blue nightgown. She saw his bare upper chest and started jumping around the room saying, "Daddy's boobies! Daddy's boobies!" Trevor began to laugh uncontrollably. It felt good to end this unrecognized one-year anniversary with a laugh and the hope for better things in the future.

At the hospital the following day, I received a note from the speech therapist saying that Trevor had declined to participate in the session that day. I was disappointed. I felt as if I was working my butt off to get him better and he was just sitting on the sidelines. There was only one speech therapist for two floors of patients in this major downtown hospital, and her time was extremely limited. I gave Trevor hell for letting down our team. I could see that maybe he had blown off speech therapy because he didn't recognize it as exercise, but I was outraged when Cynthia told me he had also refused to participate in physiotherapy on two separate days. Failing to participate in physio could jeopardize his chances of getting into a rehab facility, so I asked Cynthia not to give him a choice about participating when I wasn't there.

Grace seemed to sense that her father needed motivating. When we visited one day in early March, she said, "I need to talk to Daddy." I hoisted her up on the bed, but when she didn't say anything, just started laughing, I put her back down again. Then she said, "I need to kiss Daddy." When I hoisted her up again, she slowly leaned over and kissed him on the cheek. It was the first time she had ever kissed him.

I decided I wanted Trevor in on a discussion with his doctor so he could decide for himself whether to take out the trach. The neurosurgeon reiterated the risks involved in taking it out and said he thought it should be left in long term for Trevor's own protection. I also had some reservations about taking it out, but if we didn't do it, Trevor would never get to a rehab centre and we'd never know his potential. Trevor told the doctor that he wanted it the trach out. The doctor said he would put in the order, even though it was against his recommendation.

In the middle of March, the trach came out for the last time without blood or drama. The hole closed over completely within two days, leaving only a puckered scar. But my optimism was tempered by the thought that we'd put Trevor's ability to breathe at risk. Still, I expected him to be accepted into a rehab program now that the trach was out. After all, he was able to participate in physio for at least thirty minutes and could communicate better with the team. He was even making incremental gains. We were excited, for example, to see movement in his thumbs. After months of work, he was able to lift his left thumb up twenty times and his right five times. And when Trevor began training on an arm bike, it took two of us to keep his hands on the handles while we moved them. Even with a slight rotation of the wheel, his hands weren't able to grip and hold against the strong muscle tone in his arms. Weeks later, his muscles extended enough that he could keep his hands on the handles and do three rotations with assistance.

One day in physio, Trevor asked to stand. I think Cynthia agreed because she thought it would help him become aware of the extent of his disability. It had been more than a year since his feet and legs had borne weight. His feet were now so badly contracted that we had to stand him on his heels on the edge of the mat in a standing sling. After a few seconds, we knew he couldn't tolerate the pain in his groaning muscles, tendons and joints anymore. He had no control over any part of his body, and his feet, legs and back hurt. After this failure, he didn't want to do anything else. But when I brought it up again later in the day, I was surprised to learn that he didn't even remember the session. He often couldn't remember specifics when I asked him about things that had happened days or weeks before—and sometimes even five minutes earlier.

After a few trips home with Trevor riding backwards in a taxi, I realized that I needed to find a better means of transport. Since Trevor had become part of the civilian medical system on his arrival back in Canada, the hospital recommended the public HandyDART bus. I listened to the whine of the hydraulic lift as it raised Trevor into the bus. Although Grace enjoyed the ride because she sat higher than in my car or the taxi, I wasn't so sure about Trevor. From my seat, I could see his head whip back and forth like a rag doll's, even more than it had in the taxi. The closer we got to home, the more dazed Trevor looked. When I asked him if he was okay, he said he needed a Gravol but the ordeal had been worth it to get out of the hospital. He spent the rest of the day sleeping in the living room. When I went to the hospital to bring him home again the next day, I was disappointed to hear him say that he was too comfortable in bed and couldn't do the ride again that day. I was astounded when he said, "Next weekend, let's leave the wheelchair at the hospital and come home in the car." To avoid upsetting him, I just told him that it was easier to use the chair for now.

In the following weeks, I would hear Trevor say again and again that while he was perfectly able to do things like dress and feed himself, it was easier for the nurses to do it because "that was their job." I thought at first he was just taking to heart my advice about being positive. But one Tuesday afternoon while Trevor napped, I seized another opportunity to sit back and watch TV. As I flicked through the channels, I came across the story of a man who'd suffered a devastating brain injury from a car crash and was in a wheelchair. Like Trevor, this man thought he could walk and run and do all the activities he'd done before the car crash. The narrator explained that because the man lacked insight into his injury, he wouldn't have the motivation to recover. I couldn't believe what I was hearing! For the first time, I realized that Trevor wasn't just being positive—he didn't have any awareness of his condition.

The next day, the psychologist confirmed my fears when we discussed the results of Trevor's neuropsychological assessment. I couldn't help thinking how amazing the brain is to have developed this incredible coping mechanism. Trevor probably wouldn't be able to handle the truth if he knew it. The psychologist said that some people do regain awareness, but it can be spotty when it comes back. For other people, it may never come back. I was already formulating a plan as he spoke. I thought that if I kept challenging Trevor to show me these things he said he could do, maybe I would get him to a point of realization. I would have to strike a balance, though, between helping him gain awareness and pissing him off.

When I arrived later that evening, I asked Trevor how his day went. He told me that although he was able to get out of bed and get dressed on his own, the nurses did it because that was their job. When I asked him why the nurses used the lift if he was able to get out of bed on his own, he replied, "It's more convenient and I'm lazy." I left the subject there for the night, but on my ride home, I felt overwhelmed by the realization that we were dealing with not only massive physical challenges but also psychological issues I had somehow missed.

During the next physio session, I took Cynthia aside and told her about Trevor's lack of insight. She said she had known all along and had tried to talk to me about it a few times, but I just didn't get it. It had taken a TV program and a neuropsychological assessment for me to grasp that a person can have totally normal conversations and yet still be completely oblivious to a fundamental disability.

After one of Kelly's craniosacral sessions, she asked if it would be okay to bring in a friend of hers to meet Trevor. We agreed, and the next day Kelly and Helen came in together. When I first saw Helen, I was struck by her classic beauty. She looked about sixty and was tall, with shoulder-length impeccably coiffed grey hair, and she wore a beautifully tailored white suit. She glided gracefully into the room with poise and purpose. She introduced herself and said she was a psychologist who also worked on the energetic level.

Helen put her hand on Trevor's chest near his heart and sat

quietly next to him with her eyes closed. When she opened her eyes, I told her about Trevor's inability to forgive his attacker. She suggested I change the word "forgiveness" to "compassion" and come at it from that angle. When I told her about his lack of awareness of his injury, she said the brain would give the body only as much information as it could handle. She recommended not pushing Trevor too hard because severe depression could set in, and that would be devastating for him. She suggested asking him what he had left on the earth to do.

Later that night as I was stretching Trevor's arms, I asked him what he still wanted to accomplish in his life. He told me he still needed to raise children and advocate for peace. I told him about all the complications he had overcome and explained that God undoubtedly had a plan for him—and it wasn't to fester in a long-term care facility. "You were chosen because you are a natural leader and can handle this enormous challenge," I said. "The world needs strong people like you to be role models. You are the perfect person for this task."

About six weeks after Trevor had the seizure at home, we had him on his knees in physio and were stretching his back when his face suddenly went expressionless and his eyes blank. I screamed, "We're losing him! Put him down." When we got him on the mat, I hovered anxiously over his face and asked if he was okay. Through tight lips he muttered, "Post seizure." We got him back to bed and he slept the entire day.

Afterward, I replayed the morning's events in my mind. Ray from spiritual services had dropped by and played the guitar for about an hour. Trevor's sister, Suzanne, had arrived that morning, and the three of us chatted while Suzanne and I massaged Trevor. He had rested for only half an hour, instead of the hour I normally gave him before physio. When we got up to the gym, we all chatted loudly to Cynthia and the two physio assistants.

It occurred to me that by the time we got Trevor on the mat, his circuits had been completely overloaded.

While Trevor slept, Suzanne and I made the hour-long drive to the suburbs to check out a rehab group home he could be transferred to when he was discharged. I was surprised how normal the house looked from the outside. It was a rancher in an established neighbourhood surrounded by large evergreen trees—a welcome change from the sterile environment of the hospital. The manager met us at the door and took us on a tour. The house was old and outdated, but it had a beautiful back patio surrounded by flowers, grass and trees. The room that would be Trevor's was bright and resembled a typical bedroom.

The three other men in the house had once been ordinary people with families and jobs. One day, a random act had damaged their brains so much that they were now forced to live out the rest of their lives being cared for like addled children. Two of the three had physical and mental challenges and were long-term patients. They would likely need care for the rest of their lives. One man's wife had taken away his two kids after a car accident had left him angry and frustrated in a wheelchair. Only his parents visited him now. The other car accident victim, formerly a successful business owner with five hundred employees, regularly made the walls shake with his uncontrolled screams. It wasn't the modern, cheery home I was expecting, but it would be the change we needed.

While I was waiting to hear if Trevor had been accepted at the house, I received word from our assisting officer, Dave Gilmour, that the Chief of the Defence Staff, Gen. Rick Hillier, would be visiting. I was fortunate to have Dave assigned to our case. He was a tall bear of a man in his fifties with a sarcastic sense of humour. He was just what I needed: a sympathetic sounding board who would do anything and everything I asked. When Trevor said he needed a shave and a haircut, Dave immediately found a mobile barber to clean up his overgrown head of hair and scraggly goatee. An hour after the barber arrived, Trevor was completely transformed. He looked thinner in the face, which I thought made him look somewhat vulnerable, but it felt wonderful to run my hands over the smooth skin after weeks of fur.

On the day of the general's visit, we struggled to get Trevor's dress shirt and pants on, since he'd lost a lot of range of motion in his arms and legs. I sensed he was nervous about the visit, but as soon as the general arrived, he put everyone at ease with his good nature and humour. Seeing the rugby jerseys hanging around the room, he asked Trevor why he played. Trevor whispered, "It's from the heart."

When he asked Trevor if there was anything he needed, he answered, "I need a job."

"Trevor, your job is to get yourself better, then we'll talk about a job," he replied with a twinkle in his eye.

After the general left, Trev and I had dinner together while Suzanne spent some one-on-one time with Grace. Perhaps because he had just met with the top man in the chain of command that had sent him to Afghanistan, Trevor had a breakthrough in the corral visualization. He allowed himself to do the entire exercise, including metaphorically speaking to his attacker. When he opened his eyes, he said he had forgiven his attacker but not his act. He looked at me and said that while he still felt angry, he also felt a bit more free. It was a defining moment in our journey—the first since he'd said my name—and it gave me a sense that Trevor was also releasing himself from responsibility.

CHAPTER 21:

SAYONARA

In early April we received word that Trevor would be discharged to the group home we had toured at the end of March. Suzanne, her husband, Andy, and their boys spent the afternoon with Trevor before flying home. During their short visit they remarked on his lack of motivation, which was so out of character for the active man they knew. I tried to explain his lack of awareness to them, but it was a difficult concept for them to grasp when they had just spent the past four days having otherwise normal conversations and playing games with him.

Before leaving for the airport, each one went in to talk to Trevor alone. Suzanne told Trevor to keep focused on rehab because she didn't ever want to visit him in another hospital. Andy talked to him about being part of "Team Canada" and said that Canadians wanted and needed success stories from this war. He said to focus on one part of the body at a time, even if it was just a thumb. Trevor's teenage nephews, Matthew and Brayden, who had idolized him, came out of the room in tears.

Now that I realized there was a problem with both awareness and initiation, I started reading about the executive function of the brain. It controls, among other things, task initiation. This is the function that compels you to do something instead of waiting for someone to tell you to do it. In Trevor's case, it seemed to be impacting his ability to complete his physio homework. Cynthia would ask him to work on tasks such as reaching for something in bed, but he would rarely do it. He just didn't seem to think about it, and worse, he didn't even think it was necessary. On the evening before workdays, I would remind Trevor to do his homework. The next night, when I asked him if he had done it, he'd always say that he didn't think to. I eventually resorted to putting up "Do homework" signs around his room, but to no avail.

One afternoon shortly after his sister's family returned home, Trevor insisted he was able to get out of bed on his own. When I asked him why he didn't use the bathroom if he was able to get out of bed, he laughed and said that it was the nurse's job to help him. To coax him through this fog, I asked him if he didn't think it was unreasonable for the overworked nurses to do things like dress people and brush their teeth if they were able to do those tasks on their own. To my surprise he agreed, so I suggested that he give the nurses a break and go to the bathroom on his own.

It was difficult for me to believe he wasn't consciously denying the problem. I knew his brain worked well on many levels, so I was becoming frustrated with his constant denials. Later that day, I heard him call me "Bee" completely out of the blue. I hadn't heard him say my nickname since the day he left for Afghanistan. It made me temporarily forget my frustration. I bent over him and said I hadn't heard him say that in over a year. He looked me in the eye and started singing, "Have I told you lately that I love you . . ."

"You had me at Bee," I said to him, smiling.

"I don't want to go to the group home. What do I need to do to come home?" he pleaded.

"You need to get stronger and regain enough function in your arms to be able to move yourself around," I said with a lump in my throat. "That way, you would just need to focus on your legs and walking."

"My arms work fine," he said.

I leaned over his bed, put both hands on his arm and said softly and purposefully, "Honey, there are areas of the brain that control awareness and initiation. Those parts of your brain were damaged. Your brain is protecting you from realizing how badly you are hurt. Do you want to know the full extent of your injuries?"

"No," he answered, averting his eyes.

I wasn't ready to have this conversation either, and the tears started to well up in my eyes as I spoke. "You need to take ownership of this recovery and fight harder for it than anything you've ever fought for in your life," I said in a taut voice. "Not just for yourself, but for Grace and me. We need you to come home a whole person. She needs to know what it's like to have a father in her life."

"I will," he replied.

At lunch the next day, I asked him if there was anything else he wanted. "I want your hand in marriage," he said. I was taken aback but took his hand and said, "Yes, absolutely. I can't wait to walk down the aisle with you one day, but we have to get you home first." He told me he would be out in five months. I had a sinking feeling it would be much longer.

...

I knew I needed help to make Trevor aware of his disabilities. When I found out that Trev's military case manager was Rick Hansen's cousin, I asked her to try to arrange a visit. Twelve years after being paralyzed at age fifteen in a car crash, Rick had wheeled himself around the world, raising $26 million for spinal cord research on his Man in Motion Tour and millions more since then. I was hopeful that a visit from one of the most inspirational men in the world could help Trevor realize his deficiencies.

Trevor was plainly star-struck when Rick wheeled up to his chair and introduced himself. He listened intently as Rick talked about how critical it was to set small goals and stay focused on important things in the future. I found the visit extremely motivating and thought Trevor would, too, but after Rick left he turned to me and said, "I get the impression that he thinks my injury is worse than it is." I smiled at him and replied, "I didn't get that impression."

Two weeks before moving Trevor to the group home, I spoke with a doctor at the rehab centre in Alberta. We had sent videos of Trevor's therapy sessions, trusting that we would be accepted. My hopes were dashed when the doctor said my goal of an independent life for Trevor was unrealistic given the severity of his injury and the time elapsed. She said the rehab centre would take him on a two-month medication trial only, to see if he regained any active movement in his limbs. If the medications didn't improve his movement, the centre would have to discharge him. I knew the videos showed only passive therapy and little active movement, but he was alert and trying to participate. The doctor's decision was a severe disappointment, to say the least. I wanted to tell her that Trevor would be different and would prove them wrong. I figured we would just have to show her when we got there . . . hopefully.

Ten days before leaving the hospital, we met with our military case manager. She informed us that Trevor would be medically released from the military on the day he returned from the rehab facility. When Trevor asked if he had to be released, she flatly said, "Yes, because you won't be able to return to normal duties." She went on to say that Trevor was not classified as a rehab candidate and would go to the first long-term care bed in the community when he left rehab. It was difficult for me to hear all this and even harder for Trevor to be told that the organization he had been a part of for so long didn't want him anymore.

There was some good news, though. After weeks of jostling Trevor home in the back of a taxicab or minibus, I'd finally found a private wheelchair transportation service. When I mentioned this to the case manager, she immediately set up an account for us. The service operated only on Saturdays, so we resigned ourselves to just one day home on the weekends to avoid the exhausted Monday stupor. The long-awaited discharge day was just over a week away. But the move to the group home in the suburbs would mean that the next two Saturdays could possibly be our last at home. If Trevor's classification as a long-term care patient was never upgraded, he would forever remain a resident of a group home or long-term care facility.

The second-to-last home Saturday was sunny, so we all sat outside. For the first time, Grace was content to sit on Trevor's lap in the wheelchair. I felt as if our time together was critical and precious. When she napped, we worked on Trevor's cognitive abilities. All his old knowledge seemed to be there, but critical thinking and abstraction seemed to be lacking. If I asked him what day it would be three days from Saturday, he might say Friday. I wanted to maximize his time home and, ultimately, his function so we could change the long-term care classification and he could eventually come home for good. We did stretching and worked on crossword puzzles and on picking up and dropping coins. When he went back to the hospital after a few hours, he was mentally exhausted from the work we had done at home.

With only six days left in the hospital, Trevor showed strong emotion for the first time since his injury. He was angry with the nurses because they'd chatted loudly all night and kept him awake. I suggested he take a deep breath and return the favour, yelling at them in the middle of the night. It would grab their attention and give him a good lung workout, too. I also mentioned it to the night nurse.

I had to stop for groceries on my way home that day, so it was after 11 p.m. when I walked in the door. I was looking forward to getting to bed because I had a meeting with the rehab doctor first thing in the morning. Before taking a shower, I checked on Grace, as I do every night when I get home. But this time, I must have startled her. When I put my hand on her stomach, she half woke up and said, "Pray for Daddy in the rocking chair." Then she rolled over and went back to sleep.

The next morning, Dr. Reebye tested Trevor's cognitive functions and memory. He quizzed him on different objects and their purpose, challenged him to count backwards from a hundred by sevens, and asked him to stick out his tongue and close his eyes, then open them while keeping his tongue out. He also tested Trevor's memory. The doctor was very impressed with how much he had improved since his first assessment. As we walked outside, he said we must have been working hard and congratulated me. He said he would come out to the group home to do another assessment in a few months.

Three days before Trevor's discharge, I arranged a little surprise going-away party with his team of therapists. I got a cake that read "Trevor, keep the faith. Anything is possible. You can make it happen." That morning, Trevor didn't want to do physio. I think he was mentally done with the hospital. After lunch, I said we were going for a walk and should drop by the gym one last time. The whole team was there. Trevor looked shocked but pleased, and even smiled for all the pictures. Everyone brought food for the party. Trevor was tired but managed to stay awake to talk to everyone as best he could. There were a lot of teary eyes in the group. For thirteen months, this dedicated team had stretched, casted, coaxed and prayed for him. It was a particularly emotional time for me. I had become friendly with everyone, especially Cynthia, who was always realistic but hopeful about Trevor's recovery. She said that while it would be a long road, a lot of recovery could still happen. I felt that she went above and beyond the call of duty for Trevor. Although I desperately wanted to get out of the hospital, it was daunting to be moving into the unknown.

On his last Saturday home, Trev told me he had to go to the bathroom and could do it on his own. I said to let me know if he needed any help and headed to the kitchen to make lunch. When I came back after a few minutes, he said that his hands and arms worked fine but his legs were weak. When I asked him to show me, nothing on his body moved. He still insisted that the nurses did everything for him because it was their job, and that I did it because I loved him. I said it was quite the opposite. "If I loved you, I wouldn't do things for you because I would be taking the learning opportunity away from you." When I asked him why nobody fed me when I was in the hospital after giving birth to Grace, he said sternly, "Back off, bitch." It was totally out of character for him to speak like that, but I felt satisfied to have pushed him to that extreme. I hoped to help him attain awareness faster by keeping this up. When I took him back to the hospital, I could tell he was still mad at me. I was pleased that I was leaving him to sit and stew about it.

...

In the days leading up to the departure from the hospital, I boxed up the rugby shirts and pictures from the walls and ceiling. I made sure the rugby ball would stay with Trevor at the group home in the suburbs. The room was back to the same drab grey-beige that had welcomed us thirteen months earlier.

Discharge day was emotional for us both. Trevor still didn't fully comprehend why he was leaving the hospital and not coming home. We both wanted to put all the sadness and complications behind us and move forward. I hoped the stay at the group home would be short while we waited for a spot at the rehab centre to come open. I knew the listless atmosphere at the group home wouldn't be good for him, especially since he would see less of me and Grace. But on a positive note, I was told that being around other people in wheelchairs could help his awareness.

Thirteen months and two weeks after arriving at the hospital, we left Trevor's empty room on 5B with little fanfare. As I drove behind the van transporting him, I thought about the moments of disappointment and dread, as well as the moments of joy and tenderness. Trevor was medically stronger than when he first arrived and almost fully conscious now, despite his lack of awareness. I thought about how hard we had worked to get him to this point, spending every spare moment on his hand, arm and voice exercises, head control, stretching and range of motion. I cherished the long conversations we shared about life's purpose and forgiveness.

Over the past year, I had developed an enormous respect for physio, occupational and speech therapists. I wondered if I would have the patience to work with someone for weeks or months just to see him hold up his head or move a finger. I'd experienced first-hand how an underfunded health care system overworked nurses so much that patients suffered.

I was also grateful for the holistic healers who, for the most part, had donated their time to help Trevor. For the first time, I had observed work on a level that couldn't be tangibly felt or seen. It bordered on the mystical, yet it was becoming more perceptible and very real. These people gave their time out of love and compassion, knowing that they were a just a conduit to the universal energy field or a higher power. The things I had seen made me question whether Trevor's injury was part of a greater plot to show us that we were made up of not just a mind and a body but, equally important, a soul. It was Trevor's soul that allowed him to forgive the young man who had tried to kill him.

And of course, I felt gratitude to our friends and family. I had thought that as Trevor's hospital stay dragged on, people would simply move on with their lives. But none of our friends neglected us, especially not the guys on Trev's rugby team. They had experienced tragedy before, with the suicide of one teammate and the near-fatal injury of another. This group had become acquainted with epic life-and-death experiences. The trust and support they showed one another on the pitch carried over to the hospital, but to a much greater extent. I never once felt alone on the journey.

CHAPTER 22:
NO TURNING BACK

Trevor's first night at the group home wasn't good. The evening staff woke him at midnight to turn him and start the night tube feed, which supplemented the solid food he ate during the day. Between that and the bright light above the bed, he was awake for another hour and a half. After breakfast came craft time at the associated group home next door, run by a private company for the care of people with brain injuries. I thought a change of scene would be good for Trevor, so we went next door, but when we got there, he said he preferred to sit outside on his own. I left him on the sunny back patio and went inside to watch the rest of the group make pompom chicks.

It was a surreal experience, to say the least. I had never been around a group of mentally and physically challenged people before, but I found myself really enjoying their energy and camaraderie. They were having a great time, as were their caregivers. They seemed to have an almost child-like enjoyment of life.

Most of the people in the group had been fully functional before they were injured. One fellow had suffered a severe brain injury in a car accident while on a trip to Germany as a university student. Another had once been a semi-professional snowboarder. Some would never live on their own, but others had a chance to get home, depending on their family circumstances. The one thing they all had in common was that they were free of the responsibilities and challenges of everyday life. I went back outside to Trevor and asked him if he wanted to come in for a bit. He didn't. He'd spent a total of about five hours outside in thirteen months, so I couldn't blame him for wanting more.

A few days into his stay, we had a heart-to-heart chat. He said this was all too much for him and he wished he hadn't survived the attack. I told him that by surviving, he got to watch Grace grow up and could help guide her life. "You've come too far to turn back now," I said. "And besides, I'm not going to let you give up."

I had wanted everything to be perfect for Grace's first visit. When I brought her out after a few weeks, she acted very shy with Trevor. She would bury her face every time she looked at him. When I asked her if she wanted to give some of her blueberries to Daddy, she shied away and buried her head in my shoulder. We ended the day with me reading to Trevor in the warm air outside as Grace napped. As we said goodbye, he asked me to take him with me. I reminded him that I couldn't bring him home because he couldn't get in and out of our small car. He grabbed my hand and said, "Watch." Then he bent his head down and wrinkled his brow in concentration. Nothing moved. Watching him try to prove to me that he could get out of the chair broke my heart.

...

After Trevor had been a few weeks at the group home, I got a call from a staff member, Maggie, who said an ambulance had been called for Trevor because he was neither talking nor responsive after two successive seizures. "What!?" I screamed. The ambulance had just arrived, and the EMTs were loading him onto a gurney.

"They are taking him to Langley Memorial," said Maggie. "Don't worry, I'll be there with him."

"I'm on my way." I dropped the phone and ran upstairs to tell Regina what had happened. She said she would watch Grace and pray for Trevor. I told Grace I had to go because Daddy was sick, grabbed my purse and dashed out the door. On the way to the hospital my stomach churned and I said out loud, over and over, "Please let him be okay. Please let him be okay."

When I arrived at the hospital an hour later, Trevor was lying comatose on a gurney in the emergency room. His chest sounded gurgly, like water running down a sink. He was having a hard time breathing and moaned heavily through the respirator. Maggie stood next to him holding his arm. I asked her what had happened.

"Trevor had just finished supper when he started to shake, his head swung violently to the left and his eyes fluttered," she said. "I timed it at three minutes. After it was over, I gave him an anti-anxiety pill. He had just finished shaking when another seizure gripped his body. This one lasted six minutes. When it was over, he was totally unresponsive. The ambulance arrived within two minutes. On the way to the hospital, Trevor had four more seizures and vomited."

My first thought was to phone Eve to send distance Reiki energy and prayers to Trevor. She said she would start as soon as we were off the phone. I hung up, turned to Maggie and said,

"We need to help clear Trevor's lungs. I need you to put your hands on the left side of his chest and visualize the fluid clearing from his lungs. In your mind, imagine the fluid evaporating with each breath he takes. I'll be doing the same on his right lung. Let's start now." She nodded and her hands darted to his chest. I closed my eyes and imagined a flame burning up the fluid in Trevor's right lung. I opened one eye and glanced over at Maggie, who looked like she was concentrating hard.

After about fifteen minutes, the nurse came by to take Trevor's vitals. We moved out of the way, and I thanked Maggie for stepping out of her comfort zone. Within about thirty minutes Trevor's breathing sounded clearer. Maggie looked at me and said, with a large smile, "I would never have believed it if I hadn't seen it with my own eyes."

Maggie had a real soft spot for Trevor and opened up to me about her son. She was told when he was born that he would be a vegetable his entire life, and she'd worked incredibly hard to prove the doctors wrong. He was now in his teens, she said, and led a full and active life. She stayed with me until after 11 p.m. I didn't want to go, but I felt that Trevor was in good hands with his own nurse in yet another ICU. He was resting comfortably but was still unresponsive.

The next day, I arrived at the hospital early. Bonnie, another caregiver from the group home, was with Trevor. His eyes were open and he was able to talk. Not surprisingly, he didn't remember coming to the hospital and was in a daze all day. Maggie arrived like a hurricane at 4 p.m. She was mad about the noise in the ICU—specifically the moans from the man in the next bed space, who was suffering from a shot liver and half-functioning kidneys because of an overdose of Tylenol and alcohol. Maggie and I both stayed with Trevor until after 9 p.m., when he was soundly asleep.

I called at six o'clock the next morning to talk to the night nurse before her shift ended. She said Trevor's chest didn't sound very good. My heart dropped. I called Suzanne, Dick and Bess to tell them about Trevor's lungs. I asked Suzanne to visualize his lungs clearing and asked his parents to pray. Eve also continued to send Reiki to him throughout the day. Trevor's wheezing steadily got lighter. He slept the entire day while I held his hand and visualized clear lungs. At nine that evening, I left to get some rest.

The doctors said the seizure could have been triggered by an infection at the feeding tube site, but the CT scan indicated there was no bleeding in the brain. Then one doctor took me aside to tell me he had never seen two more compassionate caregivers in his life than Maggie and Bonnie. With each day that passed, Trevor became more awake and more alert. After five days, he was discharged.

After dinner at the group home one night in early June, Trevor asked about some things he thought had gone missing: blue-and-white basketball shoes, a Day-Timer and other items. He said he'd just bought the shoes a few weeks ago and had used them on the court. I suspected his mind was playing tricks on him, so I said everything was safely at home and not to worry. It was heartbreaking for me to see the tricks Trevor's brain played on him, but he never seemed too bothered. In this instance, as soon as I told him his things were safe, he seemed to forget about them.

I managed to persuade Trevor to try the weekly music therapy session. "It will be good for your voice," I said. When we got next door, though, Trevor again said he preferred to sit outside in the sun. I think it was his way of avoiding interaction with the other residents, since he thought he was perfectly normal and was just killing time before going to rehab. Inside, a group of about ten residents sat in a circle shaking their music makers while the leader, Michael, sang and played the guitar. Michael was pretty good and played a variety of songs, but Trevor stubbornly refused to have fun, despite my attempts to get him to sing along with me. When I asked him if he was going to participate, he said, "No, this is gay." I told him that it was music therapy for the voice and insisted that he sing along to just one of the songs. He finally mouthed along to Johnny Cash's "Ring of Fire."

After the failed music therapy session, Trevor admitted to me, for the first time, that he couldn't get out of the chair. I could sense he was feeling very anxious about it. He bemoaned his inability to be more of a father to Grace. I told him that she would get by without him right now. "You will be there for her when it really matters," I said. "Right now, she's only concerned with her potty, panties, books and Dora."

Over time, Trevor's anxiety began to build. A psychologist specializing in anxiety disorders was brought in to meet with him. The two of them talked for about thirty minutes, then the doctor called me in and said that Trevor had consented to my being a part of the conversation. I sat down across from the doctor. He spoke at length about Trevor's anxiety and his fear that I would leave him. I turned to Trevor and told him the thought had never crossed my mind.

"You are everything I've ever wanted in a man, and I'm certainly not going to give that up just because of a brain injury and a wheelchair. We are a family, and we don't abandon our family when things get tough. We have to get tougher to survive."

That didn't seem to alleviate his fears. When I asked him what I could do to help, he said, "Get married." I said I would love to get married, but I wanted to wait until we were back from rehab so all our friends and family could be with us to celebrate. "I agree," he conceded.

That night, the evening news ran a story about Afghanistan that mentioned Trevor's name. He said it freaked him out because the injury had happened over three weeks ago and it was still in the news. "It's been longer," I said. "Four weeks?" he asked. I watched his face fall as I told him it had been more than fifteen months since the attack. Shock spread over his face. We turned off the TV, and through tears and laughter, I told him everything in detail from day one. "Do you still have a fear of me leaving you?" I asked. He said no.

When Grace and I arrived the following Sunday for Father's Day, she handed Trevor a card in bed. "Here, Daddy. Happy Father's Day." Trevor whispered, "Thank you, Wabbit." While Grace amused herself in the room, Trevor insisted he wasn't getting into the wheelchair. He said that he was going to walk that day. It didn't seem to make a difference how often I told him that it was going to take time to start walking again. He worked himself into a frenzy trying to get out of the bed. All he wanted to do all day was get out of the bed and walk. It created so much anxiety that his body became rigid from all the messages firing from the damaged motor neurons in his brain. I thought he was determined to get up for Grace, and to show his parents, who were due to arrive the next week, that he could walk.

After lunch I dropped Grace off with my father, who lived nearby, so she could nap and spend the afternoon with her grandfather. When I came back, Trevor was lying in bed with his shirt soaked in sweat. He said, "I did it. I stood up." I asked him if he could do it again and he said yes, so I gave him time alone to stand. When I came back, he was still lying in bed. I overheard him saying, "Engage," a term a rugby referee uses for the scrum to come together. This was his trigger to get himself moving. I told him that he was great at engaging but the connections still needed work. After that, we stayed in his room most of the day. He was so exhausted I kept him away from any noise and activity to avoid a seizure. He kept looking anxiously at the clock as it got closer to the time I had to leave. "I don't want to go," I said, "but Grace needs one of us, and for now that person is me."

When I got home, there was a message from Sue Ridout, an independent filmmaker and a friend of a friend. She was interested in doing a documentary on Trevor's recovery. We talked it over the next day, and Trevor thought it would be good to show what injured soldiers and their families go through. I thought it would be a good way to motivate him, since he appeared to be bored when the physiotherapist worked with him. Sue and her crew began filming the following week. The documentary would eventually be titled *Peace Warrior*.

The morning when his parents arrived, Trevor asked Bonnie if she wanted to see a trick. She said yes, of course. "See? I'm standing," he said. Bonnie could only see him lying in bed, so she asked him if he was standing vertically or horizontally. Almost as soon as she said it, though, she regretted it. Trevor didn't seem bothered by her question, but she didn't want to upset him just before he saw Dick and Bess, who were waiting in the living room.

The following afternoon, I told him I was going out for a run while he rested. He said, "Why don't you make it a power walk and I'll come with you?" I told him that it was very important for him to get some rest, and that maybe we would go for a walk after dinner. I never mentioned it again. That night as I was tucking Trevor in before leaving, he said to me, "You are so strong and I am so weak."

"A lesser man wouldn't have made it as far as you have. My faith in you gives me the strength to keep up the fight. I know you won't let me down," I replied.

A week later we went next door to the "discussion group," where clients from all the group homes in the area get together. The moderator had brought a stack of cards with questions like "What's your favourite memory of your father?" and "If you could be any animal, what would you be?" Everyone in the circle was expected to choose a card and then respond to it.

On the couch sat two middle-aged women. One was missing her two front teeth and chain-smoked; the other was addicted to Pepsi and soap operas. Next to them was a Chinese fellow who smiled whenever he didn't understand a question. Another young man, who also sported a permanent grin, would put up his arms and mumble "Whatever" to most questions. Another fellow responded to each question with "I don't know. Nobody's ever asked me that before" and yelled "Oh, Jesus" every time laughter erupted. I was proud that Trevor had agreed to stay and participate in the discussion. It showed me he was trying to make the best of it.

As I was leaving at suppertime, Trev begged me to take him with me. He said the place was a "loony bin disguised as rehab." I desperately wanted to bring him home, but it just wasn't logistically possible. Maggie called me later to tell me she had found him crying in his room. She said she had given him a hug and a speech about sticking with it.

In the middle of July, after three months at the group home, we received the long-awaited news that a bed had come available for Trevor at the rehab centre in Alberta. The Canadian Forces began planning for the trip on a government jet usually reserved for the prime minister. The Challenger had been adapted to carry wounded soldiers and medical personnel. I was so relieved to be moving on because the drive to the suburbs was physically and emotionally tiring. It took precious time away from Grace, and I felt helpless watching Trevor sink into a state of sadness and anxiety. I was eager to get him settled into an intense exercise routine that would occupy his thoughts.

The day before we left for the centre in Alberta, Trevor said he thought we were getting married the next day. He was worried he wasn't going to make it for the ceremony. I told him that if we were getting married, I would make sure he made it.

The night before Trevor left the group home, Dave Gilmour, our assisting officer, picked up his wheelchair, which was too big to go on the plane with us, and drove through the night to have it waiting at the rehab centre for him the next day. He had helped me on a number of occasions, going over and above the call of duty, and he also brought me into the fold of the military family. We had developed a kinship over the past year that I would sorely miss.

At 5:30 a.m., the attendants wheeled Trevor into an ambulance for the trip to the airport. Once there, I was surprised to see two lines of kilted soldiers forming a guard of honour in the pelting rain. The skirl of the bagpipes rang out above the whine of the idling jet engines.

CHAPTER 23:
FIRST MEMORY

Trevor

I t is said that all the images we see and all the sounds we hear are stored somewhere in our brain and need only a trigger to come to life again. Shortly after I arrived at the rehab centre in Ponoka, Alberta, a snippet of bagpipe music on the radio conjured my first new memory since the attack: the guard of honour at the airport in B.C. The doors of the ambulance had flown open to a sight I thought I would never see: soldiers standing at attention in the pouring rain on either side of my stretcher. I recognized the faces as belonging to soldiers from the platoon I had commanded in my highland regiment prior to deploying to Afghanistan. As I was transferred from the ambulance to an airplane for the trip to Alberta, bagpipe music swirled in the heavy rain and wind. The drone of the bagpipes raised goosebumps on my skin, as it always had. I was reminded of the First World War pipers, who would leap from the trenches and courageously lead their soldiers into battle through a hail of bullets.

233

PART 3: PRECIOUS, FABULOUS LIFE

We would never learn to be brave and patient if there were only joy in the world.

—*Helen Keller*

CHAPTER 24:
PONOKA

Debbie

I watched Trevor being winched up into the jet on a stretcher like an oversized piece of luggage. After an uneventful one-hour flight, he was hoisted back down from the plane and into an ambulance for another hour-long ride to the rehab centre. Once we hit the highway, I was amazed by the unrelenting flatness of the terrain. The ruggedness of the coastal mountains and oceans seemed worlds away. The dry, dusty rural smell in the air was a sharp contrast to the salty moistness of the coast.

Finally the Halvar Jonson Centre came into view in the tiny farming community of Ponoka, about halfway between Edmonton and Red Deer, more than a thousand kilometres from home. The ambulance stopped at the front entrance to reveal a modern, one-level complex sprawling across the dusty prairie. We rolled Trevor down the long hallways, which were bustling with movement and flooded by natural light. Trevor's single room, in one of four residential wings, overlooked the park-like grounds. The room was starkly functional and devoid of embellishments: just a single bed, desk, and closet unit. Trevor whispered, "It looks like my room in basic training. I hope there's no inspections."

After meeting a few of the staff, Trevor wanted to sleep, having been on the road for more than five hours. While he slept, I put his clothes away and once more decorated an institutional room with pictures and mementos, hoping it would be the last time. On the corkboard next to the bed, I hung a large picture of Grace and one taken of our family on the day Trevor left for Afghanistan.

When Trevor woke up, he was hoisted back in the wheelchair for suppertime. We went to the unit's cafeteria and joined residents eating with varying levels of assistance. Some, like Trevor, had to be spoon-fed, while others were working on feeding themselves. Everyone seemed to have an air of purpose that bespoke a strong dedication to rehab. After a basic institutional dinner devoid of taste, Trevor had his first bath in years. A look of pure bliss spread across his face as he was lowered into the tub, and I could feel my apprehension washing away.

Having finally reached the only brain injury rehab facility of its kind in the country, I could at last let out a deep breath. I had been awake since 4 a.m. and was bone-weary and emotionally spent. At eight o'clock that night, I tucked Trevor into bed and called a cab to take me to the basement suite I had rented. It was two days since I had left Grace behind with my parents and I missed her fiercely. I looked forward to their arrival in a couple of days and Regina's a few days after that.

During the first week we met Trevor's team and a "before" video was taken for posterity. The first person we met was his doctor. From our phone conversations months earlier, I had expected her to be abrupt and direct. But I was disarmed by her warm and welcoming personality. She tested Trevor's limited range of motion and function and explained the medications she would trial over the next couple of months.

Next was the psychologist, David Winkelaar, who learned from Trevor's murmuring that he thought his arms and legs worked fine, and that he was at the centre solely to rehabilitate his voice. He tested Trevor's cognition and insight. He asked him to say a sentence while conveying happiness and then the same sentence conveying anger. Trevor's expression and tone were identical. David showed him a "No Smoking" sign and asked what it was. Trevor had no problem. David then showed him a "No Lemons" sign and asked what he thought it meant. Trevor laughed. This was good news, since David was testing his funny bone.

Leah, the speech pathologist, analyzed Trevor's swallowing ability, which she found to be normal. Physiotherapist Lori and occupational therapist Kunle arrived with their goniometer to measure Trevor's meagre range of motion. Lori examined his feet and said they would be tough to work with.

Three days after Trevor and I got to Ponoka, my stepfather, Bill, arrived in Ponoka with my car, which was packed to the gills. After a twelve-hour journey, he picked up my mother and Grace at the Calgary airport, and they drove the final two hours to Ponoka. When they pulled into the driveway of our suite, I could see Grace looking around at the unfamiliar surroundings from the backseat. She started screaming and waving her arms around as soon as she spotted me. My heart felt like it would burst. It had been about a week since I'd last touched her, the longest time we'd ever been apart. I ran to the car and whipped open the back door. We wrapped our arms around each other and she pressed her baby-soft cheek into mine. I felt divine love surrounding us as I squeezed her like I could make her a part of me.

After unloading the car and enjoying supper together, we all went to the centre. I hadn't told Trevor that Grace was arriving that day, so when we walked into his room, his face lit up. "Hello, Little Wabbit," he said softly. Trevor watched in awe as Grace jumped all over his bed. His grin slowly faded as he soberly said, "She has a little-girl face now." Grace was so wound up from the flight and seeing Trevor for the first time in weeks that she was restless through the night in the bed we shared. Just like Trevor, she would have a hard time getting used to sleeping in a new place.

The first week in August, Kunle and Lori took Trevor into the gym for the first time. To me, the gym wasn't just a collection of weights and rehab equipment; it represented hope for our future. When I saw the other patients lifting, stair climbing and walking with the parallel bars or on the treadmill, I knew the athlete in Trevor would get suited up and go to work.

His first session focused solely on head control. More than a year in hospital had wreaked havoc with the postural alignment from his pelvis to his head. His head hung forward from his weak neck as if he were waiting to be decapitated.

"Without proper head control, rehab will take forever," Kunle said in his deep, radiating voice. A former professional body builder from Nigeria, he was like a smartly dressed, dreadlocked Chris Rock. He competed in death races, running incredible distances through wild terrain. Trevor, oblivious to reality, thought Kunle would make an excellent training partner and asked him one day if they could start working out together. Kunle gently demurred, saying, "I get up at 5 a.m. and work out close to home."

That weekend, we decided to go the centre's lounge, the Rendezvous, where we were told they sold pie and ice cream. The centrally located lounge was the hangout for psychiatric and addiction patients. We passed them in the halls, shambling like extras in the movie *One Flew Over the Cuckoo's Nest*, before

taking our dessert outside in the fresh farm air to anchor ourselves in reality.

By the end of the second week, the medications to help with
muscle tightness had started to take effect, and I noticed Trev-
or's muscles begin to loosen. By the end of the third week, his
alertness had improved, thanks to Ritalin, and he was awake
for most of the day. His schedule started to fill up with physio,
occupational, speech and pool therapy, rounded out by sessions
of recreation, relaxation and psychology. I was happy to see
that he would finally get a chance to progress and prove himself.

Stretching was the first order of business in physiotherapy. All
the muscles in Trevor's body had atrophied and shortened. His
arms were clenched across his chest and his legs were so tight
that his hips and knees were nearly impossible to bend. I knew
Trevor would respond to Kunle's enthusiasm and toughness
just as he would to a coach in the gym. Kunle explained that
the apparently simple movement of reaching out and grabbing
something requires complex tasking of muscle movements by
the brain. Trevor's brain had to reprogram all these movements
with gruelling repetition. It started with Trevor working at picking up a rubber dog toy from his lap and trying to reach out
and drop it in a bucket. I could see he was intensely frustrated
that his muscles refused to obey the commands from his brain.
His biceps were so strong from being constantly clenched that
they easily overpowered his triceps when reaching out. He was
mentally and physically spent after each session.

In order to stay at the centre, Trevor had to be evaluated
according to the Functional Assessment Measure. The FAM
tracks improvement in self-care, systemic health, mobility and
locomotion, speech intelligibility, comprehension, reading and
writing, psychosocial issues and cognitive functioning. This
would be the basis for determining whether Trevor would

remain at the centre after each three-month treatment period.

In August, the team met to discuss Trevor's one-month assessment and to set rehab goals to work toward in the next three months. Bed space was at a premium and the waiting list was long. I hoped and prayed the team would find some goals to work toward. Unfortunately, Trevor's lack of awareness still stood in the way of any real recovery. The doctor's words rang in my ears: there can be awareness and no recovery, but no recovery without awareness. When I heard the news from our social worker, Bev, that the team wanted to work with Trevor for another three months, I felt vindicated. I immediately sent out an email to the family to let them know of our victory, and I couldn't wait to get home and tell Grace and Regina.

To extend our stay at the centre, I needed to somehow pull Trevor into full awareness. I would usually arrive at the centre in time to help him with breakfast and stay until after his last program, which was typically around four o'clock. Every morning I would run through my litany of questions, hoping they would jar him into reality, but I kept hearing how he could do everything for himself. He wasn't grasping it, even after failing to show me what he could do himself.

By the late afternoon, I usually needed a break. When Trevor rested, I would go home to spend time with Grace and make supper. We would usually take it back to the centre to eat together as a family in the common area.

One evening, I put Grace across the table from Trevor. When she looked up at him, she said, "It's good to see you, Daddy." I could tell he loved having her full attention for a fleeting few seconds.

"It's good to see you, too, Wabbit."

Trevor's seizures continued after we arrived. I knew a seizure was imminent when his left hand began to shake. I guessed that the seizures were triggered by fatigue and overstimulation. On a Sunday in September, he was rattled by two seizures. One hit just after lunch in front of Grace, who didn't notice anything was amiss; the other struck after supper, while he was on the phone with his mom and dad. Both lasted only two to three minutes.

The doctor changed Trevor's medications to try to control the seizures, but I felt a little concerned when I read a user blog that said the drug was effective but craziness was a side effect. Still, avoiding the seizures in exchange for a little craziness seemed like a good trade-off. Besides, I had always liked that Trevor was a bit crazy. It made life interesting.

At least seizures were a medical condition that could be treated with drugs. There seemed to be no cure for Trevor's lack of aware-ness. We would see the other residents propelling their wheelchairs down the long hallways with one foot or walking on the treadmill in the gym. Trevor thought they were in rough shape—at least he could walk, or so he thought. In fact, these patients had an acute knowledge of their disability and could work toward overcoming it. Trevor did not and therefore could not.

I found an article one day about how some people with brain injuries don't even realize they have any deficiencies. I read it to Trevor and told him again that his brain wasn't ready for him to accept his physical limitations. I told him that I was trying to help him become conscious of his deficiencies so he would have a chance at recovery and we would have a chance for a decent life together.

That all changed around week seven in Ponoka. One evening when I asked Trevor if he was going to brush his own teeth, he answered, to my surprise and excitement, "No, you know I can't brush my own teeth." He even admitted that he needed help to get into bed. I explained to him again how important it was to recognize what he couldn't do for himself. I pleaded with him to remember our conversation in the morning.

After rushing to the centre the next day, I nervously asked him if he had got out of bed on his own and was elated to hear him say, "Of course not." To test his burgeoning awareness, I asked a few other questions. Did he need help with breakfast and brushing his teeth? "Of course," he answered. Unsure if this was truly the day of awakening, I started his morning exercises. Struggling through a few simple arm movements, he said, "My body is fucked," and then, "I can't believe I thought I could walk."

"Trevor, you have just made the mental step that will change the course of our lives," I told him as I stood holding his shoulders. "Please remember this conversation," I pleaded.

He chuckled to himself at the memory of believing he could walk the day before. "I'm not in denial anymore," he said.

Eighteen months and a day after the axe had crashed through his skull, Trevor finally knew what sorry shape he was in. I prayed it would kick his rehab into overdrive. I knew he would never settle for life in a wheelchair if he could do anything about it. I was laughing and crying at the same time. It felt like a huge weight had been lifted from my shoulders, and his awareness stuck from that day forward. He could finally dedicate himself to his new mission: to walk again.

"You have no idea long I've been working to help you get your awareness back," I said. "For the longest time, I thought you were just being positive. Sometimes I felt like shaking you to wake you up."

"I can't believe it either. How could I not have known?" he asked.

"Your brain was protecting you. I tried everything I could think of, but I eventually had to rely on faith."

"I'm glad you did."

CHAPTER 25:
A FOLD IN TIME

Trevor

That night, as the nurses put me in bed, I felt the canvas sling cold and clammy on every inch of my body for the first time. I heard the hydraulic gasp of the lift as it hoisted and lowered me into bed, and I knew the nurses weren't just doing it because I was lazy and it was their job. I knew it was a necessity. I felt like I did when I woke up in the field after an exhausted sleep when all hell was breaking loose around me. A year and a half of my life was gone, as if there were a fold in time, and I would never get those months back. The pages of the calendar since March 2006 were blank for me.

Everything was harder for me in the days following. I was right-handed, but because my left hand and arm were ever so slightly more functional than the right, I had to use them to feed myself. Eating was a frustrating struggle because my hands didn't feel like they belonged to me. It was awkward as hell and reminded me of shooting with my non-dominant hand in basketball practice. Fortunately, Debbie was usually at the centre in time to help me practise feeding myself breakfast. The harder I tried, the more my muscles would tense because my brain had lost the movement pattern for eating. I willed the fork to my mouth, but my brain couldn't get my hand and arm to perform the task. After breakfast we struck a deal that if I attempted to brush my teeth, Debbie would let me rest if I didn't have any programs that morning. I couldn't believe I needed a nap after breakfast, like an old man. But Debbie explained it was because the loss of the brain matter I had left behind in Afghanistan made even the most mundane of movements mentally taxing.

It bothered me that Grace would sometimes act afraid when she looked at me, like she was seeing an ogre. Debbie reassured me that she was just getting to know me again after a year, and that seeing me every day would make her more comfortable. We started a routine of going for pie and ice cream on Friday nights after dinner. Grace would often ride on my lap, but as she settled in for the ride, she would caution, "No yawning, Daddy," since yawning caused my legs to go straight and rigid and she would become uneasy. I loved making her laugh uncontrollably with funny faces.

Debbie and Grace would often come up in the evenings for a swim. I knew Debbie was trying to keep me involved in normal family activities, but it was tough not t o be actively engaging with them. I would sit grumpily in my chair on the side of the pool watching them frolic in front of me. I had always thought it would be me who taught Grace to swim. That made it bittersweet to hear Grace yell, "I did it, Daddy," as she jumped in from the side of the pool. I knew I would be starting pool therapy soon, and I looked forward to being free and joyful like Grace.

Sometimes Debbie would put a beach ball on my lap for me to push into the pool for Grace. As she waited impatiently in front of me, I struggled tortuously to push the ball with my finger. Kunle said my brain needed to get the "sequencing" sorted out; otherwise it was like pulling out the wrong file from the filing cabinet. When I found the right file after a couple of agonizing minutes and my outstretched finger started the ball rolling, Grace would immediately yell, "Throw it again, Daddy," as soon as it hit the water.

Soon enough, I was in the same pool with Rebecca, my petite, gregarious recreational therapist. I was transferred into a chair several sizes too small with my feet balanced on a small utility cart and was wheeled gingerly down a ramp into the warm pool in a massive red life vest. I revelled in my weightlessness as Rebecca and Debbie slid my rigid body out of the chair like a mannequin. It was years since I had last been in a pool, and I expected to be supple and strong in the water as I had been before. But I was stodgy and stiff and had to be helped just as I was in my dry land workouts. I had thought the weightlessness of the pool would make every movement easier, but I was still restricted by my tight muscles, my limited range of motion and the damaged filing cabinet in my brain. After my stretching exercises, the workouts were limited to perfecting an awkward parody of the backstroke and grabbing and releasing the edge of the pool, which was truly exciting for all when it occurred.

On the evenings Debbie and Grace didn't swim, we usually hung around together at the centre. Grace had been given a Play-Doh set by Linda, one of the nurses, and would sit quite contentedly across from me playing with it. Now that I could communicate better with her, she was responding better with me. When Grace occasionally sat on my lap as Debbie wheeled us around the centre, I wanted desperately to put my arms around her, but they didn't obey my commands. Sometimes

Debbie and Grace would stay late enough to tuck me in. Grace would help brush my teeth and would often shave me with the electric razor. Debbie would pull the covers up, leaning in to give me a kiss goodnight and an "I love you, honey." Grace would follow with "I love you, Daddy" as they left the room.

In September, we had our first family meeting with my team of therapists. Debbie didn't want me to go, but I insisted I wanted to hear about my progress as a whole. The therapists all talked about goals they would be working on in the next three-month period. At the end of the meeting, our military case manager, Steve Stawiarski, who was visibly moved by all the positive comments, tearfully thanked everyone for their work on behalf of the Canadian Forces. I was glad to have attended but found it hard to stay focused for the entire meeting.

Because of the importance of standing and weight bearing to the brain and body, Lori and Kunle knew it was critical for me to be upright. But I had been horizontal for more than eighteen months, so my body had forgotten what it was like to be on my feet. The challenge was that my badly contracted feet wouldn't fit into standard orthotics. An orthotist was brought in to design special boots that would give my feet critical contact with the ground. It would also mean I could focus on working on the core muscles of my trunk with my feet planted firmly on a solid surface.

We laughed when we saw the specialized boots with the large black-wedged heel for the first time. If they had been made of black leather and adorned with glittery stars and satanic symbols, they would have been mistaken for those worn by the 1970s heavy-metal band KISS. A few times a week, I would be strapped to a padded tilt table in my boots and raised up gradually as my body could tolerate it. If I went up too quickly, my head would spin from all the blood rushing to my feet. Over time, I was able to tolerate being fully upright for longer periods.

I loved it whenever Debbie would stand on a chair in front of me and give me a kiss. After a few sessions, Lori started working on my trunk strength by loosening the straps and leaning me to either side. I would try to use my negligible core strength to right myself, nearly an impossible task.

A lot of rehab focus was put simply on reaching, but because my bicep muscles were just too tight, the team recommended Botox injections to loosen them. The strong muscle tone made movement as difficult as trying to drive a car with the brakes on. The Botox would paralyze the bicep muscles for about three months, allowing time to build up strength in the opposing muscles—in my case, the triceps. When the centre's physiatrist, Dr. Shaun Gray, injected the Botox into my biceps, we joked about reserving a little for the face.

During the three-month period, Debbie would bring in dark chocolate and latte as an incentive for me to reach out. For weeks, I reached forward under Kunle's guidance and with Debbie's delicious dangling carrots. Within three months, my left arm was able to slowly reach forward and bring a latte—with a little assistance to avoid disaster—to my lips.

CHAPTER 26

WE'LL DO OUR BEST
TO HAVE TREVOR HOME
FOR CHRISTMAS

Debbie

Trevor insisted on going to the first family meeting despite my attempts to dissuade him. I was worried he would hear something that would upset him or take away his hope, but he insisted on coming. Most comments were positive, but the psychologist was of the opinion that Trev's awareness was spotty. I pointed out that his awareness hadn't wavered since the previous week.

One Saturday morning, I took a different route to the centre so I could check out our new town. I made a mental note of the wellness centre on Ponoka's main street and thought I would check to see what kind of wellness a tiny farming community of six thousand had to offer. As I turned a corner, I spotted a For

Sale sign on a small house with a beautiful fenced backyard. My wheels started turning. I knew it would be impossible to keep Grace and Trevor entertained every weekend at the centre. The house would be perfect for our family, and the backyard was ideal for Grace.

I impulsively called the realtor to have a look at it, and she said that she'd just put up the sign. When I took a tour the next day, I was enchanted by the little girl's bedroom and the swing set in the backyard. There were two bedrooms upstairs for us and two downstairs for Regina. I fell in love with the house almost immediately and, dreaming about our perfect life together, planned my offer. When I told Trev about it later, he said to do it, but I struggled to reconcile my dreamy vision of a Beaver Cleaver lifestyle with the brutal reality of a conditional two- to three-month rehab extension that would take us into the winter. For us, though, the impetus to get the house was too strong to resist. Two months after our first tour of it, Grace, Regina and I walked through the door with our bags.

With his awareness back, Trevor started to become more anxious. He was convinced he couldn't catch his breath despite the 99 percent reading he saw on the oxygen monitor. I tried to get him to take slow, deep breaths, but it didn't always work. We would even have to leave relaxation therapy because he couldn't calm himself down.

"I'm probably the first person to fail at relaxation therapy," he quipped one day.

"Don't be so hard on yourself," I said. "Relaxation doesn't happen the minute you walk into the room. It's a state of being you have to develop."

I started to do a mind-clearing technique that our massage therapist, Jennifer, had given me from her healing touch book. The various hand positions on the head and neck helped Trevor relax and clear his mind, but he soon became obsessed and couldn't relax without this technique.

By late November, he was having panic attacks on a regular basis. There were no warning signs, just a radical mood shift and a sharp tensing of his body. He irrationally begged me to bring him home with us. I told our case manager, Steve, about the situation. I told him I thought it would help if Trevor were able to come home on weekends. The problem was that our house was not accessible. I asked if there was anything he could do to help get Trevor home, particularly in time for Christmas. Not only would we need transportation to get him to the house, as there were no wheelchair-accessible taxis in our small town, but we also needed a porch lift to get him in the front door. Steve said a military family-support organization could help with the van, and the army engineers might be able to install either a porch lift or a ramp to the front door. I was reassured as I read the final words in his email: "We'll do our best to have Trevor home for Christmas." I hoped and prayed that home life would be the antidote for his increasing anxiety.

On December 11, I swung into the driveway of the centre in a van with a wheelchair ramp that folded out the back, and I picked up Trevor for the first time since coming to Ponoka. It was exhilarating to finally have the freedom to leave the centre or go for a drive whenever we wanted. I drove him past the front and back of our new house and described the interior. I pointed to the exact spot where his recliner would be waiting for him, in the living room by the large picture window. Soon all the accessibility modifications would be complete and our home would be ready to welcome Trevor.

CHAPTER 27

THE RATS GET HUNGRY

Trevor

Ever since I had learned to read as a little boy, I had been dissecting long words into short ones. For example, I would break down "reincarnation" into "rein" and "carnation." My mind would casually play the game at odd moments, but now a tornado of words swirled by in my head. The game droned on and on anytime I wasn't occupied, and especially when I was trying to relax. Physiotherapy sessions would usually leave me winded, but more and more I struggled to catch my breath other times throughout the day as my anxiety sucked the air out of my lungs.

In early October, Debbie and Grace moved into the house. I immediately asked to see pictures of it—big mistake. As I lay awake, cold and lonely in my bed, I thought of them warm and snuggly in a cozy home that might as well have been at the

North Pole. Debbie and Grace finally had a home, but there was no way to get me there. And even if I reached the house, there was no way to get me up the steps to the front door. Ever since I had regained my awareness, I felt trapped in my wheelchair. I was a prisoner in my own mind, and my healthy appetite began to wane.

My good friend Clare and Debbie's mom, Judy, visited for my birthday in mid-November. Judy gave me a Christie Blatchford book about stories of Afghanistan—the story of my attack included. Now that I was actually reading about the gruesome attack first-hand, my reaction was more visceral and panicked. As the weeks progressed, the anxiety got worse, to the point where I would become extremely agitated if I saw any semblance of any uniform on TV.

By December, the anxiety had gripped me so hard I couldn't keep anything down. I was throwing up so regularly that Debbie had to stand by with a bucket during physiotherapy sessions for the inevitable breakfast or lunch discharge. I became irrational and demanding and lost control over my body as it stiffened in response to my mind's ever-increasing agitation. I instituted a moratorium on newspapers and TV to avoid any mention or sight of Afghanistan. A mere glimpse would trigger a sudden surge of terror, causing my body to go as stiff and straight as a board. A sharp pain would shoot around my abdomen as my chair's seatbelt dug in from the violent stretch. Starved of images and current events, my mind delved into my storehouse of memories—the most vivid of which were from Afghanistan. In my mind, I would once more be nauseated and claustrophobic in the dusty belly of the LAV, trying to peer through the thick armour for signs of an IED.

Psychological trauma due to combat has always had the tinge of cowardice associated with it. In the First World War it was known as shell shock, and the injured were sent to field hospitals that specialized more in injuries to the flesh than to the mind. In the Second World War it was known as battle fatigue, and the injured were immediately pulled from combat and sent home in disgrace by the first available means. Now we call it post-traumatic stress disorder, or PTSD. The specific military name is operational stress injury, or OSI. It is as insidious and damaging as a wound to the body. Many of our soldiers return from Afghanistan more or less physically whole but emotionally, mentally, psychologically and spiritually shattered. Many commit suicide. My OSI was compounded by the reality of my situation—I couldn't do anything for myself, couldn't go for a run to blow off steam, and didn't know if I'd be in the wheelchair for the rest of my life.

The episodes of deep anxiety started with a feeling of helplessness, as if I were hearing Grace scream from the inside of a burning house and there was nothing I could do about it. Then came a feeling of rats gnawing at my stomach, their heads shaking violently as they greedily ripped my tender flesh. When they started on my heart, it felt as if I would never breathe again. I begged Debbie and the staff to get me to the house so I could crawl up the porch steps to the front door.

The OSI seemed to take over my body and my mind. It was like a cloud of despair settled around me. I hoped that spending five days at home with Debbie and Grace over the Christmas holidays would cure me.

One of the nurses at the centre offered to buy a Christmas present for Debbie for me. I told her I wanted to get her a diamond ring. With the help of my recreational therapist, Jamie, I made a teapot in the ceramics room, then arranged for her to put the ring in it and place it under our tree. I had originally proposed to Debbie on my knees in 2005 at her grandmother's house, and I'd promised her a ring when I could get one. I liked the idea of proposing marriage in two parts: kneeling when I could and buying a ring when I could. The thought of giving Debbie the ring and spending my first Christmas of memory with Grace kept the rats at bay temporarily.

I was overjoyed when Debbie and Grace picked me up to go home four days before Christmas. I looked forward to living together in the same house again so I would be a permanent fixture in Grace's life. I loved the house the minute Debbie pushed me through the front door. It was adorned with Christmas knick-knacks, and the undecorated tree stood in a corner of the living room. I looked forward to christening my new recliner and being close to my family over the holidays. That night we had dinner together, and Debbie and Grace decorated the tree under my ornament placement guidance.

On Christmas morning, Grace crawled up on my bed and we opened our stockings. Because I couldn't open my small wrapped presents, she joyfully opened them for me. Later, as we unwrapped the gifts under the tree, I felt Grace's joyful squeals sink into my bones. I willed Debbie to tear her gifts open quickly so she could get to the one that would finish off a proposal I had started two years ago and a million miles away. As she carefully unwrapped the box and pulled out the teapot, I was overwhelmed by thoughts of what she had endured to stay by my side. Many times I had worried she would leave me. I couldn't think of a greater test of compassion and love than what she had been through. I had practised over and over the words I would use to ask this wonderful woman the most important question of our lives. I ended up winging it.

"Bee, when I could kneel, I fell to my knees and begged you to marry me. I said I would get you a ring when I had the money. Now that I have the money but can't kneel, I want you to picture me on my knees and promise you will marry me." As she wrapped her arms around me, I whispered in her ear, "I promise you I will walk down the aisle one day with you."

I managed to act the part of a cheerful holiday daddy all morning, but the rats found me even in the sanctuary of my home. Throughout my five days there, I alternated between swimming with joy and drowning in despair. I had been given a fuzzy black hat with fold-down flaps that covered the ears and face. I coped by pulling the hat over my head to shut out the outside world and seek serenity in the darkness.

Chapter 28

DARK VALLEYS AND
TEAPOTS

Debbie

The military engineers soldiered hard for three days, readying the porch for the lift installation. The recliner was delivered four days before Christmas and would allow Trevor to sit comfortably when he was home. When a rented hospital bed went into the bedroom across from Grace's room, we were finally able to be a family again. Steve had made good on his promise, and Trevor came home for Christmas. I looked forward to Saturday, December 22, when he would arrive at home and stay for five days straight, but I was worried about his anxious outbursts and how they would affect the peace of our household. I was also concerned about caring for Trevor at home on my own. I was practically one of the staff at the centre, but at home I would have both Grace and Trevor to look after full time.

On the Saturday when Grace and I picked up Trevor, I also brought home fast-acting anti-anxiety drugs to combat his mood swings. He loved the house and felt immediately at home surrounded by all things Christmas. He was blissfully happy the first day in his big recliner in front of the TV watching videos with Grace. A few hours later, this high was submerged in a very dark valley that made him slump in the recliner and shut himself off from the world and from us.

I don't think it was the joyful reunion Trevor was expecting. He was at home, but he couldn't be a loving husband to me or a doting father to Grace. All he could do was sit in his wheelchair or be transferred to the recliner or the bed. He couldn't change the channel on the TV or feed himself, and he still spoke in a loud whisper. The highs and lows happened every day but peaked on Christmas.

After opening stockings in bed with Grace, we ate breakfast together and then went after the presents under the tree. Grace was giddy as she opened the stacks of gifts the family had sent out. One, from our friends and former landlords in Ponoka, was a classic black trapper's hat, fuzzy on the inside with long flaps over the ears and forehead. Having just moved from the big city, where nobody would be caught dead in a hat like that, we all laughed uncontrollably when I put it on Trevor's head. The trapper hat would come to be a symbol of his darkest days as he pulled it completely over his face and shut out the world for hours on end.

Trevor told me to leave one present, the size of a shoebox, until the end. A couple of weeks before Christmas, Trev had asked me to give Jamie, one of the nurses, a large cheque so she could buy Christmas presents for me. I was surprised to open the wrapping paper and reveal a beautiful blue teapot and two matching teacups that Trev had made himself. I thought I knew everything he was involved in at the centre, but I had stopped going to his arts-and-crafts sessions with his recreational therapist, also called Jamie, so I could run errands or spend the time with Grace. Trevor and the two Jamies had conspired to make the tea set for me by Christmas but disguised it by working on a jewellery box for Grace whenever I came by. Inside the teapot was a small, unwrapped ring-sized box. Inside was a beautiful princess-cut diamond solitaire engagement ring. I looked over at Trevor, who was grinning from ear to ear. He was very emotional as he asked me to picture him kneeling as he had done in my grandmother's backyard two years earlier. "Promise you will marry me," he said with a smile. I sat on his lap in the recliner and promised to marry him. I had no idea what our future would be like and I didn't care. I had had no doubts from early on in our relationship that this was the man I would spend my days living with and looking up to. All the while, Grace was happily playing with her new toys, oblivious to the love that filled the room.

Within the hour, all the joy was sucked out of the air, leaving Trevor slumped in his recliner, hat pulled low over his face and completely shut down. The anxiety became too much to bear, and he refused to talk or eat anything all afternoon. At dinnertime I managed to coax him out of his recliner to eat a little, but he just sat in silence at the table while Regina, Grace and I ate a beautiful Christmas dinner.

CHAPTER 29:
A NEW YEAR

Trevor

Up to Christmas, I had dealt with my painful anxiety by shutting down and shutting out the world. In January, I cracked. The breathlessness and hunger of the rats were beyond what I could bear. Desperate for relief, I tried to make myself vomit by sticking my fingers down my throat, but I had neither the range nor the strength to reach far enough. The only outlet for my broken body and soul was my voice. My mind took over this escape valve, and foul words spewed from my lips one Saturday at the house.

Trevor: I demand that you take me back to my beloved centre. Take me back right now. I've gone completely insane. Fuck off. My brain is not rewiring. This is permanent. I'm fucking going insane.

Debbie: You're not going insane. This is part of the recovery.

Trevor: This is not part of the recovery.

Debbie: It is. I've read about it. I read it to you last weekend. This is normal, and I have to just listen and not take it personally. We have to just let it wash over us.

Trevor: This is permanent. Fuck you. Fuck off.

Debbie: Do you want to go lie down in bed?

Trevor: Yes. Fuck off. Fuck off. I'm fucked. I'm going straight to hell.

Debbie: You are not going straight to hell.

Trevor: I am, too.

Debbie: God knows that this is just a phase.

Trevor: God doesn't know anything. You're crazy.

Debbie: I'm crazy?

Trevor: Join the club. I'm going straight to hell.

Debbie: No, you're not.

Trevor: I'm trying to commit suicide.

Debbie: How?

Trevor: Any way possible. I demand you take me back to the centre. I demand it right now.

Debbie: You can demand whatever you want, but I don't have any way to get you back to the centre until Miriam comes back with the van.

Trevor: I'll walk.

Debbie: I'm not walking in this weather, and I'm certainly not pushing you up that hill to the centre.

Trevor: You have to. This is serious. I'm fucking insane.

Debbie: This is only momentary. It will pass.

Trevor: It's permanent.

Debbie: It's not permanent.

Trevor: Fuck you. Take me back to the centre right now.

Debbie: I have the benefit of perspective, and I know this will pass. Here, put this under your tongue. It will make you feel better.

Trevor: Fuck off. You've never loved me. Fuck you. Fucking bitch. Knock my head against the door. Fuck you. Fuck you. I demand that you take me back right now.

Debbie: Trust me, I want to take you back to the centre, but I have no way to get you there. Miriam has the van with Grace.

Trevor: Don't come near me. I want to go back to Afghanistan so he can finish his job with the axe.

Debbie: The guy who hit you is dead, so he can't finish you off. You're just frustrated. It's hard to be in this position, dependent on people. You're impatient and tired. You can't exercise, so verbalizing is the only way for you to blow off steam right now. You're lucky I'm a patient, understanding woman.

Trevor: I'll say anything right now to piss you off . . .

Debbie: Nothing can piss me off.

Trevor: . . . and turn you against me.

Debbie: Nothing can turn me against you. I've read about this and I've seen it first-hand in the hospital with the gentleman in the room next to you. You can't piss me off and you can't make me leave you. It's hard for spouses to understand what it's like to be overseas.

Trevor: It's not normal. It's in my soul and I'm going to hell. I'm irrational. I demand you take me back to the centre.

Debbie: You can demand all you want, but you're staying here.

Trevor: Go fuck yourself.

Trevor: Sorry, my love.

I was shocked that such violence could erupt out of me. I had never sworn at Debbie, ever. On one occasion, I even swore at my precious three-year-old Grace. Fortunately, my voice wasn't loud enough for her to understand, and Debbie deflected it expertly, saying, "Daddy said to have a good nap." It felt like my emotions and voice were not my own—just the way my whole body felt.

CHAPTER 30:
SAY IT ISN'T SO

Debbie

After Christmas, Trevor spiralled completely out of control. He wore the black hat, which we were now calling "the stupid hat," to a physiotherapy session with Lori and Kunle. Kunle took one took at him and said, "Duuuude, what's up with the hat? You look like Elmer Fudd." The psychologist at the centre wasn't experienced with PTSD, so I called our case manager to get help. Steve immediately hooked us up with two peer support counsellors, Pete Palmer and Greg Prodaniuk. They came the following week and would prove to be invaluable.

In the midst of all this craziness, my good friend Miriam came for a week-long visit. I had warned her about Trevor's panic attacks, but since he was at the centre during the day, I knew she would likely miss them. We had a wonderful visit, spending time talking over tea, playing with Grace and making fabulous meals.

On the way to the airport at the end of the week, I popped into the centre to drop off Trevor's supper. As I was rushing out, his doctor stopped me and asked if I had a few minutes to chat. Only a couple, I said. I was taking a friend to the airport.

"The team has decided they've taken Trevor as far as they can," she began offhandedly. "He likely won't regain any more function. He is being discharged in July."

I was dumbfounded. I had seen the team all week, and no one had mentioned anything about not wanting to continue working with Trevor. I fought back the tears all the way to the airport. When Miriam asked what was wrong, I broke down with the crushing news. Over dinner at the airport, she reminded me that the doctors had been wrong all along, and that a lot could happen between now and July. "I see such a phenomenal change in him since a few months ago. Have faith in him."

When I got home later that night, I felt utterly devastated, and I knew that it was too premature to even begin thinking about leaving the centre. Trevor had just started to make progress when the PTSD struck in November. It didn't seem fair that a decision had been made while he was still grappling with a psychological injury that was literally holding him hostage. My dreams of being a normal family again one day were fading, and I was finally waking up to the realization that my dream might not ever come true. I was determined that Trevor would be at home with us, even if he didn't regain any semblance of independence.

As I crawled into bed with Grace that night, I cried into the pillow. I couldn't believe Trevor had failed. He had never failed at anything, and I didn't think the brain-injured Trevor would be any different. But Miriam's words echoed in my mind: I needed to keep my faith in him. I reminded myself of the doctor's pronouncement almost two years earlier that he wouldn't come out of his coma. I decided not to tell Trevor about his discharge. He was going through his own internal hell, and he didn't need to hear that his time was up already. I could only hope that once the anxiety had passed, he would be able to focus on his physical rehab again.

On Friday afternoons when I picked Trevor up for the weekend, he would be slumped in his wheelchair, draped in a blanket with the black hat covering most of his face and head. He fit in perfectly with the mental health patients. Before and after programs, he would sit immobile in his wheelchair, wearing gloves and the hat pulled over his face like a shut-in. He said he wore the hat indoors because he was cold. I wanted to tell him to sit up straight and take the stupid hat off, but I knew it would do no good. When he became agitated, his arms and legs would splay out stiffly and tremble like he was getting an electric jolt. Seeing his body in such an unnatural state was terrifying for me, and I prayed this phase would soon pass. I could feel the fear rip through my body when this scene played out again and again.

I was shocked each time the attacks escalated to verbal explosions—three horrible times at home in January. Trevor would swear at me and beg me to leave him. Grace came up next to me during one of the verbal attacks and he swore at her as well. I had become adept at understanding Trevor's soft voice, but thankfully Grace couldn't always make out what he said. Even though I had read about this phase of brain injury recovery, his words still stung.

After each episode, Trevor thought he was losing his mind. He couldn't believe such words were coming from him. I told myself this was the injury talking, not him, since I had never heard him speak that way to anyone before. I would say to him, "Your words bounce off me because I know they are not coming from you. Your brain injury has overruled your heart, and now you have no control over what comes out of your mouth." Often when I started to see an episode coming, I would quickly put on one of our favourite movies or comedy shows and leave him alone. I would give him an anti-anxiety pill and go downstairs to play with Grace until the anger blew over. But even worse than the strain it put on me, Trevor's anxiety all but stalled his rehab.

CHAPTER 31:
BEGONE, BULLY

Trevor

Pete and Greg, the two operational stress injury peer counsellors, had both soldiered in volatile Croatia. They talked
about the challenges of manning a machine gun in the face of
an army one day and walking the peaceful streets of Canada the
next. When they came home, they were both deeply disturbed
but didn't know what was wrong or how to get help. One of
them went a year before seeking treatment. He almost got di-
vorced in the process.

I met them in early January when the psychological trauma
started to severely affect my family. Debbie was on edge every
time she came to the centre. She would anxiously scan my face
for signs of terror. Since Christmas I had made sure my desk
light was left on at bedtime, like a child afraid of the dark. I
desperately needed help. Pete and Greg told me to call them

whenever I needed to. I called them regularly. When I did, they advised me to look around to ground myself and repeat in my mind that I was home among loved ones and not in Afghanistan anymore. Through all this, I constantly thought about how Bill Turner, my CIMIC friend who was killed after replacing me, would love to have my problems.

Debbie knew that peer counselling alone wouldn't be enough to heal my OSI. She took me for a meeting with my social worker, Bev, also a former member of the military. After conversations between Bev and my doctor, the anti-depressant medication was increased and I began exposure therapy with David, my psychologist. David helped me get control over my blatant reaction to images and uniforms. During sessions, he would show me pictures and have me rate the anxiety level I felt in a safe environment. The first images were mild—of a postman in uniform, say. Over the next few weeks, the images slowly increased to show a policeman, a fireman and ultimately a soldier in uniform. Finally I felt I was ready to confront my psychoses by having Pete, one of my OSI peer counsellors, stand in uniform in front of me. One day, Pete came to David's office wearing his combats. I was extremely nervous before the meeting because Pete and I had grown close through the OSI ordeal and I didn't want to fear a friend. Fortunately, my first glimpse of Pete didn't make me want to cower in the corner. We finished the day telling war stories over coffee.

To supplement the medications and exposure therapy, Debbie wanted to try craniosacral therapy. She had found a study on the Internet about how it helped Vietnam War veterans overcome severe PTSD. She dropped by the local wellness centre and met the owner, Trish, who had studied under Deepak Chopra and also practised various forms of Reiki. Trish hooked Debbie up with Heather, a craniosacral therapist. As Heather laid her hands on me to manipulate my spinal fluid, I told myself that if this therapy had worked for the Vietnam veterans, it would work for me.

Thankfully, by the end of February, my psychological wounds had begun to heal. It felt like I was no longer afraid of the neighbourhood bully. I could fall asleep in the dark and wake up to a peaceful day. I could focus on my physical healing again, which took on a new sense of urgency for me.

With the debilitating anxiety episodes behind me, Debbie would fire me up before physio with the *Rocky* soundtrack. The immortal words of the theme song rang in my head as we headed to the gym.

By the spring, we had fallen into a comfortable rhythm on the weekends at home. I cherished my time away from the centre and dreaded going back on Monday mornings. I never said anything because Debbie chastised me with a pointy finger in the chest for complaining a couple of Mondays and threatened not to bring me home on Fridays. One Saturday morning while Debbie was taking the garbage out to the garage, I was fiddling with my chair controls, raising and lowering the back. To my surprise and horror, the back kept going forward seemingly of its own accord. I was riding an out-of-control lift chair roller-coaster to disaster and couldn't make my fingers stop the ride. As the chair and I reached the point of no return, my mind screamed, *Christ, I've done it now.* I pitched forward and kissed the living room floor with my face. Grace heard the crash and came running. She stood over me asking, "Daddy, what are you doing on the floor?" I urgently told her to go to the garage and get Mummy. A few minutes later Debbie came running in, panicked, and asked, "Oh my God! Are you hurt?"

"Only my pride," I answered.

My dash for freedom left me with only a split lip and a bit of my blood splattered on the floor. Debbie rolled me over onto the sling and hoisted me back into the death trap, keeping the controls well away from me.

On Saturday afternoons, I looked forward to a two-hour massage and range-of-motion session with Jennifer, who was quickly becoming our good friend. It gave Debbie the much-needed one-on-one time she looked forward to with Grace. Afterward, we would sit and enjoy tea and conversation together while Grace napped after their walk to the playground.

Throughout the spring and summer, I worked hard with Kunle and Lori in the gym. The two of them were a powerful odd couple, and Lori was the perfect foil for Kunle. Where he was gregarious, she was demure and understated. Kunle was black and muscular; Lori was white, a petite girl-next-door type in her late forties with piercing blue eyes and a careful voice. I respected them immensely and worked hard to reach their targets, which they constantly raised to challenge me. I naturally gravitated toward Kunle, with his huge smile and big laugh. We easily bantered back and forth during the workouts. He would joke about how he normally had to prod people on to reach ten repetitions, but athletes insisted on doing *at least* ten reps and often more. "But you crazy military guys are the worst," he joked. "You want to do at least a hundred reps."

Once I was able to hold up my head in line with my spine, rehab focused on strengthening my trunk. Our sessions began with cobra-pose push-ups to activate and strengthen my back muscles. I loved feeling the burn that spread from my forearms to my lower back. Afterward, I was rolled onto my back to work on reaching my hand up toward my chin. From there, I searched for my forehead and eventually was able to reach the top of my head. It was eerie to feel the bumps and ridges of my rebuilt skull. With my feet and lower legs firmly in my KISS boots, I would sit on the edge of the treatment table and practise balancing myself while sitting. My legs felt like wooden stumps. My entire right side was less sensitive to touch than the left—as if there were a thin layer of nylon draped there from my chin to my toes. My trunk muscles were so weak that without Kunle and Lori holding me upright, I would have flopped around like a 6'4," 190-pound ragdoll.

Twice a week, Kunle's assistant, Roger, would lead me through an arm-bike session to improve my range and strength. At first, Roger had to stand next to me and coax my right arm through the rotations. My right arm would lock when stretched out fully, and my left arm couldn't overpower it to complete the rotation. By the end of the summer, though, I could "peddle" with only a little help. Therapy was frustrating for me because I couldn't see any week-to-week progress, but friends and family who visited often would rave about the changes they saw in me. What really mattered to me was that I was making progress for my girls. I needed to show them that their faith in me was justified. I adored Debbie and looked forward to showing her what I was capable of. She always said that she fell in love with my strength, and I needed to prove to her that I was still strong and would walk down the aisle one day.

CHAPTER 32:
PRAYING TO STAY, PLANNING TO LEAVE

Debbie

At the next family meeting in March, the team talked positively about Trevor's progress. He was finally making noticeable gains, but in the background, discussions were taking place about our discharge. During his physio and OT sessions, he was clearly getting stronger, reaching farther, speaking louder and being upright longer. But I learned that unless there were tangible, functional improvements, his FAM score probably wouldn't change. The parameters were just too narrow to register his small gains. He would need to show that he could eat totally unassisted or transfer from his wheelchair without the lift. The harsh reality was that he was not progressing fast enough. I was still hopeful that Trevor's FAM score would somehow improve enough by the next evaluation date to get further extensions.

I was terrified to leave the centre because then Trevor would go to the first long-term care bed in the community back home. As long as he stayed here, his rehab would continue and he could come to our temporary home on the weekends. If we were kicked out of the centre but remained in town, Trevor would have no rehab. I felt my only option was to make a strong case for staying at the centre beyond July. The crux of my argument was that Trevor was showing potential with his therapists— enough to warrant at least one more three-month period to prove himself. His doctor didn't dispute my claims, but she said that everything Trevor was working on at the centre could be done with therapists in our hometown.

It would be hard to go back to the city after enjoying the charms of small-town life, but the highly specialized therapy Trevor needed was available only in a larger city. I had enjoyed living in a town with a population of just six thousand. It was a community where you felt comfortable leaving your door unlocked. Our eighty-year-old neighbour, Werner, would race out in the winter and shovel our walkway. In the summer, we borrowed his clothesline for a country-fresh scent on our city clothes. Since November, I had been working part time at a close-knit family-owned accounting firm and was starting to put down roots and make friends. I golfed on Wednesday nights with ladies from the office and took meditation classes at the wellness centre. Grace and I could choose from a multitude of playgrounds, most of which were often empty, and she had made a few friends.

Ponoka had become home for me. The small-town rhythms and routines were predictable and comforting. I felt that for the first time in a long time I had a say in our future. I feared the instability that would inevitably sink in if we broke our bucolic bubble.

CHAPTER 33

PRAYING FOR A MIRACLE

Trevor

There was never any possibility that I would be able to wheel myself in a manual wheelchair, so my therapists brought in a power wheelchair for me to trial. I had just enough hand movement to work the joystick control, but my brain couldn't work fast enough to keep me from running into everything and everyone. Wheeling down the hallway on the lowest speed, I would weave with frequent juddering stops like a child who has stolen the family car, so I was relegated to the large, open gymnasium with Roger. I thought it would be easy to navigate the empty gymnasium, but I still managed to charge down the walls despite Roger's best efforts to coax me to avoid impending disaster. One day, Roger set up an obstacle course of chairs. I was meant to practise turning around them, but I ended up herding them like cattle. Debbie told me to think about the cursed wheelchair as a means of independence. But to me the chair represented submission, and I didn't want anything to do with it. Roger's exhortations didn't help matters.

In the empty hours between therapy sessions, I reflected on the irony of going to war with a superbly trained army equipped with sophisticated weaponry only to be almost killed by a teenager wielding a Stone Age weapon. Choosing to train for and go to war meant I was taking a soldier's chance. My cruel twist of fate came the moment I removed my helmet and became a target for a young man's axe. Seeing the other patients made me reflect on the unpredictable nature of fate, and how a life can be utterly transformed in an instant. One man had developed an innocuous cold sore that had travelled treacherously through his bloodstream and left him with the inability to find words to common items and places, such as where he lived or the names of his kids. An electrician had had hundreds of volts pass through his body while he was stringing Christmas lights. We met others who had just reached adulthood when tragedy struck. Remy was a young professional mountaineer who said he always enjoyed the adventure of climbing and accepted the risks gladly. He just never expected to be grounded from his passion by something so commonplace as a stroke. Mandy had been in her last year of high school when the car she was riding in was T-boned. Years later, she still struggled with balance issues.

Another young girl of seventeen would sit in front a blaring TV in the communal space for hours on end while food was pumped into her stomach to keep her alive. A brutally raw scar encircling her neck like a grotesque caricature of a smile marred the white skin. The tragedy of her case reads like something out of a bizarre short story. In the grip of a dark despair, she had decided to commit suicide. At the last minute, she sent her mother a text message. For better or for worse, the paramedics who found her hanging from her kitchen ceiling were able to save her life. Her mother, two young children in tow, was told she would be fine. She came to the centre badly brain damaged and an infection ultimately ended her life shortly after we left.

The team at the centre tried in vain to unlock my hideously contracted ankles. Even Botox couldn't help get them out of the permanent ballet dancer's position. Our case manager, Steve, arranged for a consultation with an orthopedic surgeon who specialized in trauma to the feet and ankles. We'd have to see the surgeon at the closest military base, which was in Edmonton. I looked forward to hearing the timeline for fixing my feet so I could stand and eventually walk.

When I heard that my feet would be examined at the base where I had done most of my training for Afghanistan, I was glad to have this chance to show Debbie where I had spent half of 2005. Two and a half years earlier, I had walked confidently out of the base clinic with a clean bill of health for deployment. That time, I was confident my strength and stamina would be judged more than adequate for the mission. This time, I was helplessly wheeled in without any strength or function, praying for a miracle.

We were led into a sterile examination room and a surprisingly young female surgeon walked in with my chart. After introducing herself, she twisted and turned my deformed feet for a couple of minutes and dispassionately pronounced, "What I'm seeing here clinically is that not only is your Achilles tendon tight but everything that fires into your foot is contracted. The amount of release that needs to be done is quite enormous."

Debbie spoke up first and asked if the doctor could get my feet in a position to stand on.

"Multiple surgeries will result in a slightly better position, but with all the surgical incisions, he may end up with a chronic pain type of syndrome." After a few minutes, the surgeon casually asked if we had any other questions.

"Am I going to be able to walk?" I asked.

"I don't think so," she said flatly. "Not given where we are in the course of your recovery, and even though you have made enormous gains, given the info the docs in Ponoka sent along, I don't think you'll be walking." After a long pause, she asked, "Is that the expectation that was given to you guys?"

Debbie jumped in and said, "It's a long-term goal we have."

The doctor went on, "No one ever says it's a never thing, but to be honest, I don't think it's a realistic expectation."

I had come here expecting to get a date for surgery, not a bombshell declaration that I would never get out of the wheelchair. I knew that without my feet being straightened, my rehab would eventually plateau.

When we left the room, a young man in combats was waiting in the hallway to talk with us. He nervously approached me with hand extended and said in a quavering voice, "How are you doing? Shaun Marshall. I was the platoon medic the day you were attacked. You look fantastic, sir."

I realized that I was finally looking into the eyes of the man who'd saved my life. Without him, I would have bled to death while the platoon looked on helplessly. He had kept me from being the eleventh ramp ceremony in the tour. Shaun explained that he had just been posted to the clinic a few weeks earlier and happened to notice my name on the roster.

"The last thing you said when we were sitting around the campfire that morning was you didn't think we'd need a medic that day. At the last minute, I ended up jumping on."

"I'm glad you came along," I said.

"I was glad to be there, sir. It definitely had a huge impact on me and the person I am today," he said.

"Thank you," I replied as I grasped his hand in gratitude.

"Thank you, sir," he said, suppressing his tears at the sight of the man whose skull he had held together, trying to keep its contents from spilling further into the Afghan soil.

With tears in her eyes, Debbie asked Shaun if she could give him a hug. "Thank you for going that day and for saving Trevor's life," she said as she hugged him. It was an emotional chance meeting for both of us, and it dispelled the gloom from the surgeon's prognosis. After we said our goodbyes, Debbie leaned over while wiping away tears and asked if I was okay.

"I got a chance to thank the man who saved my life. I'm more than okay."

After leaving the base clinic, I showed Debbie the officers' mess and we sat at the table where Gwen, Tony, Jay and I would have beers after supper. Right beside the table hung the phone that I used to call home. She asked me to show her where I had stayed. I led her over to a huge three-storey brick building with two long wings. Down both wings was a multitude of rooms with closed doors on either side. I pointed down the right wing and said my room was the last door at the end on the left. It was early afternoon and everyone was either at work or out training, so we wandered down the hallway. When we got to the room, the door was slightly ajar. Debbie tapped lightly and a soldier came to the door. She introduced us and said that this room had been assigned to me before I deployed to Afghanistan in 2006. After the soldier invited us in, I pointed out to Debbie which of the two beds was mine and showed her where I hung my clothes. The same grey blanket with the black stripe was at the foot of the bed. With that and thanking the man who saved my life, the surgeon's dire prognosis faded into the background.

Shortly after I returned from the meeting with the surgeon at the base, I had the opportunity to see two other men who had played a critical role in saving my life the day of the attack. I had wondered what my reaction would be when I saw them. Rob Dolson and Kevin Schamuhn had instantly shot my attacker, preventing a lethal second axe blow. As they ambled into the common area at the centre, I unconsciously scanned their bodies for signs of injuries. I was both disappointed and relieved to see none. Disappointed because it meant I was the only member of the platoon to be badly wounded, but relieved they'd made it out intact. As I searched for words, Kevin broke the tension. "Hey, buddy," he said, "is it okay if I give you a hug?" He leaned in and hugged me, followed by Rob. "You look great," they both said, almost as one. The last time Kevin was home, I was in no shape to receive visitors, so Debbie met up with him the night before my second bone flap surgery. I'd expected to be on edge seeing them for the first time and hearing first-hand about the attack, but I was relieved at our light-hearted banter as we caught up on one another's lives and reminisced about the tour. Finally talking about the tour with my fellow platoon mates was like finding people who spoke the same language and had survived the same wicked storm.

CHAPTER 34:
KEEP YOUR HEAD UP,
DADDY

Debbie

A power wheelchair would soon arrive, requiring adjust-ments and practice, neither of which we could get easily at home, so I was happy to hear that Trevor's doctor had agreed to allow him to stay almost two extra months.

In June, I listed our little house and arranged to meet with a realtor to look at houses in Nanaimo, a small city on the West Coast where my family lived. We planned to tour eight level-entry houses in our price range. I would have one day to make a decision. The narrow hallways of each house knocked them off the list one by one. Finally, the realtor convinced me to check out a house I had eliminated because I thought it was too small. When we walked into the bright, spacious home I was impressed with its wide hallways, hardwood floors and large patio overlooking the backyard. I walked down the hallways with my arms outstretched, certain that this was indeed the house for us. I flew back to Ponoka tremendously excited that our family time wouldn't be restricted to weekends and visiting hours at a facility. I drove directly to the centre to tell Trevor the news and show him the video I had taken of the house.

As the weather got warmer, we spent more and more time outside and tried to make the most of our remaining days in Ponoka. We walked along the paved river path and visited playgrounds every weekend. We ate dinner at a picnic table in the backyard in the late afternoon sun. We roasted marshmallows over our small firepit and watched Grace play on her swing set.

Even on weekends at home, the rehab continued. To restore Trevor's dignity and reduce the burden on me, I was determined to have him feed himself. Because of the limited range in his arms, Trevor would flop his head down practically to his chest to meet the fork. Kunle had warned us that if we kept this up, Trevor's head would bob down to meet his food for the rest of his life. So every meal at home, I helped his arm bring the food up to his mouth, all the while reminding him to keep his head up. Grace got into the spirit of the exercise too and would prattle, "Keep your head up, Daddy."

CHAPTER 35:
SNAP

Trevor

"Have a look at this," Debbie said as she held up a camera with a video playing. She had just returned from a house-hunting trip and was excited to show me the house she had chosen. She pointed out the various features, but I didn't care about them. This would be home at last after two and half years. When the camera wandered out the glass doors onto the deck, I saw myself walking over to the railing and gazing out to sea. In the gleaming kitchen, it was me standing there cooking. I knew this would be the home where I would begin walking again.

In early August, six weeks before leaving the centre, I was having a Thai massage session with one of my outside therapists. As she stretched my right leg perpendicular to my body, my hamstrings twanged. I heard a crack like a branch being snapped over a knee and felt a warm bulge in my leg. I had broken fingers playing rugby but had never actually heard them break. I deluded myself by imagining a muscle tear, but in my heart I knew my leg was broken. The therapist dashed out the door of my room calling for staff, and they immediately called 911. Debbie arrived at the centre within ten minutes of a phone call from one of the nurses. As I waited for the ambulance, my thigh throbbed, but the pain was surprisingly mild.

When the two paramedics arrived, they asked my white-faced therapist what had happened. "I was just stretching his leg when I heard a pop," she stammered. As they slid me from the bed to the stretcher, I immediately felt white-hot pain flash through my body, and I heard the bone crunching while a nurse immobilized my leg. We all agreed that it could just be a dislo-cation, and that an X-ray would confirm it. Debbie followed behind the ambulance in her car for the forty-minute drive.

At the hospital, I was taken for an X-ray and then wheeled into a small curtained-off area in the emergency room to wait for the doctor. "You have an interesting medical history accord-ing to the records sent by the centre," said the ER doctor. "It's not often we get an Afghanistan veteran in here. Anyway, your leg is broken at the top of the femur. But if you have to break a leg, tonight is the best night to do it. There is an extra surgeon on before the long weekend, so you will probably be operated on tomorrow." Debbie stayed by my side until I was moved to a room and I dozed off to sleep.

The following day, the surgeon attached a metal rod to the shaft of my right femur and a pin to the head of the femur to stabilize the bone. The surgery was tricky because the break was close to the main femoral artery, which supplies blood down the leg. The surgery cost me two litres of blood and five days in the hospital. Fortunately, because of the long weekend I didn't miss any physio or OT sessions. The next day Debbie brought in

Grace, who immediately began to crawl up on the bed. Debbie pointed to the large bandage and told her, "Daddy has a big owie on his leg." When Debbie found out how much blood I had lost, she loaded me up on iron-rich foods every day until my hemoglobin levels recovered. Back at the centre early the following week, I got right back into my rehab, albeit gingerly, while Debbie planned our trip home.

As the move got closer, Steve and our new military case manager, Lise Bardon, were lining up therapists in our new community so the continuity of rehab wouldn't be broken. It was customary to throw a going-away party for patients who were leaving the unit. As patients and staff gathered in the common area the day before I left, a large cake with the words "Best Wishes, Trevor" was placed in front of me.

As I gave my farewell speech, I looked around at the faces of the people who had guided, encouraged and cajoled me to excel over the past fourteen months. "My army comrades helped me win my war," I said, "and you, my rehab comrades, helped me win my peace. I thank you from the bottom of my heart."

Lori and Kunle hung around after the crowd had dispersed. Kunle slapped my shoulder and said, "Keep pushing hard, my man." Lori leaned in and squeezed my hand. "It's been an honour to work with you," she said with tears in her eyes. After they left, Debbie sat down next to me. I could tell it was hard for her to say goodbye to these people we had befriended. "I love you," I said. "Thank you for being on this journey with me."

"I love you, too," she said as she leaned in close. "We've come so far since March fourth. Let's keep going."

Living in institutions had become tiresome, and I longed to sleep in the same bed with Debbie every night in the sanctuary of our own home. But I wondered if it would feel empty and useless to be unable to even take out the garbage. Still, I knew that helping Debbie with the parenting would make up for it. I had visions of Grace crawling into bed with us on Saturday mornings or when she'd had a nightmare. And I also worried about the burden I would impose on the household and wondered if Grace would look on me as an outsider, in contrast to the close relationship she had with Debbie. For years I had been a part-time father to Grace, and now I'd be living with her. I was afraid I wouldn't know what to say or how to draw the line between playmate and disciplinarian. But I knew Debbie's love was unconditional, and I hoped Grace's would one day know no boundaries.

That night, the unit staff came in one by one to wish me a melancholy farewell. As I shook their hands and hugged them, I was reminded about how I had got to know them, listened to their jokes and heard stories about their lives. I looked around the bare walls and wondered who would take over my room and how much of that life would be recovered.

CHAPTER 36:
ONE JOURNEY ENDS . . .

Debbie

Grace and I flew back to Nanaimo in late August to pick up the keys to our new house. I left Grace there with Grandma Judy and Grandpa Bill so she could start at her new preschool with the rest of the kids. Trevor and I would follow two weeks later. The porch lift would arrive in days, and the overhead tracking to lift Trevor would be installed in the bedroom, bathroom and family room in time for our arrival on September 12.

With the keys in my hand, I walked through our new house and thought about what life could have in store for us. I would miss the hustle and bustle of the centre as patients and staff rushed off to programs and back for meals. And I would miss the staff, who had become part of our social fabric; we had spent more time with them over the past fourteen months than we had with our own friends and family.

I felt triumphant that Trevor would not be living in an institution, but I was scared about how I would cope with our permanent life together. I was starting to realize just how much I had processed since Trevor was injured: I had moved twice, left my job, separated from friends and, for the most part, become a single parent also caring for a totally dependent husband.

The safety net that had surrounded and protected Trevor for the past two and half years was about to disappear, and I knew I would have to build another. I also knew I would have to assume the roles of manager of the household and protector of the family. Having Trevor home on weekends in Ponoka was one thing, but the prospect of being his full-time caregiver was daunting. I worried that my caregiver responsibilities would overshadow our romantic relationship. Even though we'd been together for nearly seven years, we were still passionately in love, and I didn't want to lose that. I was also concerned about how I would keep him mentally and physically stimulated. His mind was strong and needed to be challenged, as did his body.

CHAPTER 37:
HONEY OR MAGGOTS?

Trevor

I felt a slight thump as the Learjet touched down at the small airport in Nanaimo. I couldn't wait for the doors to open, completing my two-and-a-half-year journey to get home. I could see Debbie's parents smiling and waving frantically from outside the gate with our van to take me home. As my stretcher was lifted out of the aircraft, I could smell the salty sea air and feel the warm late summer breeze on my face.

I reached down, felt the rough, warm tarmac and knew I was finally home. Fourteen months earlier, I had left with bagpipe music ringing in my ears, convinced the only part of my broken body that needed rehab was my voice. I knew now that I still faced a long, hard road that stretched far into the distance. But with Debbie and Grace by my side, I could do it—I *had* to do it.

My military family was waiting to welcome me home as

well. From the ground, I looked up into the faces of the new commanding officer of the Seaforth Highlanders, Lt.-Col. Paul Ursich, and the regimental sergeant major. "Welcome home," they chorused. They had come in uniform, as is customary to welcome a soldier back from a mission.

"Thank you, sir. It's good to be home," I replied.

I was lifted from the stretcher to my wheelchair and wheeled into the back of our van to go home. For good. On the way, we stopped to pick up Grace at her new preschool. As Debbie entered the school, Grace's eyes widened and she shrieked with joy. Her face was pressed against Debbie's and her arms were wrapped tightly around her mother's neck as they joyously crowded into the van.

We spent the first week settling in and arranging the house. I felt a tranquillity and stillness slip over me every night as we read bedtime stories to Grace. My sister, Suzanne, flew out to help with the transition. Debbie joked about how Suzanne spent the whole week flying around the house with a drill in one hand and a screwdriver in the other asking for her next job.

I enjoyed the week off with Suzanne, but I was looking forward to meeting my new team and getting back into rehab. For fourteen months at the centre, every day was game day. My games were only sixty minutes long: physio and OT sessions. The incremental gains didn't give me the immediate gratification of a hard rugby tackle or a smooth, powerful rowing stroke, and the PT game never ended. There was always another game or another race—another day. Same teams. Same struggle.

The following week, we met my new occupational therapist. We were impressed with Lila Mandziuk immediately. A tall, athletic woman with little patience for idle chatter when there is work to be done, she was the perfect replacement for Kunle. After our first session, Debbie and I saw her to the front door. After the door closed, we looked at each other and said, "Score!" like we were celebrating a first victory. Two weeks later, we were equally blown away by my new physiotherapist, Bonnie Lamley, who had a thirty-year career specializing in brain injury. She read my body as if she were part of me and could tell which muscles were firing by a light touch. After our first workout, we knew the two-hour round trip each week to Bonnie's clinic would be worth it.

The only piece of exercise equipment we had to start with was an arm bike that Suzanne had cobbled together. Twice a week, I sweated on the bed lifting Lila's weights to strengthen my upper body and arms. When our treatment mat arrived, Debbie improvised a gym in our empty garage. A few months later, a universal gym arrived, and we were in business. But while my upper body strength improved, my ballet dancer feet kept my legs weak and my recovery limited.

In early December, *Peace Warrior*, the documentary about our journey, aired. Dr. Norgrove Penny, a local orthopedic surgeon, saw the show and got in touch with us through a journalist who had written an article. He wanted to offer another surgical opinion after hearing the gloomy prognosis offered by the surgeon at the base. We later learned that Dr. Penny had started a program of correcting bad deformities in children with neglected clubfoot in Uganda, where it's seen as a curse.

At a consultation in his clinic on December 31, Dr. Penny demonstrated how he planned to correct my feet by lengthening the Achilles tendon. He sketched an ankle on a piece of paper and made two slashes at the top and bottom of the tendon, like stretching out a Z. Dr. Penny scissored with his fingers on my bare foot where he would be making the incisions. He also said my toes, the tibial tendon and the plantar fascia, which runs along the bottom of the foot, would all need releasing.

The best-case scenario would be to get ninety degrees of flexion from the surgery. If ninety degrees could not be reached by surgery, plan B was to attach an Ilizarov apparatus. These bulky, stainless steel frames, invented in the Soviet Union in the 1950s using bicycle parts, are screwed into the bone with pins that are attached to three rings. The rings are connected with rods threaded through adjustable nuts. A slight turn of the nuts moves the rings closer together, stretching the tendons and muscles. Because of a cancellation, Dr. Penny was able to book me in for surgery right away in the middle of January.

January 15 was a crisp, sunny creature born of early winter 2009. The 5:30 a.m. alarm buzzed in our room. We were to be at the hospital at 6:30 a.m. Debbie rolled over and put her arm around me and smiled. "Everything is going to be fine today. You don't need to worry. Dr. Penny is a world expert and has worked miracles on feet in worse shape than yours." She leaned over and kissed me. "Let's get on with it. I want to see you standing at the altar one day."

Despite her words, I had a hollow feeling in my stomach. Surgeries hadn't been very kind to me in the past: I'd had my skull rearranged four times since the axe fell at Shinkay, and I had dumped a bathtub of blood during leg surgery. But Dr. Penny had impressed me as soon as I shook his hand and looked into his kind eyes. And most important, he was confident he could fix my feet. This time at least I was mentally, physically and medically stronger than ever before. The most serious risk of the surgery was respiratory complications due to my compromised lungs.

Dr. Penny was all smiles when we met him at the hospital. He explained the surgery again and said he expected it to take about two and a half to three hours. Debbie stayed with me until just before I was taken away. She looked me in the eyes and said, "I love you so much and will be waiting here for you when it's over. You will have beautiful feet again."

It seemed to be minutes later when I woke up in the post-operation room. Looking down, I saw huge mounds where my feet should be. My calves and feet throbbed like I had danced with a lawn mower. When I was wheeled into my new hospital room, Debbie was waiting for me as she'd promised.

"I'm so glad to see you. How are you feeling? Have you seen your feet yet?" she asked.

Dr. Penny came in the room just then and lifted up the sheet to check on his handiwork. I looked down at my feet and saw stainless steel rings suspended on spokes that had been drilled into the bones of my calves and feet in thirty places. Bright yellow disinfectant was splashed all over and punctuated by bubbles of dried blood. My feet weren't pointed straight down anymore, but it looked like two torture machines had been clamped down on them. Dr. Penny said the surgery had brought my feet halfway and the frames should stretch them the rest of the way.

As he spoke, he grabbed one of the rings and lifted my leg up off the bed. Seeing the look of alarm on Debbie's face, he said that the rings were very sturdy and wouldn't pull out of the bone. "There's no reason to be afraid of them." Debbie rolled her eyes at me when he encouraged her to swing the frames around. Then Dr. Penny handed her two ten-millimetre wrenches. "To start, you'll need to undo the top nut below the four-sided turning nut." He pointed to it and then went on, "At least one full turn. Then tighten the locking nut. You'll need to do this four times a day. This will stretch the underlying tissues one millimetre a day. If Trevor's pain is increasing, slow the rate to a half turn four times a day. Do you have any questions?"

"Just to confirm, I unlock here, turn one full rotation, then lock the nut?" she replied, looking a little overwhelmed.

"Yes. You'll be fine," he said.

Although the angle of my foot had come up, my toes still curled down like bat claws despite a complete tendon release. Two occupational therapists came by to build small toe slings that would attach to the frames to stretch my toes back to neutral. All day, every day, Debbie would be working the wrenches and slinging each toe for as long as I could tolerate. She would literally be stretching my feet straight over the next few months. Three days later, we left the hospital with all the delicacy of carrying newborn twins—bundled in cages.

Once I got over the psychological baggage of having steel rods sticking out of my legs and feet, I learned to live with the constant ache. The nut tightening was so slow and gradual that the pain level didn't get worse. Debbie became comfortable with the cages and could even lift and swing them around to show friends how solid they were. They had the same incredulous look on their faces as she did the first day.

Two weeks later, our home care nurse, Mike, a former British army medic in his late fifties with a sharp, sarcastic wit, removed the staples from the incision. Left in their place was a fifteen-centimetre partially healed scab. The skin around my ankle had been stretched from the surgery and was being pulled even farther by the tightening frames. The incision gaped to an angry red, pulpy two-centimetre wound with blisters that oozed yellowish liquid. Debbie slowed down the adjustments to a quarter turn to allow the skin to settle down. Mike came twice a week to clean the pin sites and the steadily widening incision. There was little circulation and blood flow to my ankles because I wasn't able to bear weight on my feet or move around, so the wound stayed raw.

To help heal the open wound, Mike gave me the delightful choice of maggots or medicinal honey. Despite Mike's assurances that maggots had been curing wounds since the days of the Mayans, Debbie was too squeamish to have little worms eating my flesh, so we opted for the honey, a common remedy in ancient Egypt. Sure enough, under the honey the wound started to close and healthy pink skin tissue grew.

With the exercise mat now taking up a corner of our gym, Lila took advantage of my heavy Frankenstein feet. Lying on the mat, we draped my knees over a padded cylindrical bolster. Lila guided the cages like they were free weights while I strained to lift my legs. The cold winter weather and grotesque appearance of the cages kept me cooped up for weeks. Debbie and I ventured out only for our weekly physio sessions at Bonnie's.

After fourteen weeks, it was finally time for the cages to come off. My feet looked like they were in a much better position, but with the cages on it was difficult to tell for sure. I needed to hear Dr. Penny say that my feet were now flat enough to stand on. Before I went in for the surgery to remove the cages, Debbie leaned in for her usual pre-surgery hug and kiss. "I love you," she said throatily. Dr. Penny assured us it was a simple procedure to remove the cages and put on casts.

When I came out of surgery, I looked down to see bright lime-green casts on my feet up to my knees. Debbie gave me a funny look as she asked if I had picked out the colour myself. "I requested green. I guess I should have been more specific," I replied, laughing. Dr. Penny came by and was impressed with the position of my feet. "Your ankles are close to ninety degrees," he said. When the casts came off six weeks later, I gloried in the sight of my fresh, flat feet sliding into my first pair of orthotics, which would keep my feet flat and my ankles supported for weight bearing.

Three years and three months after Shinkay village, I felt the unfamiliar tightness of a shoe sliding over my foot. Debbie looked on approvingly as if I had just given birth. The oversized black sneakers with unsexy Velcro straps would affectionately become known forevermore as my "birth control boots." The right shoe was even sexier, with a three-centimetre lift that compensated for my shortened leg—a legacy of the broken femur. But they would allow me to stand again, and I wasn't too worried about dressing to impress.

I had been waiting well over three years to get off my arse and stand on my legs. Now that my feet were flat, it was long past time to get up on them. Lila and Debbie sat me in a hydraulic frame that gradually lifted me to standing. About halfway up, I became dizzy and breathless, so they lowered me until I got my breath back. I had expected to feel intense pressure and pain in my feet, but there was no feeling at all; it was like standing on cotton balls. Lila explained that my brain was trying to process a deluge of signals that it hadn't received in over three years.

We worked on the standing frame for weeks until I started to have sharp pain in my right foot. We assumed that the bones were groaning from the 190 pounds of new weight they were carrying. My foot was becoming redder each day, even after being iced, and it grew tender to the touch. Eventually a dark bulge that looked like the evil womb of a hairy purple critter formed on the side of my foot. Debbie was worried about an infection in the bone, so she took me to Emergency. The doctor pronounced it to be a boil and said he would have to lance it. Not knowing what was involved in lancing, Debbie sat close by and watched as the doctor poked the purple critter with a scalpel. She was horrified to see blood and pus gushing out like a tap had been turned on.

"Don't look at it!" she blurted.

The critter hole looked like a bullet wound in my foot. The doctor sent us on our way with gauze stuffed into the hole and advised us to consult with the infectious diseases specialist.

Dr. David Forrest reviewed the scans and prescribed a six-week course of home antibiotics. "Bruce," as we called the IV bag, lived in a fanny pack around my waist and spewed drugs into me throughout the day and night. After dragging cages around for three months, I found living with Bruce a breeze. The critter eventually was put to rest and my foot healed.

By August, Bonnie wanted to get me upright without the standing frame. She parked me in front of the wall ladder in her clinic and told me to pull myself to standing. With the help of Bonnie and her husband, Tony, I grabbed the highest rung I could reach, nearly tearing my arms out of the sockets in the process. I pulled with all my strength and felt my bum rise ever so slightly. I willed my legs to push me higher, but it was as if they didn't know what to do. Bonnie said that my upper body didn't know how to live with my lower body anymore. With her and Tony on either side of me hauling on a waist strap and Debbie pushing mightily at my rump, they hoisted me the rest of the way up to standing. I clutched the ladder like I was dangling off the top of a skyscraper while they braced my knees to keep me from crumpling. I hung on—trembling—as long as I could, until I had to collapse back into the chair, exhausted and breathless. Standing was almost too much for my brain and body to manage all at the same time. I felt numb and nauseated. If the mere act of standing was this difficult, I thought, relearning to walk would take a lifetime. I had expected my newly flat feet to magically galvanize my ponderous body into doing what it was supposed to do.

Lila said aquatic training was the next step. The buoyancy of the water allowed me to engage my legs and do squats for the first time. Debbie and Lila steadied me as I gripped the rough concrete ledge and emerged from the chest-deep water. Each week, Lila would move us to shallower water, until I was springing up from only thigh-deep water. She rolled a wheel-chair deep into the pool so I could practise pushing up to stand-ing. Debbie would guide my hands to her shoulders to aid my balance. These movements were exhilarating in the pool but very difficult to replicate in the gym. Lila reassured us that the gains made in the pool would eventually translate to land.

As summer turned to fall, the crimson leaves withered and fell and we needed a portable heater in our gym. The cool water in the pool constricted my muscles and I couldn't perform as well. By winter, we were pulling on thicker sweatshirts and cranking up the heat in the gym. Debbie's uncle Doug built a ladder into our garage wall and we worked on getting me up to standing and keeping me there as long as I could manage. By November, I could stand for three full minutes. By April, I was up to five.

In October, I received a letter from our Governor General's office. I was invited to come to the nation's capital to receive the inaugural sacrifice medal two days before Remembrance Day. The medal had been created to recognize soldiers and their civilian colleagues who had been wounded or killed by hos-tile action. My first thought after reading the letter was relief. The forces had watched over us for the past three years and provided for my every need. But it meant so much to receive a medal acknowledging that what I had lost was something more than a handshake and a wound stripe. It symbolized gratitude and sympathy—gratitude for the decision I had made to serve overseas, as well as the sacrifices my family had made in sup-porting me, but sympathy that the decision had left me hunched in a wheelchair in the prime of my life.

Debbie, Grace and I flew to Ottawa for the ceremony. That morning, as Debbie rolled my deadweight body over in bed to position the sling underneath me, I thought about how the day would unfold. Debbie pulled on my black socks and blue suit pants for the occasion. I watched her tighten the laces of my birth control boots over my orthotics and felt the familiar tug as I was lifted out of bed and lowered into the wheelchair. Debbie looked stunning in her tailored black suit and heels. I didn't often get to see her dressed up anymore. At home, we had talked about me wheeling myself up to the Governor General, but I had neither the strength nor the coordination to pull it off gracefully and efficiently. Besides, I was glad Debbie would be behind me, because in my mind she deserved the sacrifice medal as well. The medal would be presented to me, but we had both earned it.

After tightening my tie, Debbie took my Afghanistan service medal out of the box and pinned it above my heart. "I am so proud of you. You deserve this medal," she said emotionally.

"No," I reminded her, "*we* deserve this medal."

A pounding at the hotel door and excited squealing from Grace abruptly signalled it was time to head out for the ceremony. Grace, who'd been staying down the hall with my parents, burst into the room in her best dress, followed closely by her grandparents. At four and a half, she was excited about the day's events but oblivious to what they represented. She was more pleased to be spending time with my parents.

At Rideau Hall, we were ushered into a private room with other injured soldiers and the families of the fallen. When the time came, we walked, wheeled and limped into the main hall and down the aisle past invited family members. Without delay, the throng of media at the front began filming. I spotted Grace and my mum and dad waving subtly on the right. We formed up in rows along the left. Debbie was directed to sit a few rows behind me.

Governor General Michaëlle Jean opened the service by speaking passionately and emotionally about the sacrifices of the injured and fallen and their families. Then she invited each person forward, sharing a private moment in an empathetic embrace, especially with the mothers and children. She held the mothers in her arms and wept with them before handing over, almost reluctantly, the engraved wooden box that held the medal.

When my name was called, Debbie pushed me to the front of the hall. Madame Jean placed her hand on my arm and told me that she was very impressed with my recovery. After handing me my wooden box, she guided me to Prime Minister Stephen Harper and the new Chief of the Defence Staff, Gen. Walt Natynczyk. The general shook my hand firmly and said, "I have a new mission for you, Captain. Get yourself better. We'll all help you."

"Thank you, sir. I intend to," I replied.

As Debbie led me away, a wave of emotion washed over me. I caught sight of Grace and my parents across the room, full of big smiles. As expected, Mum was wiping away her tears. I couldn't see Debbie behind me, but I knew she would be struggling to hold in her emotions. I felt a sense of closure in receiving the medal. My country had looked after me well since the injury, and now its leaders had recognized our sacrifice.

After we returned home, I looked forward to completing my new mission from the general. Debbie and I were already looking at rehab as a mission with one goal to achieve: walking. Between appointments with Bonnie and Lila, Debbie and I spent our mornings weight training in the gym. When we weren't training, I was visualizing myself doing the movements over and over. I had done this before in competitive rowing and was confident I could do it again now. The only problem was that I wasn't working with all my equipment. I was missing some of the grey matter that helped control my legs, and what I had left was prone to acting haywire.

A few days after getting home, we received an email from a neuroscientist, Dr. Ryan D'Arcy, who specialized in functional imaging of the brain. He had some ideas about our goal to push the limits of rehab further. Dr. D'Arcy explained that changes in the brain invariably precede changes in behaviour, and he wanted to conduct a two-year study to examine how my brain was reorganizing. The study was set to begin in May 2010.

My rehab seemed to be improving all around. Progress was measured in baby steps, but it was at least consistent. One night as we lay in bed, I faced Debbie and said, "Almost a year ago, you promised to be my wife. I'm not walking yet, but I will do everything in my power to walk down the aisle with you. Should we set a date?"

With a smile, she responded, "I would love to set a date. What are you doing next July?"

"Marrying the woman who saved my life," I said.

We had talked about marriage for years but something had always taken precedence. Before I left for Afghanistan, we'd agreed the best time would be once my tour was over and before I started my next career assignment. My next assignment had ended up being chosen for me, so to speak, and had consumed the next four years of our lives.

In between physio and OT sessions, Debbie and I worked hard in the gym together, doing weight training, leg lifts, stretching, breathing exercises and electrical muscle stimulation. We were so focused on our goal that even during our downtime, we talked about and planned our next workout. The strength in my arms was building, as was the motor control, but my legs still lagged behind. Another challenge was my upper body's lack of coordination with my lower. My waist felt like it was an accordion, but at least I could finally activate my legs to get me to standing.

In addition to being my full-time cook, driver, lover and the mother of my child, Debbie also became my coach. She gave up her career for me and asked nothing in return but hard work. Not many women would have done what she did. I watched her do literally everything for four years. She had to deal with toddler tantrums, sort out appointments, do laundry, drive everyone everywhere and try to squeeze in time for herself. I had been the family chef before I went overseas, but now I only watched impotently as she planned and prepared all of our meals and cleaned up afterward.

I wanted and needed to show her how much she meant to me. I would spend the rest of my life justifying her faith in me. I was in awe of how she intuitively seemed to know how to handle every phase of my recovery. It was as if she had written the book on what to do if your fiancé goes to war and is severely injured.

I felt like I owed Grace, too. She had lost years of her father and much of her mother's attention since my injury. But I finally felt like I was becoming a father to her again. After preschool, she would look for me in my recliner, where I rested after my workouts. I felt important to her. When Debbie was preparing supper, Grace and I would often play school in her room. She was always Miss Margaret, the teacher, and I was always Thomas, forever on the verge of getting in trouble. She "read" to me and often scolded me: "Thomas, don't interrupt." I walked on eggshells for the whole class but looked forward to the inevitable nap and snack because I knew Thomas couldn't possibly screw that up.

Often after supper, she would sit in my lap laughing gleefully as we watched the videos I had recorded before I deployed. Friday nights became her night to sleep with me after our customary movie and pizza. Her breathing would soften as Debbie laid her down next to me. I loved being there to see her open her eyes in the morning and look at me. "Morning time, Daddy," she would say, then the inevitable, "I spy with my little eye . . ."

We had chosen Debbie's sister Toni's large and secluded backyard as our dream wedding venue. Debbie had reserved a large white marquee and white chairs, and she'd secured a popular caterer immediately after we set the date. In the months leading up to July, I was still working on strengthening my stand as we were putting the finishing touches on the preparations for the day.

By June, seven weeks before the wedding, my upper body still wasn't coordinating well with my legs, and my balance was too wobbly to let go of the parallel bars. We had long ago resigned ourselves to the fact that I wouldn't be walking down the aisle. I was disappointed, but at least, I reasoned, I was alive to be disappointed.

CHAPTER 38:
YOU SAY IT BEST

Trevor

On the day before the wedding, my best friend, Barb, arrived. Almost six feet tall in heels, she created a vortex that swirled behind her as she swept confidently across the parched lawn in a tailored white pantsuit. "Bubba! Deb! God, you're beautiful! This place is gorgeous, and perfect for the wedding of the century!" she shrieked.

She bent over to give me a hug and ardently hissed in my ear, as she had for the twenty-five years I'd known her. "I wouldn't have missed this day for the world," she said. "You woke me up. After you were injured, I promised you I would continue your mission. I realized that the lives of Afghans could be improved and the women empowered if they were growing legal crops instead of poppies for heroin. So I bought orange-blossom oil directly from women in Jalalabad and developed it into this perfume for the

North American market." She handed me a bottle of the finished product. "For your incredible bride," she said.

"I always knew you would do it, Babsie."

That night, my mum and dad threw a pre-wedding ceilidh for all of our guests. As Debbie and I entered the room, I thought I caught a glimpse of my long-time friend Mud, of Carpfest fame. I brushed the thought off because it couldn't possibly be him. He had been living in Argentina for years, and we hadn't even heard back from him and his wife after sending them a wedding invitation—or so I thought.

"How's it hanging, Tree?" Mud ambled over and said in his mild Southern drawl.

I was speechless. I had no memory of his visit to the hospital three years earlier, so in my mind, I hadn't seen him in more than fifteen years. I was incredibly happy to have him at my wedding. Mud's wife, Maria, had had a plane ticket waiting for him when he got back from sea. Debbie had been in contact with them all along. He wasn't sure if he would get the visa in time, but he had confirmed a week earlier. Seeing Mud again was like getting a brother back, and it made my wedding complete.

On the morning of the wedding, Debbie was up early to do last-minute arranging and set up the backyard. I was power-less to help but knew she had a crowd of family and friends at her disposal for the day, including her maid of honour, Miriam, who had been out all week practising my stand with us. Debbie rambled off all the things on her to-do list and flew out the door, giving me a hurried kiss on the way. "I'm not sure when I'll be back, but I'll see you before the ceremony. Don't forget that Karin's coming at noon to give you a massage," she yelled as the door slammed shut behind her.

As Karin worked her magic on me, I mused about my chance meeting with Debbie nearly nine years earlier. Back then, I had quickly realized that she had all the qualities I was looking for in a wife without knowing I was looking. I felt satisfied that I had found the perfect partner. She was kind to a fault, compassionate, beautiful, an incredible mother and seemed always able to handle anything life threw at her. I knew that she loved me to distraction, as I did her. Equally important, she had supported me in my decision to deploy to Afghanistan and carried me when I came home broken. She had kept faith in me when most women would have walked away. And she was willing to risk years of her life and Grace's to make me whole again.

In no time at all, my massage and the day flew by. As he had done countless times in the hospital, Dad came by to shave me. This time he did it slowly, as if drawing out the moment. "Are you ready to go, Trev?" he said gently as he examined his handiwork. "Mickey is here to drive you over. He promised me he wouldn't go by the pub first."

The late afternoon shadows crawled across the lawn as my cousin Mickey and I drove in the van along the side of the house to a tool shed to meet Lila and warm up my legs for standing. After five carefully supervised stands, I was wheeled into the backyard.

I was awestruck and expecting a director to call "Action." The backyard had been transformed into a bucolic, flower-filled sanctuary. The beautiful sunny day, the magical white canopy tent and chairs—all were set against a backdrop of live guitar melodies.

Lila manoeuvred me onto the parquet dance floor outside under the marquee, where a waist-high silver bar stood waiting for me. Our guests erupted in a stupendous cheer that Debbie later said she heard upstairs in her sister's bedroom as she was getting ready. I looked at the faces of my parents, who sat proudly on the left side of the aisle. They never thought the day would come. Mum and Suzie had always thought I was incapable of settling down and joked about me being a bachelor forever.

An air of expectation settled in as the musicians paused and guests took their seats. The live strains of *Andantino in G* by Ferdinando Carulli, a romantic classical melody, signalled a start to the procession. Debbie's nieces, in matching white dresses, walked delicately down the aisle dropping flower petals. Grace came next, besieged by 130 sets of eyes and cameras as she clutched her white ring-bearer's purse.

Then I caught sight of Debbie as she came out of the house with her parents on either side. She looked poised, elegant and more beautiful than I had ever seen her. I knew then why she had never let me get a glimpse of her dress. The floor-length white gown hugged her body like I used to and showed off her curvy figure. There was a rustling as our guests rose to their feet, but my eyes stayed locked on Debbie's. She took in the crowd but kept her focus on me as she walked across the lawn radiating peace and total contentment. I followed her with my eyes as she came around the parallel bars and stood next to me.

We had chosen our long-time friend Robin Gibson to perform the ceremony in front of a justice of the peace. He started things off by saying, "Ladies and gentlemen, please take your seats. Trevor, please take your place." This was our cue. Miriam and I guided Trevor to a place few people had thought he would reach: standing tall by my side. It felt so natural to have him next to me. Since the day he was taken down, I'd only ever looked at him as the man I knew him to be: tall, brave and strong. With him next to me, I felt the past four and a half years slipping easily away. I looked around at the smiling and tearful faces of our family and guests as Robin continued with the ceremony.

"Let me first say that it is with great humility that I stand in front of you, Trevor and Debbie, and presume to tell you anything about love, loyalty and commitment. For all of us gathered here and many people across this nation, you two have shown us what these words, these ideals, really mean . . .

307

"The vows that Trevor and Debbie will make before us here today are not promises of what they will become, but rather the declaration before their family, friends and community of what they have already created and embody together."

I heard only scattered sentences. My mind was obsessed with keeping my back straight and my chest high. I gloried in knowing that Debbie was finally looking up at me instead of looking down to the wheelchair. I felt so proud to stand next to her in front of our family and friends, as she had done for me in front of countless doctors, nurses and therapists. My palms were sweaty inside my gloves from gripping the bars with all my strength to stabilize my torso, but I had all the confidence in the world. I measured each breath carefully to keep from going woozy.

Debbie and I stood facing our guests, and I felt the soft summer breeze wrapping around us as Robin continued: "I would like to share a favourite quote of Trevor and Debbie's from *The Little Prince*: 'Life has taught us that love does not consist in gazing at each other but in looking outward together in the same direction.'"

I knew that when we were to exchange rings, I would have to sit, a movement I had practised for months. This time it was different; 130 people were watching, and I could feel every eye on me. When I heard the words "Trevor, would you please be seated," I prepared myself to sit by loosening my fingers one by one and softening my knees. Debbie and Miriam guided me down from my perch and Debbie slid onto my lap.

We had told Grace she had the most important job of the whole ceremony: carrying and handing over the rings. So when Robin asked her to bring up the rings, a proud smile played across her face. With all eyes on her, she reached into the small white purse she was carrying like a baby bird and gingerly passed the rings to Barb.

"Trevor, place the ring on the third finger of Debbie's left hand and say your vows."

I slid the ring onto Debbie's finger and spoke directly from my heart. "My darling love, because of you I laugh, I smile, I live. I look forward with great joy to spending the rest of my life with you, caring for you, nurturing you, being there for you in all life has for us, and I vow to be true and faithful for as long as we both shall live."

"Debbie, place the ring on the third finger of Trevor's left hand and say your vows."

I couldn't take my eyes off Trevor as I slid the ring past the tip of his finger. "Trevor, I promise to encourage and inspire you, to laugh with you in good times and struggle with you in bad." I paused and took a deep breath as my voice began to quaver, then continued, "I promise to always push you beyond your limits so that you can reach your fullest potential. You have shown me the true meaning of life and love, and for that I thank you. I consider it an honour and a privilege to be your wife, and I will stand by your side and love you always."

After signing the register, I asked Trevor if he was okay. He had a dazed look on his face and stared at me like he was about to cry. "You look so beautiful," he said, smiling.

After cocktails, an incredible meal and a few speeches, I took the microphone. "Today, you are all witness to the power of hope and love. They are said to be the pillars of the world, and together they create miracles. There is an African proverb that says: 'Love is like a war: easy to begin, hard to end.' It was a war that separated us, but the same war united our souls forever. There are many people I have to thank for keeping me alive and well. A wife, several doctors, our families and friends, and therapists." My voice had become weak and was barely audible to anyone beyond our table, so Debbie stood and took over. She did a fabulous job of recognizing and thanking everyone who helped make the day a reality. When it came time to toast Kevin Schamuhn, I needed him to hear it directly from me. I wanted everyone to know how much it meant to me to have him at our wedding.

Looking around at our guests, my gaze rested on Kevin's face as he stood at the back. I asked Debbie for the microphone, sucked oxygen deep into my lungs and spoke. "The man standing at the back is Kevin Schamuhn, my good friend and platoon commander in Afghanistan. Next to him is his incredible wife, Annalise. I am honoured to know a man who carried out our mission with courage and integrity. No words can ever express how grateful I am to him for saving my life on the battlefield. Please join me in raising a glass to Kevin." One hundred and thirty glasses clinked to a chorus of "To Kevin."

Kevin cleared his throat and, with glass raised, replied, "You can tell the calibre of a man by the people who are close to him. Trevor, there is a whole battle group of soldiers who stand with you today."

The sun was setting as Debbie gave our final toasts of the night and marshalled the crowd onto the dance floor. "The first dance will start when everyone is on the floor with us." I had arranged with a couple of the rugby guys to move the parallel bars to the centre of the floor. The energy surrounding us from our friends and family was palpable. Most couples spend hours choreographing and practising their first wedding waltz, foxtrot or rumba. Debbie and I had spent close to four and a half years working on our first dance. She looked at me with excited anticipation as she and Lila helped launch me to standing. From the corner of my eye, I could see Debbie looking up at me and smiling like I had just been awarded a medal for bravery. When the DJ saw me towering over the crowd, she kicked off the night with our lively first dance to "You Sexy Thing" by Hot Chocolate.

The crowd erupted as if a game-winning goal had been scored. I felt as if I were being lifted even higher by the power encircling us—a combination of love, camaraderie, triumph, friendship, laughter and unbridled excitement. The dance floor was alive the rest of the night. Grace and a few of the other kids even jiggled and bounced until close to midnight. Partway through the night, I snuck away, as much as it is possible to sneak away in a large wheelchair, to drink moonshine and howl with the boys under a full moon in our traditional kilts. It was just like old times and exactly what I had expected from my rugby mates at my wedding.

All too soon, the DJ announced the last song of the night. I had brought a CD with a song we'd always talked about having as our first dance, but once the proceedings started, I had completely forgotten about it. I had become so attached to the song when I first heard it because it talks about connecting to the heart without speaking. I felt this so strongly in the months when Trevor wasn't able to speak yet I felt we could still communicate. The song got us through some rough times at the centre when Trevor was having severe bouts of anxiety. I would play it for him and we would imagine ourselves happily dancing at our wedding. I couldn't let the night end without hearing the song, but I had only minutes to get the music to the DJ. I bolted out of the tent, across the back lawn and up the stairs to my sister's bedroom, where my bag sat on the floor. I grabbed the CD and flew down the stairs and across the lawn like Cinderella about to turn back into a peasant at midnight. "Can you play 'When You Say Nothing at All' for the last dance, please?" I panted as I handed over the CD. My dream wedding was complete as Alison Krauss's words drifted through the night.

By this time, Grace was getting wobbly from all the dancing, so Debbie leaned down and put her on my lap. I reached my arms around both of them as Debbie perched on my knee and held us both. When I looked up, a crowd had gathered arm in arm and was circling around to the music in a spontaneous show of love.

When we got home after midnight, Grace crawled into our bed. Too tired to move her, Debbie hoisted me in next to Grace and fell in on my other side.

"Is this how you expected to spend your wedding night?" Debbie whispered, a warm smile playing across her face.

"I wouldn't have it any other way. I'm next to my two favourite girls in the world. Thank you," I said to my new bride.

"You don't have to thank me. It's my pleasure to marry you," she replied with a wry smile.

"That's not what I meant. Thank you for not giving up on me."

"It was all worth it to see you standing at the altar today," she said.

"Let's do it all over again when I can walk down the aisle."

"Let's do just that," she said as she dozed off to sleep in my arms.

CHAPTER 39:
I HAVE SOMETHING TO SHOW YOU

D ebbie and I are sitting on a secluded patio that gives on to a wide swath of lush green grass. To our left, a bench crafted from gnarled driftwood waits under an oak tree. Farther on, small waves gurgle listlessly onto a scruffy beach of pebbles and flotsam. The air is redolent with the sweet seaweed perfume of the land meeting the sea. We are finally able to relax and breathe. No rehab for five days. I am at peace and, for the first time in a long time, completely content. Debbie breaks her gaze away and says, "This is the perfect place for a honeymoon."

"A perfect place to wind down from the wedding of the century," I said.

"It was even better than we imagined, wasn't it?"

"Yeah, it was the kind of wedding I would have wanted to be a guest at."

"Me, too." We both laughed, pleased with ourselves.

"Do you ever wonder what our life would be like if this hadn't happened to us?" she asked as she stared out at the setting sun.

"We would probably be plodding on day to day in the rat race, not fully appreciating life."

After a long pause, Debbie said with a serious expression, "You don't talk much about your tour. I want to know, would you do it all over again—go to Afghanistan—knowing what would come?"

"I don't remember much from my time, mostly vague images and scenes, like from a movie. If I had played it safe and stayed home or taken the UN job, I think I would be a bitter, empty man impossible to live with. I suppose I lived my entire life in preparation for Afghanistan. Yes, I would do it all again."

After a long pause, Debbie smiled at me and said, "I have something to show you."

She went inside and came back with five tattered notebooks. "I started writing a journal the day I was told you weren't coming out of your coma. One night a few weeks later, I told you I was writing it." She wiped her eyes and continued, "You said to me in the faintest voice, 'Keep writing.' I knew then you were still there, so I kept writing, and writing, and writing. Are you ready to hear about the last four years of your life?"

EPILOGUE

The elders' laughter at the discussion of education for girls had always rankled Trevor, but he chose to hear it as a call to action. That call to action is taking root with us sharing our story.

When Trevor deployed, we knew the experience would profoundly change our lives. We thought it would set us on a path to a new life. We never imagined we would be confronting a life of major physical disability—a traumatic brain injury, no less.

It wasn't hard to find the good arising out of this attack. We have a renewed sense of the wonder and shortness of life. The injury strengthened our love and solidified a bond that began to form the day we met. Most important, we have been given a forum from which to speak about the social injustices in the world and the adaptability and power of the brain to recover from injury.

In 2006, Debbie was told by one of the doctors that Trevor might regain enough movement in a couple of fingers to run a power wheelchair. At the time of writing, in June 2011, Trevor has just started back in the kitchen again. His specialty is preparing our evening salad. It's a long way from what he used to cook for us on a regular basis, but no less appreciated and enjoyed. His formerly dominant right arm is regaining its strength and mobility, which makes it easier for him to do everything, including eating and wheeling his own chair.

Trevor's successes don't seem to faze Grace. She's wrapped up in her own little six-year-old world. She is very protective of her father and loves one-on-one playtime with him. When she asks about the "bad man" who hit Daddy, we tell her that he was just an uneducated boy easily swayed by a group of bad people.

Rehab is far from over. Pushing the limits of a brain injury is still the main focus of our lives and a full-time job. Every day we get closer to our goal of walking. In March 2011, Trevor began using a machine to help him relearn how to walk. The Lokomat is a four-hour round trip from our house, but we make the trip almost weekly so that Trevor can remember what it's like to walk, to help his brain rewire. Partway through his fourth session on the Lokomat, he said something clicked for him, almost like the muscle memory was coming back.

We have experienced first-hand that the brain can be retrained and rewired. We hope the muscle memory will be reflected in the neuroplasticity study that began in May 2010. Dr. Ryan D'Arcy and Dr. Stephen Lindsay say the study so far shows that Trevor's brain is making new connections and that other parts of his brain are taking over for the damaged or missing grey matter. The study gives us hope that changes still happening in Trevor's brain will translate into physical changes. We hope it will inspire those living with a brain injury to keep pushing beyond the limits imposed by others.

Trevor's tour was not wasted and the devastating brain injury he suffered was not in vain. Life has improved for girls in Afghanistan since Trevor was carried out of the desert, but the oppression remains and the risk of terrorism on our doorstep still looms. Eradicating terrorism will take generations. During workup training, Trevor realized that education was the key to restoring democracy, and he made the education of girls his personal mission. The desire to complete that mission hasn't waned. If we can teach Afghan kids the benefits of democracy, we will create a whole generation that isn't beholden to the Taliban for a future. The first place to start is educating the young women and men, providing them the tools to become future business owners and leaders.

Trevor believes it was the right decision for Canada to pull out of the combat operation. Our expertly trained army is small, seventy-fourth in size in the world, and has punched well above its weight for years. We've paid a heavy price to help bring peace and stability to Afghans.

Kevin Schamuhn and his second-in-command, Justin McKay, led One Platoon through seven scorching months of combat patrols, firefights and ambushes. Of the guys in the platoon, Trevor was thankfully the only one to be carried off the battlefield, despite heavy fighting and a friendly fire incident in which an American F-15 mistakenly dropped two laser-guided bombs on the platoon's position. Watching from the rear, Kevin thought his command had been destroyed as he saw the thunderous explosion leave behind two massive craters. Miraculously, the platoon was unscathed. During the tour, an invisible white curtain hung over the platoon, presided over by Kevin's mother, who prayed every day for each member of One Platoon by name. As the CIMIC officer, Trevor was attached to the platoon later and therefore wasn't on that list. The story of One Platoon is but one of the many miraculous survival tales of the Afghan war.

In 2010, Task Force Orion was awarded a commander-in-chief commendation for "Exceptional determination and courage during relentless combat in Afghanistan."

Rob Dolson, Kevin and Trevor still keep in touch. At the time of writing, Kevin is a squadron commander at the Royal Military College of Canada and Rob is an instructor at the Combat Training Centre in Gagetown. Rob and Trevor have made a promise to sip beers on our back deck and watch their daughters play together. Trevor will forever be indebted to the platoon for saving his life and encouraging him to hang on as he lay bleeding in the desert. We have met, by coincidence and planning, the first three people to care for Trevor after the axe fell: the platoon medic, Shaun Marshall; Gary Adams, the medic in the Medevac helicopter; and Maria Streppa, who was serving as a nurse at the hospital in Kandahar. She shared with us the dire situation confronting the trauma team in Kandahar and said the Medevac crew members were reluctant to transport Trevor to Germany because they thought he might not survive the flight. Fortunately, she convinced them that Trevor wouldn't survive if he stayed at the Kandahar hospital.

Throughout this test of our spirit, we've felt the hearts of Canadians and people all over the world reaching out to communicate with us. We couldn't possibly respond to every message, but we've kept them all. Canadians may not have always supported the mission, but we thank them for supporting us during our recovery and the troops during their hard-fought deployment.

In 2010, we received what we thought was a prank call from a man informing us that $100,000 had been left to Trevor in a will—with no strings attached. We had never heard of the man who died. Six months later, that money was in a trust fund awaiting disbursement. We talked long and hard about the best use of the funds and decided to set up an annual scholarship to educate young Afghan women to be teachers. Part of our proceeds from sales of this book will be donated to that cause as well. Instructions on how to donate to the Greene Family Education Initiative are at the end of this epilogue. We hope to create an endowment that will continue to train teachers long after we're gone. Our hope is that these teachers will return to their villages to pass on their knowledge to the first Afghan generation in over thirty years to grow up untouched by war.

The Greene Family Education Initiative

Mission: To train women in conflict zones as teachers to enlighten and empower future generations.

HOW TO DONATE

Online:
www.vancouverfoundation.ca/GreeneFamily

By mail:
Suite 1200–555 W. Hastings Street, Vancouver, BC V6B 4N6
*Make cheques payable to the Vancouver Foundation—
Greene Family Education Initiative. Tax receipts are issued for
all donations.*

AFTERWORD

Canada's longest war began in early 2002 in eastern Afghanistan, when Lt.-Col. Pat Stogran led his 3rd Battalion PPCLI into battle alongside American troops in Operation Anaconda. The objective of the mission was to capture Taliban and Al-Qaeda fighters in the mountains of the remote eastern province of Paktia. During the operation, Cpl. Rob Furlong broke the record—twice—for the longest sniper shot in war.

Our first casualties came on April 18, 2002, at Tarnak Farms, the former home of Osama bin Laden. U.S. Air Force major Harry Schmidt, on a combat air patrol in his F-16 fighter, mistook a live-fire exercise on the designated range at Tarnak for a Taliban attack. Schmidt dropped a 227-kilogram laser-guided bomb on the range. The first Canadian soldiers to die in Afghanistan were Sgt. Marc Leger from Lancaster, Ont.; Cpl. Ainsworth Dyer of Montreal; Pte. Richard Green of Mill Cove, N.S.; and Pte. Nathan Smith of Porters Lake, N.S.

In February 2005, Defence Minister Bill Graham announced that Canada would double its troop commitment to twelve hundred soldiers. That spring, Parliament decided to move the focus of operations south to the volatile and deadly Kandahar Province, which is roughly the size of Croatia. Gen. Rick Hillier, then Chief of the Defence Staff, argued to keep our troops in the relatively safe areas in and around Kabul to work on the rebuilding of the airport. But by the time General Hillier returned in autumn 2004 from a stint as commander of NATO's International Security Force, planning was already largely under way to move to Kandahar.

That made 2006 a bad year to be in Kandahar for a Canadian soldier. The Taliban were massing there and in Helmand

Province to the east in preparation for a violent spring offensive. The Taliban surged up to two thousand fighters in the area and, atypically, dug in for a conventional battle. In heavy fighting, Canadian and Afghan forces quickly defeated the enemy and the Taliban withdrew. But this war would become a long decade of frustrating battle against an enemy that faded seamlessly into the local villages after firefights. Finally, on July 7, 2011, at 11:18 local time, our combat mission ended in a simple handover ceremony near the spot where, nine years earlier, the members of 3PPCLI became the first Canadian soldiers to set foot on Afghan soil.

I think the decision to redeploy to Kandahar was misguided. It's true that our success in counter-insurgency war often surpasses that of our NATO allies and is enhanced by our extensive experience in difficult peacekeeping operations in places like Kosovo. But Kandahar's complex web of tribal loyalties and byzantine power struggles took time to figure out and navigate effectively. It was fortunate the axe fell relatively early in my tour, on my fiftieth day in country. If it had come much later, I'm sure I would have been too exhausted to survive.

Like a good officer, General Hillier has taken a personal interest in my welfare. After visiting Shinkay with Lieutenant-Colonel Ian Hope, the commanding officer of the 1st Battalion and Task Force Orion, the general directed that I receive the best possible care.

I don't know what is in store for Afghanistan. I don't know if peace and prosperity can once more reign after so many years of war, but I am hopeful it will happen in my lifetime. I think Kandahar, where over half of the targeted killings in Afghanistan took place in April and June 2011, will definitely be the last province to be tamed. Within two weeks in the summer of 2011, both Ghulam Haider Hamidi, the mayor of Kandahar City, and Ahmed Wali Karzai, President Hamid Karzai's half-brother and the most powerful man in southern Afghanistan, were assassinated by the Taliban. It's impossible to predict what NATO will achieve in Afghanistan, or to understand what unique contribution Canada made to the mission. I do know that more women are out in public with their faces uncovered. I do know that water is once again gushing down irrigation canals that have been dusty for years. I do know that there are more girls going to school than ever before. And another milestone was reached on July 17, 2011, with the transfer of control of relatively peaceful Bamiyan Province, which got worldwide attention in 2001 when the Taliban blew up two enormous sixth-century Buddhist statues. The handover to the Afghan government was a low-key ceremony that New Zealand troops, who played a key role in stabilizing the province, finished with a traditional haka dance made famous by their rugby team, the All Blacks.

When two journalists from the *Toronto Star* were embedded with our platoon, I was reminded of my university thesis, in which I mused on how war reporting could be improved if journalists accompanied troops on operations. That way, they could get the soldiers' perspective instead of merely reporting the facts like any other story.

When Kevin found out I had been a journalist, he put me in charge of the two newest members of the platoon. At first, I was peeved at the babysitting job. Then I noticed how Mitch Potter and Rick Madonik moved like soldiers on patrol, carefully watching their step and constantly scanning all around. I was particularly impressed with how Rick negotiated the rocky ground with his bulky camera gear. He told me he was a yoga enthusiast and had made several trips to India on six-month sabbaticals to practise yoga morning and evening. My job was to bookend Potter and Madonik with another soldier. On foot patrol, I walked either in front of them or right behind them in case of an ambush or IED strike. On the day of the attack, they would have been at the *shura* with us as usual, but their editor had told them the *Toronto Star* was holding an unprecedented twelve pages for their next story. On the night of March 4, Potter and Madonik plugged into the LAV's power to file their pictures and copy. Potter sat his laptop on a rations box in the dimly lit, dusty LAV, and by the light of his headlamp, he crafted ten thousand words of the most incisive, compassionate journalistic prose I have ever read.

The seasoned, savvy journalists selected to cover the Afghan War are at the top of their game. But I think the Western news media is being played by the superb Taliban PR machine. By quoting the Taliban instead of Afghan civilians, reporters are reinforcing the notion that they speak on behalf of the people. This is not balanced reporting. In the wake of my attack, the Taliban put out a press release purporting that coalition troops had killed an innocent boy. A Canadian Forces public affairs officer, Cmdr. Albert Wong, had to quickly issue a press release giving the facts.

More than 125,000 Canadians have soldiered in nearly fifty peacekeeping missions since 1949. In the fifty-two years prior to the Afghan war, Canada suffered 116 deaths in peacekeeping missions. Canadian generations tend to be known for the wars they fight. Our great-grandfathers are defined by the First World War, our grandfathers by the Second World War. Our fathers and mothers, aunts and uncles are known for the many peacekeeping missions in which our country has participated. Canada has contributed more troops to UN peacekeeping missions cumulatively than any other nation. Past generations battled totalitarianism. We fight extremism. My generation and the one to follow will be forever entwined with the Afghan war. We held the line shoulder to shoulder with our NATO allies against an evil, intractable enemy. We sacrificed and struggled to help restore peace and prosperity to another nation in its time of desperate need. And that, along with many other things, is what Canadians do best.

ACKNOWLEDGMENTS

Writing this book was a labour of love and many late nights. Sometimes we had to hash out the story from memory, with only a few "gentle disagreements"—usually as we breached midnight. We have many people to thank, especially our parents, who always left the light on. You helped your children through the most difficult time of their lives with undying love and support.

And of course our thanks to our extended families . . .

Our rugby mates from the Rowers and Forgotten Islanders, who kept the dark clouds at bay with their jokes, songs, stories and memories. Gregory, Frenchy, Spud, Alex, Francis, Jay, Mikey, Gibby, Rudy, Relic, Angus, Swee'pea, Superdubya and Remmer, take a bow. You got stuck in on the pitch and stayed stuck in at the hospital.

The members of One Platoon, Alpha Company, 1st Battalion PPCLI, who saved Trevor from being the eleventh Canadian ramp ceremony of the Afghan war. And medic Gary Adams and the crew of the Black Hawk, who medevacked Trevor out of bandit country.

The Department of National Defence and particularly Gen. Rick Hillier, the consummate soldier's solider, who took a personal, compassionate interest in Trevor's welfare and that of all his wounded soldiers. Thank you for directing that he receive the best possible care. Maj.-Gen. Steve Bowes and Chief Warrant Officer Kit Charlebois, who made us feel like we were still a part of the Canadian Forces family. And Maj. Kirk Gallinger, for writing such a thoughtful and difficult letter explaining what had happened to Trevor.

Rick Cameron and Steve Basaraba for making the long Alberta winter a little warmer with your visits, and Greg Prodaniuk and Pete Palmer, Trevor's OSI counsellors, who soldiered with him through a psychological hell.

Col. Rob Roy Mackenzie, Trevor's commanding officer at the Seaforth Highlanders, for setting the example of an exemplary officer and gentlemen, and for his frequent visits to the hospital in the difficult early days. And our Seaforth assisting officer and gentle giant, Dave Gilmour, who went beyond the call of duty for a wounded warrior and his family.

Jim Gifford, our talented, wise editor at HarperCollins, for his compassionate guidance. And our first editors, Bill Inglis and Jamie Moore, who helped us separate the wheat from the chaff.

The many surgeons and doctors who made the difference time and time again along the way, including Dr. Homer Tien in Kandahar, Drs. Sorini and Johnson (and team) in Germany, Dr. Norgrove Penny in Victoria, and the doctors and nurses at Vancouver General Hospital and the Halvar Johnson Centre for Brain Injury. Thank you for making a difference in the dark early days.

Our talented alternative therapists, Eve, Kelly, Joy, Trish, Heather and Andy, who always stayed the course, and especially Adam McLeod and Anita Lawrence, for their healing beyond the parameters of modern medicine.

The many passionate therapists who refused to give up on us: Cynthia Wilson, Kunle Akinyode, Lori Gartner, Bonnie Lamley, Lila Mandziuk, Jennifer Davidson, John Blasevic, Lesley Lawrence, Karin Jacobsen, Joel Corlazzoli, Edna Ricafrente and all the gals at Neuromotion Physiotherapy.

Mitch Potter and Rick Madonik of the *Toronto Star*, who breathed the same dust and braved the same dangers to tell the story of One Platoon with heart, great skill and honesty.

Sue Ridout for bringing light to Canada's injured soldiers and brain injuries in the Gemini Award–winning documentary *Peace Warrior.*

Drs. Ryan D'Arcy and Stephen Lindsay for taking an interest and pushing the limits of science of the brain.

And Trevor's good mate and mentor, C.W. Nicol, who first saw the spark and fanned it into flame.

Trevor's good friend and best person, Barb Stegemann, for continuing his mission to empower war-torn and impoverished countries. Barb purchases raw materials from countries like Haiti and Afghanistan to make perfume. Afghanistan Orange Blossom debuted in March 2010.

Most important, Grace, who sometimes went without an extra story and snuggle at bedtime when deadlines loomed. We really, really super-duper looooove you!

From Trevor
To my one true love, Debbie Anne, whose fortitude and courage made our happily ever after come true.